Raising Brighter Children

Raising Brighter Children

A program for busy parents

Sidney Ledson

Walker and Company
New York

First published in the United States of America
in 1986 by the Walker Publishing Company, Inc.

Library of Congress Cataloging-in-Publication Data

Ledson, Sidney.
    Raising brighter children.

    Bibliography: p.
    Includes index.
    1. Domestic education. 2. Child rearing.
3. Education, Preschool. I. Title.
LC37.L35 1986   649'.68   86-15716
ISBN 0-8027-0924-9

Printed in the United States of America

10 9 8 7 6 5 4 3 2 1

Acknowledgments

This book has benefited from the comments and criticisms of several friends and associates, chief among them: Starling Lawrence, of W.W. Norton & Company, who suggested the present format of the book; Dianne Luciani, Gifted Children's Coordinator for Mensa Canada; Margaret Woollard and Ann Holloway of Macmillan Company of Canada, and Jennifer Glossop of McClelland and Stewart, who made many valuable contributions.

Others contributed over the years, generally or specifically: Joyce Devonshire and Herta Fletcher of the Ministry of Community and Social Services; Wendy Priesnitz, president, Canadian Alliance of Home Schoolers; Donald Bryant; David Ibbetson; and in Ottawa, M. Audrey Voitkus and Paul Harris.

My thanks to all the tutors, who then ranged in age from eight to sixteen, whose enthusiastic support made our home-learning program so successful.

Lisa Stone	Lana Toole	Diane Gervais
Cathy Stone	Vivian Bibby	Katherine Neuspiel
Shelagh Burke	Karen Davidson	Debbie Brown
Karrin Wright	Susan Hemsley	Margaret Wood
Sandy Wright	Kathryn Davidson	Sarah Wayne
Marg Rita Wright	Liz Barker	Sandra Salmins
Judy MacDonald	Debbie Cameron	Tal Gilboa
Danielle Murray	Lynn Rivett	Ada Howie

Contents

Raising
Brighter
Children

1

Home, the Center of Learning

Whenever the question of educating children is raised, thoughts usually turn to schools and to schoolteachers—an unfortunate association of ideas, for parents are, and have always been, their children's first and most important teachers. What parents teach, or fail to teach, intentionally or unintentionally, profoundly influences their children's entire lives. Home is, in a practical sense, currently and traditionally, a child's first school. Here, a child's learning pattern is established; here the seed is planted, or not, for advanced education. And here each child acquires an assortment of strengths and advantages, or handicaps and vulnerabilities, that predispose him to success or failure, to happiness or unhappiness.

Today, we tend to divide children's education in two: home education and school education; social and moral instruction being thought best suited to the home, and scholastic or academic instruction best suited to the school. But this is merely a hold-over from the days when only schoolteachers had easy access to teaching materials. Today, all manner of school supplies, kits, devices, and various educational activities are available to the general public. And parents who use these materials are finding that children's academic education flowers no less well—and often better—at home than in school.

Those who have troubled to educate their children at home have often been surprised by what young minds can comprehend, and they have taught various intellectual matters to children as young as two: reading, foreign languages, mathematics, and sciences among them. Not that there is anything wrong in stimulating a two-year-old's intellect. To the contrary. But parents have sometimes failed to realize that children's first needs are emotional and social, not intellectual; that love, affection, and a sense of fun are of infinitely greater worth in predisposing a child to happiness than is any program of academic study; that children's proper first need is to be able to attract affection, respect, and lasting friendship from those inside and outside the household: an ability that depends for its success upon several learned traits; among them, the ability to share with others, to wait one's turn without complaint, to be courteous, mannerly, and respectful of others' rights, and to possess, generally, those social habits we routinely associate with good breeding.

A child trained and fashioned thus—likeable, mannerly, and emotionally secure—might be likened to a well-made, well-baked cake, one we can then top with an icing of rare intelligence: a minor task, for, as we will see, in every recorded instance where parents have troubled to stimulate their children's thinking, their youngsters have acquired high intelligence; many, in fact, have risen to eminence. Consider, for example, Albert Einstein, whose parents (and uncles) guided and encouraged the boy in the study of mathematics, music, and science. And consider Thomas Edison, whose mother, a former schoolteacher, patiently instructed the youngster at home after he had been dubbed "retarded" at school. How different might the careers and accomplishments of Einstein and Edison have been had their parents and relatives simply sat back and left the youngsters' education to the schools, as so often happens.

But, as most parents will agree, high intelligence, in itself, is of questionable value. Some people with acknowledged high intelligence haven't had even horse sense for getting along with others. Einstein and Edison were both brilliant, but Einstein alone was socially competent. Edison, an egocentric—rated a tyrant by his employees—was able to attract grudging praise from them, but not affection. The thousands of hours Edison's mother gave to her son's education yielded a genius who could solve staggering scientific problems, but who couldn't deal with the simple task of getting along with others.

Our goal here is high intelligence, yes, but not a socially unfastened sort of braininess that bangs like a noisy gate in the wind, annoying everyone within earshot. Most parents are rightfully more concerned that their children will be accepted and welcomed by others than that their children will have high intelligence. But why not have both? High intelligence doesn't deter friendship. Bright children, no less than average children, gain ready acceptance not by being the *same* as others, but by possessing traits that are commonly admired; among them, honesty, kindness, generosity, modesty, a sense of restraint and of discretion. So important is the question of sociability that an entire chapter of this book is devoted to guiding children in ways that will win them respect and affection.

The premise throughout the book is that human intelligence is alterable; that parents can, by following a program of instruction, equip their children with a better-functioning brain, one that will help their offspring face life's problems with confidence and solve them effectively.

What then is the case for heredity? Aren't intellectual limits influenced by genetic transfer? Yes, unquestionably. Differing as we each do in external appearance, and in the size and performance of our internal organs, we can hardly believe that our brains are uniquely exempt from natural variation. However, each of us functions so far *below* our respective upper intellectual limit that any concern about difference of intellectual potential or quality of brain is pointless. As we will see in Chapter 3, the potential of your brain and mine is truly phenomenal, yet we habitually fail to use more than a fraction of its power.

The educational program presented is one that permits all children to tap more fully the great potential of their brains. The program has, time and again throughout history, raised ordinary youngsters to great intelligence and to leadership. The only change that has been introduced to this tested program is the manner of teaching. Techniques presented here permit today's busy parents to engage their youngsters in educational activities that are pleasant and rewarding for children and parents alike. You don't have to be a university professor or a schoolteacher to follow the program. You needn't have worked with children before. All you need is the ability to read and understand, plus, of course, the get-up-and-go to engage your child in the activities described.

IQ

The terms *intelligence* and *IQ* (for intelligence quotient) appear often in this book, so perhaps a word would be in order to explain what each term is or is not intended to mean. First, the terms are not interchangeable, though they might be said to overlap. Intelligence has been described as the ability to understand and to cope with new or trying situations: a definition we will use here. High IQ, on the other hand, simply indicates skill in solving problems of a sort that can be presented on paper. People who achieve high scores on IQ tests – and who might rightly be termed, in consequence, "paper geniuses" – have proven intellectual ability in a specific area. They may not, however, be able to solve day-to-day problems involving other people. A person scoring high on an IQ test could, therefore, be a genius on paper, but a numbskull in practice.

Moreover, the imposition of time limits – a routine condition of IQ tests – penalizes those who, by nature, deliberate longer than others before making a decision. For example, the person who correctly answers only eight test questions out of ten in a prescribed ten-minute period, and does so with time to spare, would receive a higher IQ score than someone who, though able to answer only seven of the ten questions in the prescribed ten minutes, *could* have answered all ten questions correctly if time had permitted. In short, IQ tests tend to favor those who give hasty answers.

These weaknesses of IQ tests aside, a high score does, however, reveal a knack for seeing a particular type of problem clearly, for analyzing it skillfully, for mustering various possible solutions to the problem, and for choosing the best solution: abilities that permit their owner to succeed not only in IQ tests, but usually in academic studies too.

But the best news is that mental agility, like swinging on parallel bars, can be learned. In his book *Lateral Thinking*, Edward deBono reveals how even adults may achieve a springiness of mind in viewing the world around them. Why should this matter here? Because the better able parents are to use their brains, the better able will they be to teach their children how it's done. And skillful thinking is a first concern here, for, as Dr. Dennis Stott has observed in his book *The Parent as Teacher*, "Until a child is using his mind, and using it aright, no one on earth can discover how much ability he has." Dr. Stott, former director of the Centre for Educational Disabilities, University of Guelph, voiced these words in defense of mentally retarded youngsters; but they apply equally well to all children.

Horn-rimmed Excellence

The stereotype of early brilliance has, until now, taken the form of a sober-faced youngster—usually a boy—wearing horn-rimmed glasses; one who, we are led to believe, is keen about academic matters.

This is an unfortunate image, and one that would probably discourage many parents from wanting to raise a bright child. Who wants a glum genius around the house? But it's a false picture, and one that needs altering.

Early brilliance, which, as we will see, is the predictable, inevitable result of early instruction, needn't speed children into academic studies, though some parents have so guided their youngsters. Children's early education should, instead, help them to better understand and appreciate those matters that appeal to and delight *children*, not adults.

The hope here is to create a new image of early brilliance; one in which the child—whether a boy or girl—doesn't necessarily wear glasses (horn-rimmed or any other kind);* a youngster who smiles easily and frequently; and who, despite the possession of high intelligence, likes to play with toys and games, and read books suited to his or her own age.

---

*Children are sometimes thought to wear glasses at an early age because they read so much. After all, children who read a great deal often wear glasses. But what is seldom realized is that children with weak vision tend to read more as a *consequence* of their defective eyesight. The reason? Children who are afflicted with poor eyesight early in life, and who must, in consequence, wear glasses, tend to avoid—for the safety of those glasses—boisterous activities, and become more disposed to indoor activities, chief among which is reading.

Knowledgeable, Happy Children

Although early intellectual development is sometimes thought to reduce children's enjoyment of childhood, this notion isn't supported by fact. Instead, early learning is seen to open doors for children leading to a wealth of exciting new interests and useful skills, not the least of which, apparently, is the ability to get along with others. In his article "Education of the Exceptional,"* Samuel Alexander Kirk, professor of special education, University of Arizona, Tucson, concluded:

> Research on the personal adjustment of gifted and handicapped children (other than the socially or emotionally disturbed) has not shown the probability of maladjustment to be as great as "common sense" would indicate. It was once assumed, for example, that a gifted child would show exceptional talent in some area but would be abnormal in social relations. This myth has long been discarded; studies over a period of years have shown that the extremely gifted (children with IQs of 140 and above) were better adjusted than the average [child], personally, and socially, in school and in later life.

The advantages of high intelligence seem only to increase with age. Researchers Lewis Terman and Melita Oden, after studying more than a thousand bright children periodically – continuing into the subjects' fifties and sixties – concluded that their superintelligent subjects possessed, as a group, fewer neurotic symptoms, experienced fewer nervous breakdowns, and had lower divorce and suicide rates than individuals of average intelligence. In fact, members of their special group were found to be superior in every way, even in matters seemingly unrelated to intelligence, such as artistic ability and personal ethics.

Knowledge vs Facts

Of the many matters children might be taught, some contribute more than others to youngsters' intellectual growth. Ideally, we want to give children a maximum number of abilities while teaching them a minimum number of facts. Teaching children facts can be an endless task, one that may, admittedly, give youngsters a great store of knowledge, but may give them few skills. For example, although little time and effort is needed to teach a three- or four-year-old the names of the planets and their order out from the sun,† this information doesn't really add much to a child's

---

*Encyclopaedia Britannica, 15th ed., Macropaedia, vol. 6, pp. 431–34

† The names of the planets and their order out from the sun, Mercury, Venus, Earth, Mars, Jupiter, Saturn, Uranus, Neptune, Pluto, when set to the tune of some well-known song – for example, "Here We Go Gathering Nuts in May" – become easy to remember.

daily pleasure, or to his ability to deal with daily life. Similarly, teaching children to identify the various dinosaurs and early mammals, though permitting an impressive performance for relatives and friends, contributes little to children's intellectual growth or to the formation of desirable personal qualities and characteristics. We would do better to teach children elementary psychology: why people act the way they do, why they perform the duties they do, why some children behave better than others, why the letter carrier delivers our mail, and similar matters.

Not that there is anything wrong in teaching children about the dinosaurs. The giant reptiles are inherently fascinating for youngsters. But parents with limited time for teaching must give priority to those matters that fill children's most important needs: the ability to understand and cope with the puzzling world around them. When two-, three-, or four-year-olds have been taught to read – a simple task, as you will see – they can then begin reading about dinosaurs, planets, or any other subject that interests them.

Parental Motive

Sometimes parents who teach their preschooler "school" subjects are suspected of doing so for the attention, admiration, or envy that their child's performance may attract. Possibly there have been parents so motivated. But why shouldn't children gain an intellectual advantage regardless of what their parents' motives might be?

Consider, for the purpose of comparison, early musical education. In the Shinichi Suzuki system of musical training, children as young as two are taught to play the violin. First, the mother receives violin lessons for three months, while the infant merely watches. Then the youngster is given a miniature violin, and the mother begins teaching the child to play it. The idea is that just as mothers (or fathers, for that matter) are best suited to teach their children to speak, so they are best suited to teach their children to play an instrument; that is why the Suzuki system is called the "mother-tongue" method of instruction.

Children – even backward or handicapped youngsters – taught by the Suzuki method soon become accomplished musicians, many achieving brilliance. The first child so trained, four-year-old Toshiya Eto, eventually became the first Japanese concert violinist to achieve distinction.

When a parent teaches a child to play a musical instrument, the parent is usually said to be "encouraging" the youngster to play. Ironically, though, when a parent teaches a child to read, the parent is sometimes said to be "pushing," "forcing," or "rushing" the child to read, even though learning to read is much easier for a child than learning to play a musical instrument.

16

Similarly, no one accuses the Suzuki-trained parents of wanting to attract attention, admiration, or envy to themselves by teaching their children to play the violin. Everyone congratulates the parents for taking the trouble to help their youngster acquire a pleasing and valuable skill. But if parents deserve praise for helping children develop musical ability, why shouldn't they be similarly praised for helping children develop intellectual ability? In the final evaluation, parental motive, whether benevolent or selfish, is unimportant. The important matter is what the children gain. If, in attempting to give their youngsters an advantage they themselves probably never had, parents attract compliment or praise to themselves – whether sought or not – is this a valid reason for condemning their efforts?

Shouldn't we regard with greater suspicion the excuses given by other parents for *not* teaching their preschoolers? Parents have been heard to say: "I'll explain anything to him if he asks, but I don't intend to teach him. The interest has to come from his side." Parents who can't be bothered to teach a child will usually find some excuse for their inaction. These same parents are seldom slow, though, to teach their children skills that make life easier for themselves. For example, by teaching children to walk, to eat unaided, and to dress themselves, parents are spared the inconvenience of carrying, feeding, and dressing children. But parents aren't greatly inconvenienced if their preschooler can't read. So why bother? And with no one to voice the child's case, instruction in reading and in other useful skills is often left to the latest age permitted by law: age five in England, age six in North America.

But what about energetic, well-intentioned parents who, for want of knowledge, ignore their youngsters' early education, perhaps thinking that what they are doing is best for their children? Children lose either way, whether parents deceive themselves to escape the teaching task, or whether they are honest about their beliefs but ignorant of the consequences. For example, one mother was heard to say she didn't intend to teach her preschooler to read because the youngster was already showing signs of cleverness, and the mother feared that early literacy might make the child even brighter.

The mother was correct in her belief. As we will see in Chapter 6, teaching a preschooler to read is believed to stimulate neural growth in the brain. But the mother's statement was upsetting. The daughter, age three, could have no knowledge – probably never would have – of the mother's plan to restrain her intellectual growth. Were her youngster to learn, on reaching adulthood, of the mother's early decision, and of the adverse effect that decision may have worked on her present ability to think and act, would the daughter thank her mother?

Kitchen College: The True Alma Mater

Educating is implicit in parenting. Children's formal education isn't alien to the home setting: it is *initiated* in the home. Parents encourage youngsters, at a very young age, to undertake the most complicated learning project they will ever face throughout their entire lives – mastering the art of speech: a matter so complex that the distinguished mathematician and philosopher Alfred North Whitehead said of it: "What an appalling task, the correlation of meaning with sounds." Truly, parents are the first educators their children encounter.

Some educators, though, contend that infants aren't *taught* to speak, but that they learn speech merely by being exposed to it; however, this notion ignores the fact that teaching is, essentially, the hastening of learning, and that parents hasten their child's mastery of speech, first by reducing our language to sound-elements that children can more easily duplicate – "da-da," "ma-ma" – then by encouraging their child to respond imitatively, and finally by rewarding the child, perhaps unconsciously, with an expression of excited pleasure whenever the youngster approximates the desired sound: all first-rate teaching techniques. In homes where parents are unable or unwilling to patiently rehearse their children in word pronunciation, infants usually begin speaking later.

By teaching children to speak, parents acknowledge the fact – while demonstrating the proof – that raising children and teaching them are indivisible. Teaching children is as natural to the role of parenting as feeding, clothing, and sheltering children. What is *not* natural, though it is common practice, is for parents, on having taught their child to speak, to then halt intellectually stimulating instruction and oblige their youngster to wait three or four years until a Grade 1 teacher takes over.

Such a delay in teaching preschoolers simple, yet valuable, skills – reading, writing, and elementary computing – represents, for parents, the loss of a pleasurable teaching right, and, for children, an unintended insult to their native intelligence. Worse, by delaying children's participation in activities that stimulate intellectual growth, parents inflict upon their youngsters a process of mental retardation. Though steeped in tradition, this three- or four-year delay is supported, not by clear-sightedness, but by the muddled thinking of long-gone educational psychologists whose philosophies – since found to be wrong – continue to thwart educational advancement by the invisible thread of established practice.

The program of instruction described here isn't "extra"-parental at all, but merely the logical continuation of a program parents start when they teach their youngsters to speak. And, despite the fact that parents who *don't* abandon their youngsters' early academic education are sometimes considered odd, how really odd can parents be thought for refusing to stop an educational program they alone were responsible for having started; for wanting, in fact, to fill more fully what they recognize as being mere parental duty?

Finding time to teach a child can be difficult, so most of the teaching procedures to be described throughout the book draw upon moments that, in the routine care and management of a child, might otherwise be tedious for parents. The procedures are equally well suited for single-parent households, and have, in fact, been tested there. One technique (see pages 56 to 60) will virtually lengthen your day by an hour, leaving you free to cook supper without interruption, and will then provide you with a more interesting level of conversation during the meal.

If you are home all day with one or more children, the various instructional activities and diversions can add considerable interest to your day, while adding intellectual sparkle to your child's day.

Some of the educational pastimes require the preparation of materials. For example, to teach a child to read (Chapter 7), you will need to prepare lettered cards. There is, however, a way around this chore, and it, too, is described. You may find more educating activities described throughout the book than you will want to use. You may, therefore, shop, as it were, among the ideas, taking this one or that, to create a program of instruction that suits you and your youngster best.

2

The Case for Preschool Education

Early Intellectual Stability

Intellectual development is said to stabilize early in life. This early stability and the reasons for it are worth our attention because we want the level at which our children's intellectual development stabilizes to be a high one.

One prominent researcher has concluded, from extensive study of early intellectual ability and its ultimate influence on adult performance, that, in terms of an individual's measurable life-long intelligence, 50 per cent of the intellectual development has already taken place by the age of four, and 80 per cent by the age of eight. The trouble with these figures is that they lead us to believe we have been presented with a natural law, when in fact they merely describe an environmental consequence.

There can be no disputing the fact that a child's ethical values, character traits, and personality are largely formed – if not immutably so – during the youngster's first few years. But does this mean that a child's intellectual limit is also fixed? Experiments conducted at the University of California by the late Dr. David Krech and his associates seem to prove otherwise. There, an experimental group of animals, kept in a manner that discouraged thinking and decision-making, were seen to become feeble-minded: unable, that is, to solve simple food-in-a-maze problems. Yet when these animals – and the group included animals that had then reached an advanced age – were switched to a stimulating environment, they quickly began to catch up with animals that had always lived in the stimulating environment. The researchers found, in short, that the brain apparently possesses a lasting potential for development, a potential they termed *plasticity*: the ability to begin development anew if circumstances favor or encourage it.

Might the same be true for humans? Apparently it is. Research conducted in Central America seems to confirm the belief that the human brain, too, possesses a continuing plasticity for development. A Harvard team under the direction of Professor Jerome Kagan studied a primitive society living in a remote region of Guatemala. There, infants are kept inside for the first year or so of their lives to avoid disease. The parents, however, pay little attention to the infants and make no effort to stimulate their intellectual growth. By age two, the children are mentally retarded. But, at age eleven, the same children are happy, active, and alert; and their memory, reasoning, and conceptual skills are as good as those of eleven-year-olds in most middle-class American families.

Consider, too, the treatment of retarded children at the Institutes for the Achievement of Human Potential, in Philadelphia (reported in the book *What To Do About Your Brain-Injured Child*, by Glenn Doman). There, brain-damaged and mentally deficient youngsters engage in an unusual program of physical and intellectual stimulation. Many improve. Others do even better; they become completely normal. And some, astonishingly enough, rise to an above-average level of intelligence.

Brain damage occurs more often than is generally realized. About 9 per cent of all babies are demonstrably brain-damaged at birth. (Children's brains can be injured in several ways: by an incompatible Rh factor between the parents' blood, or by premature birth, late birth, too long a labor, and by other events occurring before, during, or after birth.) Even less generally known is the frequency with which brain-injured children are normalized by their parents. Such cases are seldom reported because parents, having turned a sub-normal child into a normal child, don't want anyone to know the child was ever sub-normal. A newspaper report describing seven super-bright children in one family mentioned – almost incidentally – that two of the brilliant youngsters had been brain-damaged at birth (the parents wisely didn't disclose which two).* Another child who will probably never be named in a newspaper – or here – is the son of a former neighbor. A brief account of the boy's story will serve to show both the nature of brain damage and the great plasticity of the brain for development.

The mother went to the hospital at 7 P.M. with contractions occurring every three minutes, but the baby wasn't born until twenty-one hours later. During this long ordeal, pressure was evidently exerted on the infant's head, for, when the child was born, there was merely a large dent where the back of his head should have been.

At two years of age the child had no balance and could only crawl. He could not speak. The mother sat him on her knee, sang nursery rhymes, and read to him for hours. To develop his pincer grip, she bought him a Leggo set. To help him coordinate the movement of his leg muscles, she tied the child's feet to the pedals of a tricycle and later a pedal cart and either pushed or pulled him around. In this way, the youngster eventually learned to get around on his own.

At age four, the child could barely walk, and his speech was so poor

---

* *The Globe and Mail*, November 2, 1978, p. T8.

only his mother could understand what he was attempting to say. She patiently encouraged him to learn nursery rhymes, and when he slowly—and surprisingly—did finally begin to learn them, she coached him in enunciating every consonant distinctly. Finally, the mother started teaching the child to read.

Because the family had moved to a new district, no neighbors now knew of the child's earlier disability. The mother decided to enter him in Grade 1 and say nothing about his past. He could, at that time, read and write simple sentences and count to 100. The Grade 1 teacher quickly reported that the youngster was brilliant. Since then, he has stood at, or near, the top of his class each year; and recently, the principal asked that the child—now age nine and completing Grade 4—skip Grade 5 and go into Grade 6.

His classmates, whose brains were never less than excellent (yet whose performance was never better than average), are now obliged—because of early, prolonged, parental neglect—to face life's problems with poorly functioning brains.

What irony! What tragedy!

Another mother has written a detailed account of the normalization of her mentally defective daughter (IQ 40 at age two) using the Glenn Doman-Carl Delacato method of treatment (*Brain Child*, by Peggy Napear).

What now of the belief that intelligence has become 50 per cent stabilized by age four and 80 per cent by age eight? The figures are probably correct; however, they do not, properly speaking, indicate the extent to which intelligence has been *fixed*, but rather the extent to which it has been *arrested*.

It is a child's environment and its educating power that becomes stabilized early, *not* a child's potential for intellectual growth. It is the teaching habits parents form, or fail to form, that become fixed, *not* their child's ability to learn. The richness or poverty of the educational environment that has persisted up to a child's fourth or fifth birthday isn't likely to change much in quality, though it may change geographically; and this stabilization of intellectual stimulation can lead us to think that it is the child's intellectual potential that has stabilized.

The quality of speech heard in a home, as well as the beliefs, actions, habits, and interests of the parents, their friends, neighbors, and relatives, tend to exert a "formula" influence, a conglomerate guiding force on the child; an influence that will largely determine the type of person the child feels at ease with now, and later, as an adult. And this environmental formula tends to remain constant. Homes in which books are rarely read, in which the television set, radio, or record player frequently displaces conversation, and in which the sparse conversation is usually gossip or small talk concerning personal problems, aren't likely to change suddenly into stimulating centers for scientific, philosophical, and psychological enquiry. We should hardly be surprised to find children's intellectual development becoming stabilized. But the development is not stabilized by the child's *age*—be it four, five, six, or seven; rather the development is stabilized by the *unlikelihood of any improvement in the quality and quantity of information to which the youngster is routinely exposed.*

Interpreted in this way, then, the figures of 50-per-cent stabilization at age four and 80 per cent at age eight seem valid. A four-year-long environmental molding of this sort, with its concomitant shaping of speech patterns, attitudes, and personal conduct, will tend to set an upper limit on a child's social and intellectual aspirations and achievements. The child's view of himself as a congruous part of his environment will tend to ensure that he becomes a congruous adult extension of that environment. But—and here's the big difference—remove a child from an intellectually humdrum environment, expose him to bountiful knowledge and opportunities for exploration, and we can expect to see the child emulate the sudden intellectual advance demonstrated by Dr. Krech's animals and begin catching up with other children who enjoyed these opportunities from the beginning.

It is, therefore, parental attitude and predisposition toward early education—habitual involvement or habitual neglect—that sets the level of intelligence at which children function. And, as a corollary, we now see the disservice done by those in education who advise parents to ignore or stay out of their preschoolers' formal training, asserting that education is a school matter and the rightful domain of professionals. By honoring such advice, obliging parents inaugurate a program of educational indolence that works quietly over the next year, two, or three, to reduce their children's eventual intellectual worth. Worse, parents run an unexpected risk, according to Dr. Eigil Pedersen, when they send an *un*taught child to school.

The Grade 1 Hazard

Dr. Pedersen, professor of education at McGill University, has discovered that children can be virtually programmed for success or failure by the opinion their Grade 1 teacher holds of them; but—and this is the frightening part—children can be programmed not merely for success or failure in school but for success or failure throughout their entire life.

Dr. Pedersen found that children formed attitudes about themselves and their academic abilities based upon what their Grade 1 teacher *thought* about their abilities. Moreover, the attitudes formed by children tended to become self-fulfilling prophecies, influencing not only their entire academic career, but their adult IQ rating and their ability to function in a mature manner.*

From this, we see that Grade 1 teachers can exert almost as much influence on a child's brain as a brain surgeon. Recognizing this awesome power held by teachers, wouldn't it be wise to pick your child's Grade 1 teacher as carefully as you would a surgeon? It *would* be wise, but, of course, it isn't possible in our school system. And so, having no choice in the selection of a suitable Grade 1 teacher, parents are obliged to gamble with their child's brain. They are, that is, unless they have troubled to educate their child, because an *educated* child is largely immune to a schoolteacher's adverse influence. Why? A child who has already faced various learning challenges and triumphed over them will face new challenges buoyantly and with confidence, and will, as a result of this, be more likely to succeed.

But not so the untaught, untrained child: the child having no past record of academic success or self-esteem gained from earlier achievements, who enters school perhaps with a low expectation of success (possibly because he has been repeatedly told by parents and peers that he is dumb or stupid): *this* is the child who can so easily fall victim to the depreciating influence of a thoughtless Grade 1 teacher.

Self-imagery

Once a child has formed a self-image of competence or incompetence, he becomes virtually hypnotized by the notion. The extent to which youngsters can be obsessed and subsequently influenced by their own expectation of general academic success or failure is hinted at by the powerful and curious way in which the mind controls success or failure in a specific subject. In his book *Self-Consistency*, Prescott Lecky reveals that students tend to perform poorly in subjects at which, from their own point of view, success would be inconsistent with the image they hold of themselves. Here, incidentally, is perhaps the reason males always seem failure-prone and awkward in sewing and in other "feminine" tasks; and why females are often gauche when handling tools.

Lecky reveals how, when one's self-conception (or, perhaps better, self-deception) is suitably altered, and the individual is made to realize that success in a particular subject need not stir inner conflict, success invariably follows.

Such a change in the pupil's attitude often results in improvement which is quite astonishing. A high school student who misspelled 55

Reader's Digest, Canadian edition, October, 1979.

words out of a hundred, and who failed so many subjects that he lost credit for a full year, became one of the best spellers in the school during the next year, and made a general average of 91. A student who was dropped from another college and was later admitted to Columbia was graduated with more than 70 points of "A" credits. A boy failing in English, who had been diagnosed by a testing bureau as lacking aptitude for his subject, won honorable mention a year later for the literary prize at a large preparatory school. A girl who had failed four times in Latin, with marks between 20 and 50, after three talks with the school counselor made a mark of 92 on the next test and finished with a grade of 84. She is now taking advanced Latin with grades above 80.

High school, college, and university may be a long time off for your child, but to whatever extent the problems of higher education can be seen and dealt with now, those upper-school years will be more enjoyable and more beneficial.

Random Education

When parents make no conscious effort to teach their children, youngsters' education becomes haphazard, derived mainly from random elements in their environment; from matters that are often trivial, matters that often lead to no worthwhile goal, or worse, lead to some undesirable goal: information gathered from other children, from neighbors, from chance comments heard inside and outside the home, or from television and radio. In short, children's education becomes, for want of parental initiative and guidance, *random* education, unpredictable in its content, and unpredictable in its consequence. *Failing* to educate children, therefore, is merely another way of educating them. But it is a way that can provide unpleasant surprises and disappointments.

Whatever children learn early in life determines their instinctive response and actions later in life, proof of which was demonstrated in an unusual way to a group of scientists at NASA. There, men who had studied the surface of the moon, who in fact had walked on the moon, were told they would be asked one quick question, and were asked to respond with the first answer that popped into their heads. The speaker then asked them what the moon was made of. Their instinctive answer? Cheese.

If humorous surprises of this kind were the only consequence of random early guidance we would have little cause for concern. But, as will be seen in Chapter 14, random education, besides being possibly *mis*-educational, can be malevolent and antisocial in its influence.

We hear much about inefficient teaching in schools, and teachers have faced heavy criticism. Sometimes the criticism seems justified. In a study prepared for the U.S. College Entrance Examination Board in 1978, secondary-school principals reported that their teachers were less dedicated, were less likely to enforce high academic standards, were more permissive, spent less after-school time with their students, and placed less emphasis on classroom discipline than had their counterparts in 1965.

But schools aren't the only ones to blame. Parents, too, sometimes give a disappointing performance. Consider an encounter with David, a kindergarten child, reported to me by a friend. In a bid to get David talking, she asked the youngster if he knew his nursery rhymes, then recited the first line of "Little Miss Muffet" and waited for David to burst forth with the other lines. Getting no response, she recited the first line of "Ba-Ba Black Sheep." Again, no response. And when David couldn't contribute anything to "Little Jack Horner," his mother was asked about her child's puzzling lack of basic knowledge. The mother's response was quick and indignant: "Yes, I know," she said. "They don't teach them *anything* in school anymore!"

The mother's misunderstanding of the school's role, and her own, in the youngster's early education had robbed both parent and child of many warm moments and rich memories. Such neglect is rare, but it is rare in degree only. Yes, most parents teach their children the nursery rhymes. But what *else* do they teach them? Often, very little. And children who are taught little understand little; and this, in turn, reduces their opportunities for enjoying and participating in life around them.

Ignorance impoverishes childhood in the same way it impoverishes adulthood. Keeping children ignorant, though sometimes convenient for parents – or perhaps providing parents with a source of cute humor – exacts a high price from children, not only by diminishing their enjoyment of childhood, but by reducing their eventual ability to function as mature adults.

Schoolchildren

Parents who can readily see their role in educating a preschooler sometimes fail to see their role in educating a schoolchild. Indeed, why should parents concern themselves with a child's education once the professionals have taken over? Several reasons. First, despite what the law of compulsory school attendance may lead us to believe, children's education is a *parental* responsibility, not a governmental responsibility. Schools have no obligation to educate children. They have an obligation to *try*, but they have no obligation to succeed. If children learn little in school, teachers are accountable to no one. But if teachers presume to be responsible for educating children while accepting no blame if they fail in the task, then parents are caught in a semantical pea-and-shell game. And they have no shoulder to cry on when they lose.

However, parents must do more than complain about the injustice of it all. They must accept the fact that, in the final accounting, they and they alone are answerable for their children's education both in and out of school.

The fact is that schools count heavily on parents to help in children's education, more heavily than parents realize. And parents who are ignorant of this attract only ridicule when they complain about their child's poor school performance. The Council for Basic Education nails it down thus: "Parents are sitting ducks when they take no active interest in their children's schooling. Teachers and administrators list parent apathy as one of the greatest obstacles to the effectiveness of their teaching and their school, and their professional journals are full of articles deploring it."

When Dr. Jerome Kagan saw how the intelligence of mentally retarded Guatemalan children rose to a North American standard by age eleven, he concluded that our schools give up too easily with slow learners, and that the solution could be found in the use of imaginative teaching techniques. "Every child in the United States," he contends, "–short of the 7 per cent or 8 per cent born with a biological deficit–is capable, basically, of mastering the school skills." And, as we have already observed, even the 7 or 8 per cent of biologically deficient youngsters have a pretty good chance, too, if they have the right parents.

But while we await the day when schools begin to use imaginative teaching techniques to turn slow learners (or slow teachers) into quick learners (or quick teachers), wise parents will at least supplement at home the education their youngsters receive in school; or better, they will initiate their own educational program and accept, graciously, any contribution or reinforcement that schoolteachers may make to their home program.

This book, then, is for parents of both preschoolers and schoolchildren. The procedures can profoundly influence the quality of life children lead now, and will lead later as adults (though the sooner the child is engaged in the program, the greater this influence will be). Chapter 4 is devoted to babies. Chapters 5, 6, and 7 are mainly for preschoolers. The rest of the book is for both preschoolers and schoolchildren.

Reading, the Key Skill

Many children don't learn to read well in school, and this makes the learning of other subjects more difficult for them. Two major influences have made reading more difficult to teach: the widespread use of slow, complicated reading programs that encourage word-guessing, and the advent and ascendancy of electronic entertainment. The reason faulty reading programs are widely used, and the reason they cannot be expelled from schools, is too complex a matter to be dealt with here. Readers who want the details will find them in the books listed on page 250.

The adverse influence of electronic entertainment on reading ability is more easily explained. Fifty years ago, the only low-cost entertainment available to children came in printed form. Newspaper comics and cartoons – highlights in every schoolchild's day – were savored panel by panel. The public library was a veritable palace of humor, adventure, and mystery. Teachers didn't have to prod children to read. Children couldn't be stopped from reading.

But times have changed. Pollsters report that 50 per cent of students today read nothing outside the classroom. Instead, they watch television or listen to radio or records. But how can a child become a skillful reader if he rarely reads? Reading, like playing a musical instrument, requires considerable practice between lessons if the learner is to master the skill.

Fitting in at School

Two questions are sometimes raised about children who are taught early: will they have difficulty getting along with other youngsters when they begin school, and will they be bored with schoolwork?

Children who are educated early but who haven't been allowed – or worse, encouraged – to form grandiose opinions of themselves simply because they know more or can do more than children who never had similar early training, and whose early education has stressed consideration and respect for others, will usually make friends easily in school.

In the early school grades, most of the day is taken up with activities that appeal to all children regardless of their abilities: activities such as assembly or morning exercises, show and tell, singing, story telling, watching TV or films, playing games, art, music, crafts, safety talks, hygiene, and any other subject the teacher might introduce.

Children who can already read will, of course, notice their advantage over others. But Grade 1 children are usually divided into three or four groups. Those children who can read – and an increasing number *can* read when they start school – simply form their own special group. These children read while the others are learning how to.

Boredom is more common in the middle grades, and more likely to occur among incompetent pupils than among the competent. Children, like adults, aren't keen about activities that make them look dull. Difficult subjects become, therefore, unflattering and boring subjects. On the other hand, if a competent pupil becomes bored because the pace is too slow, the teacher can enrich the child's studies with materials provided for that purpose. Of course, an unenthusiastic, perhaps untalented, teacher can make school dull for advanced children – and possibly for the slower children, too; but in this case, parents who have educated their youngsters at home can take comfort in knowing their children can't be irreparably damaged by uninspired teaching.

The possibility of boredom in school is a hazard *every* child faces, whether the child is advanced or not. Boredom is not, therefore, a valid reason for ignoring a preschooler's education. Indeed, to inhibit or thwart children's early intellectual growth simply because they *may* encounter boredom in school is as warped a course of action as locking children in their rooms for the first five years of life so they won't catch communicable diseases.

The fact that a child enters school knowing more than other children is less important than that he enters school with a well-exercised thinking organ and with confidence in himself. Putting aside, for the moment, measurable changes in brain cells brought about by intellectual stimulation (covered in the next chapter), a six-year-old who has already grappled with the requirements of learning for two, three, or four years will be better able to cope with the challenges of Grade 1; the implication being that learning is, itself, a procedure that improves with the doing; that learning is, in short, a developed skill, and one that is best developed early.

3

Reaches of the Human Brain

Passing through the checkout at the modern supermarket, we might marvel at the smartly designed computer that weighs food, deciphers coded prices, names items on the bill, and automatically keeps an inventory of stock for the merchant. But an object worthy of far greater wonder is the brain of the cashier whose fingers flick so rapidly across the computer keys.

The human brain of an adult, which weighs only about three and a half pounds, contains ten *billion* nerve cells, or neurons as they are called: enough cells to store an estimated ten new items of information for every second of an individual's entire lifetime. Furthermore, each neuron – each ten-billionth part of the brain – has a wide choice of connections; and it makes its choices not simply by stimulation, but by experience and expectation. The more we expect, the more will the neurons in our brain respond. The only limit to intercellular response is the total number of possible connections each neuron has to choose from. How many is that? The late Dr. P.K. Anokhin, neurologist at the Laboratory of Neural Physiology in the U.S.S.R. and former student of the famed Ivan Pavlov, said:

> We can show that each of the ten-billion neurons has a possibility of connections of 10^{28}. This means that the total possible connections in the brain, if written out, would be one, followed by nine-and-a-half million *kilometers* of noughts. If the *single* neuron has *this* quality of potential, we can hardly imagine what the whole brain can do. No man yet exists who can use all the potential of his brain. This is why we don't accept any pessimistic estimates of the limits of the human brain. It is unlimited.

Professor Anokhin wasn't talking about the brain of Bertrand Russell or Albert Einstein. He was talking about your brain and mine, and our children's. Each of us possesses this same phenomenal thought organ; yet we make such little use of it that, to employ the metaphor of speed, it is as if we each possessed the fastest, most powerful car in existence, but were limited, by strange social custom, to a speed of one mile an hour.

What is it, then, that limits your intellectual development and mine to the unflatteringly low level we accept as normal? First, of course, it is an ignorance of the brain's potential, plus an ignorance of how the brain's potential can be realized—though this latter ignorance is, in itself, a matter of wonder, because history is rich with stories of parents who disregarded the skepticism of others and engaged their youngsters in a program of early intellectual stimulation. And their offspring head the list in any *Who's Who* of world leaders; among them, Thomas Babington Macaulay (English historian, essayist, poet, and statesman), Blaise Pascal (geometrician, philosopher, and writer), Johann Wolfgang Goethe (poet), Hugo Grotius (Dutch jurist, poet, founder of the science of international law), Gottfried Wilhelm Leibnitz (German philosopher and mathematician).

Let's consider the early education of a few brilliant people, descriptions of which are presented here not as ideals for other parents to emulate, but merely to show the inevitable intellectual brilliance that results from early intellectual stimulation.

JEREMY BENTHAM

Jeremy Bentham, born in 1748, was educated to a plan by his father, a lawyer. The boy was taught the alphabet even before he could talk (indicating, presumably, as much by gesture as by sound, whatever letter was asked for). The boy's reading and writing skills at age three are revealed in a letter to his grandmother.

> Honoured Madam, I have been very much troubled with Sore Hands, but the Greatest Trouble was their preventing me thus long from writing to my dear Grand-Mama, indeed if you knew how bad they are still, you would be surprised at my handling my Pen at all, having only the use of my Thumb and the Tip of my fore Finger, all the other Fingers of Each of my Hands being tied up together in a linnen Bag, otherwise I shod say a great deal more besides that I am Your dutiful Grandson.

That same year Jeremy Bentham read Rapin's *History of England* and, under his father's instruction, began studying Greek and Latin. The boy started school at age seven, entering the upper second form. At ten, he passed the admission requirements for Oxford, but the authorities wouldn't let him enter until he was twelve. Bentham received his B.A. at fifteen, and returned later to pick up his M.A. at eighteen. He went on to become a philosopher, an economist, and a theoretical jurist who exerted great influence on the reforming thought of the nineteenth century.

Jeremy Bentham, when an adult, befriended James Mill, twenty-five years his junior. Mill shared Bentham's belief that the value of school education was overrated, and that education at home was much superior. Mill, like Bentham, dismissed the notion that intelligence was genetically endowed, insisting that it was instead the result of early training. A philosopher, historian, economist, and the author of several works, among them *Analysis of the Phenomena of the Human Brain*, James Mill wrote: "Whoever has power to regulate the sequence and the strength of the experiences which flow in upon a young mind, [will] decide the habits of association [that mind] will form, and to that extent [will] determine both the character and the ability of the later man." His son, John, born in 1806, provided the father with the means for proving the correctness of his belief.

Years later, the son wrote: "I have no remembrance of the time when I began to learn Greek, I have been told that it was when I was three years old. My earliest recollection on the subject, is that of committing to memory what my father termed vocables, being lists of common Greek words, with their signification in English, which he wrote out for me on cards."

But here is an interesting omission. Nowhere in his detailed autobiography does Mill tell us when he learned to read *English*. Yet, to learn Greek by the father's method of teaching it, the boy had to read English. And because he couldn't properly remember learning Greek, we must assume that he learned to read English in a pre-memory period; perhaps at age two.

By his eighth birthday, Mill's reading in Greek included "a number of Greek prose authors, among whom I remember the whole of Herodotus, and of Xenophon's Cyropaedia and Memorials of Socrates; some of the lives of the philosophers by Diogenes Laertius; part of Lucian, and Isocrates ad Demonicum and Ad Nicoclem. I also read, in 1813 [just turning age seven], the first six dialogues (in the common arrangement) of Plato, from the Euthyphron to the Theoctetus inclusive."

The study of Greek took up most of young John's day. After supper, he had mathematics (which he detested). Latin was added to the home curriculum when he was eight, and during the next four years the boy read an astonishing list of Latin and Greek authors.

Mill eventually became one of the most intellectually advanced persons of all time, achieving fame as a philosopher, economist, logician, and ethical theorist.

FRANCIS GALTON

The early education of Sir Francis Galton (Charles Darwin's cousin), born in 1822, is particularly interesting because his parents played only a small part in educating him. Instead, it was his sister Adèle, described as being, herself, "a mere child," who taught him. Adèle had an unusual gift for teaching. Her playful manner of instruction permitted Francis to correctly point to any letter of the alphabet, on request, even before he could speak.

By two and a half, the boy was able to read a small book, *Cobwebs to Catch Flies.* Before age three, he was able to sign his name. Adèle taught herself Greek and Latin just so she could teach them to Francis. His study of these languages is mentioned in a letter to his sister.

My Dear Adèle,

I am 4 years old and I can read any English book. I can say all the Latin Substantives and Adjectives and active verbs besides 52 lines of Latin poetry. I can cast up any sum in addition and can multiply by 2, 3, 4, 5, 6, 7, 8, 10.

I can also say the pence table. I read French a little and I know the clock.

Francis Galton,
Febuary 15, 1827

His only spelling error occurred in the date.

Under his sister's teaching, Francis was completely familiar with the *Iliad* and the *Odyssey* by age six, and she had him well along with entomology and mineralogy between six and seven. At eight, Francis attended a boarding school; his intellectual performance then being equal to that of children twice his age (thus giving him an estimated IQ of 200). Francis Galton eventually achieved prominence as a scientist, explorer, and anthropologist.

KARL WITTE

Perhaps the best-documented case of early education is that of Karl Witte, born in 1800. His father, a clergyman in a German village, held strong and unorthodox views about education. He contended that what children learned before starting school was most important in setting their lifelong achievement. He wrote:

Since children are essentially thinking animals, they are certain, from the moment they first use their own minds, to draw inferences and arrive at conclusions regarding everything they see, hear and touch; but if left to themselves will inevitably, because of their inability to form sound critical judgements, acquire wrong interests and thought habits which all the education of later life may not be able wholly to overcome.

Pastor Witte had such great faith in the power of early education that he publicly declared his intention to raise a superior person; and his declaration was made before the child was born. "If God grants me a son," he said, "and if he, in your opinion, is not to be called stupid, which Heaven forbid, I have long ago decided to educate him to be a superior man, without knowing in advance what his aptitudes may be."

No sooner had the youngster's umbilical cord been snipped than his education began. The father boldly asked both the city of Leipzig and the University of Leipzig to give him money so he might devote all his time to his son's education. More surprising, they gave it! (In time, the French Westphalian Government and the German monarchy contributed money, too.)

Young Karl's education began with vocabulary growth. The father wrote:

> Karl learned many things in the arms of his mother and in my own, such as one rarely thinks of imparting to children. He learned to know and name all the objects in the different rooms. The rooms themselves, the staircase, the yard, the garden, the stable, the well, the barn – everything, from the greatest to the smallest, was frequently shown and clearly and plainly named to him, and he was encouraged to name the objects as plainly as possible.

In naming each item for the child, the parents pronounced the words loudly, clearly, slowly, and repeatedly. Baby talk was forbidden. The manner in which members of the household were organized to fill their role in the youngster's education suggests a dramatic performance:

> We always spoke pure German, in other words, book German, in very simple and comprehensible – but none the less, choice – expressions, and always loudly, distinctly, and in an appropriately slow manner. We never allowed ourselves to make an improper use of intonation. We spoke as correctly, in every sense of the word, as we could. Obscure and intricate sentences and expressions, such as gave no distinct meaning, were scrupulously avoided.

By age four the boy was reading German. By age eight he was reading and speaking French, Italian, English, Latin, and Greek; and had read – with enthusiasm! – Homer, Plutarch, Virgil, Cicero, Ossian, Fenelon, Florian, Metastasio, and Schiller.

Karl entered the University of Leipzig at the age of nine, received his Ph.D. when he was thirteen, became Doctor of Laws and was appointed to the teaching staff of the University of Berlin as professor at age sixteen.

Heirs of the Witte Legacy

Pastor Witte described his son's education with great detail in a book that ran to more than a thousand pages. Among those who apparently read the book and profited from it was James Thompson, of Belfast, father of the boy who eventually became the celebrated physicist, Lord Kelvin. Another who read the book and applied Witte's teachings was A. Berle. His son, Adolf, became a child prodigy, passed the entrance examinations for Harvard at age twelve, and began practicing law at the age of nineteen. He eventually became a professor at Columbia Law School and a member of Franklin Roosevelt's brain trust.

Another to use the Witte method of early education, Leo Wiener, later translated Witte's book into English. His son, Norbert, became another child prodigy, entering Tufts College at age eleven, Harvard at fifteen, and eventually achieving eminence as a mathematician and founder of the science of cybernetics.

But it is to a contemporary of Norbert Wiener's at Harvard, William Sidis, that we must turn for the most startling comment on the reach of the human brain. The boy's father, Dr. Boris Sidis, a psychologist and psychiatrist, lectured at Harvard at the turn of the century. Dr. Sidis contended that youngsters were capable of understanding complex matters at a very early age. And when his wife bore him a son in 1898, the father began a daring experiment to prove his assertion. The baby, William James Sidis (named after the distinguished American philosopher, William James, a friend of the father), was subjected to a program of instruction, the intensity of which has probably never been equalled. By six months of age, Willie (as he was known) had been taught his letters. At two years, he could speak, read, and spell at an adult level. Before he was three, the youngster had worked out a formula for determining on which day of the week any historical date fell (the formula was patented and became widely used). At four years of age, Willie was typing letters to adult friends in excellent English or French.

At age six, Willie Sidis entered a Boston elementary school. By noon he had been promoted to Grade 3. The child graduated from the school five months later. The following year, Willie went through an entire high-school curriculum in six weeks (much of his time there was spent helping teachers assess mathematics-examination papers).

When Willie applied for entrance to Harvard, the committee thought he should take a few years off to let his personality catch up with his intellect; so the youngster filled in the next three years at home reading works in French, Armenian, Russian, Turkish, Greek, Latin, German, and, of course, English.

Willie was finally admitted to Harvard when he was eleven. The boy immediately gained top marks and that same year, by invitation, lectured at the Harvard Mathematical Society on the four-dimensional regular figures: a subject so profound that few of the mathematicians present could understand what he was talking about. We will return to William Sidis' story in another chapter; its conclusion illustrates an important point.

Alerted to the great potential of the human brain, and accepting, for the moment, the belief that children's intellectual growth can easily be stimulated, wouldn't it be fitting and proper of us, if not to create super-geniuses, to at least raise our children's intelligence a little higher than the unflatteringly low level we erroneously label "normal"? After all, "normal" children, possessing as they do an IQ of 100 or thereabouts – and standing midpoint between a moron (IQ 50 to 70) and a genius (IQ 140) – merely represent the degree of intellectual neglect, or mental retardation, our uninformed society will still rise to applaud. Sidis' father may well have earned the criticism he eventually received for the high-pressure tuition that permitted his son to read adult material by age two. But should all other parents be congratulated for ignoring their children's education so completely that their youngsters can't read even *children's* books by age *six*?

Taking Stock

As we have seen, astonishing intellectual goals are reached when parents shut their ears to the mutterings of "can't," "impossible," and "unheard-of," and proceed to stimulate their youngsters' thinking. Then, the seemingly impossible becomes possible. Children read, write, spell, and compute at a level of excellence we wrongly term *adult* while they are still preschoolers. What might the proper adult level of intellectual performance be? Some hint is found in a report on the adult Willie Sidis. A man who sat opposite Sidis at a cafeteria table was ostensibly correcting galley proofs for a book on Einstein's theory of relativity, which at that time was little understood by mathematicians; but his actions were, in reality, a ruse calculated to enlist Sidis's help. Sidis, merely an "uninvited" observer, studied the equations from across the table, upside-down, then pointed to a number and said, "Excuse me, but they've made a mistake here. This should be a six, not a seven." On checking the original manuscript for the book, the man found Sidis to be right.

The difference in IQ rating between the average person (IQ 100) and an imbecile (IQ 25 to 50) is 50 to 75 points. However, the difference in IQ between the average person and, say, John Stuart Mill (reckoned as having an IQ of 200) is 100 points. We are faced, therefore, with unflattering evidence that most people are better suited to the company of an imbecile than to that of a brilliant person: an observation that gives an impressive ring to the words of William James, who wrote:

Compared with what we ought to be, we are only half awake. We are making use of only a small part of our physical and mental resources. Stating the thing broadly, the human individual thus lives far within his limits. He possesses powers of various sorts which he habitually fails to use.

We might like to think that J.S. Mill had been touched by a divine hand and, because of it, had risen to a level of intelligence unattainable by others. But in thinking so, we'd invite the ghostly wrath of Mill's father. When young John was about to leave the environment of his home for the first time, the father thought the boy had better be prepared for this new experience. Mill describes the conversation thus:

> I remember the very place in Hyde Park where, in my fourteenth year, on the eve of leaving my father's house for a long absence, he told me that I should find, as I got acquainted with new people, that I had been taught many things which youths of my age did not commonly know; and that many persons would be disposed to talk to me of this, and to compliment me upon it. What other things he said on this topic I remember very imperfectly; but he wound up by saying, that whatever I knew more than others, could not be ascribed to any merit in me, but to the very unusual advantage which had fallen to my lot, of having a father who was able to teach me, and willing to give the necessary trouble and time; that it was no matter of praise to me, if I knew more than those who had not had a similar advantage, but the deepest disgrace to me if I did not.

Norbert Wiener's father was equally emphatic on this matter. In the son's own words:

> My father had reiterated that my success, if indeed I had had any genuine success, was not so much a result of any superior ability on my part as of his training. This opinion he had expressed in print in various articles and interviews. He claimed that I was a most average boy who had been brought to a high level of accomplishment by the merit of his teaching and by that merit alone.

In one article, the father had said:

> I am convinced that it is the training to which we must attribute the results secured with [my children]. It is nonsense to say, as some people do, that [they] are unusually gifted children. They are nothing of the sort. If they know more than other children of their age, it is because they have been trained differently.

And the parents of W.J. Sidis denied with equal heat that their son had been born with any exceptional abilities, insisting that any normal child, similarly taught, would emulate their son's achievements.

A major force for the continuing belief that intelligence is inherited is an ignorance of the several – sometimes surprising – influences that promote high intelligence. The word *gifted*, often applied to intellectually advanced individuals, unfortunately suggests a mysterious origin for high intelligence. But *gifted* is merely a label, and like many labels – *indigestion*, for example – *gifted* gives no hint to the forces or circumstances that produced the condition. Worse, the term *gifted* tends to discourage any inquiry into what caused the giftedness when, in fact, those influences in a home that promote high intelligence aren't difficult to spot when one knows what to look for. As we will see in Chapter 6, merely teaching a preschooler to read greatly stimulates neural growth in the brain. But other influences in and around the home have been found to promote intellectual growth. Let's consider what those influences are, bearing in mind, first, that there are exceptions to any rule, and second, that high intelligence sometimes results from a combination of stimulating forces.

Early Isolation

Being an only child, or being separated in age by several years from brothers and sisters, or having few playmates – either due to a dearth of neighborhood children or because of an inability to attract and sustain friendships – prompts resourcefulness in puzzling out how to occupy one's time, what to make, what to build, what to try (a challenge that, with the advent of television, is unfortunately less often faced than the TV set). Such children, obliged to exercise their imagination, their creativity, and their inventiveness, not surprisingly become more imaginative, creative, and inventive.

Studies show that first-born children are more likely to develop higher intelligence than later brothers and sisters. One reason given is that the first child in the home, being a novelty, attracts more parental interest and attention than later children. Parents are more likely to engage the first-born in play and in conversation, and to encourage the youngster to speak. But when, two or three years later, the next child arrives, the parents' enthusiasm may be less. Also, the new child is obliged to share parental time and attention with another child; a sharing that the older child was never taxed with. And, as each successive child arrives, parental time and attention are further divided; while the oldest child, obliged now to begin assuming household responsibilities, receives, by virtue of this new challenge, even more intellectual stimulation.

Being a later brother or sister does not, however, automatically doom a child to low intelligence. As we saw in the case of Francis Galton, having an older sibling can provide a child with an additional teacher. Another child who may have benefited from the company of older siblings was Benjamin Franklin, youngest son among seventeen children. Or did Franklin instead benefit from still another intellectually stimulating influence, namely, the early encounter with difficult *but not insurmountable* problems, problems that required considerable mental effort for their solution? That is our next consideration.

Early Disadvantage

We learn to solve problems by meeting problems and solving them. Not surprisingly, youngsters who face problems early in life – provided that the problems are not so onerous as to overwhelm, discourage, or defeat them – gain an early faith in their ability to solve problems; a faith that permits them to face new and more difficult problems with courage. Those whose confidence springs from a series of challenges and victories sometimes acquire a degree of determination and persistence that is less often seen in others who lead more comfortable, less complicated lives.

Benjamin Franklin, with but two years of schooling, worked as soap-maker, candle-maker, cutler, and finally, printer before running away from home at age sixteen. Franklin rose from poverty and obscurity to become an internationally famous statesman. Would Franklin – or Abraham Lincoln or Booker T. Washington, for that matter – have risen to greatness had they not faced and solved the problems that accompany early poverty? Would Helen Keller have become an eminent scholar had she not been initially obliged to overcome the disadvantages of blindness and deafness? No one will ever know. Yet who can deny that the most powerful prompter to human effort and industry is not personal advantage and comfort but adversity and discomfort?

Victor and Mildred Goertzel report, in *Cradles of Eminence*, that three-quarters of the 400 eminent people they studied had been troubled as children by poverty or by broken or upset homes or by some other hardship. In fact, one-quarter of their subjects suffered physical handicaps, and many of them regarded their eventual triumphs as the direct result of an urge to compensate for their disability.

Can we wonder that individuals who are burdened early and compelled by circumstance to improve their lot sometimes acquire sufficient self-discipline, moral strength, and problem-solving ability to be able to solve not only their own problems, but those of a nation?

And they become leaders.

Early Advantage

Homes where learning is valued, where many books are found, where academic or intellectual matters are discussed: these, too, are homes that will stimulate children's interest in learning. Consider for a moment the old-world equivalent of such a home, where, wealth aside, the heir's most valuable legacy wasn't quality of blood, but lucidity of thought and quality of speech. When Thomas Macaulay was four years old, a maid-servant accidentally spilled hot coffee on his legs. Asked about his condition a little later, the youngster replied: "Thank you, Madam, the agony is abated." Such a response, though comical by today's standards, nevertheless reveals the uncommonly high level of conversation to which the child had been exposed. And, as we will see in Chapter 9, early rich vocabulary and early high intelligence are inseparable. We should hardly be surprised that Macaulay became an eminent scholar and statesman. Nor should we wonder, considering the stimulating conversations Bertrand Russell, Winston Churchill, and Franklin Roosevelt were privy to—and occasionally engaged in as children with knowledgeable occupants of, and knowledgeable visitors to, their homes—that they each achieved high intelligence and greatness without any parental plan of early education such as is set forth in this book. The goal here is to give *all* youngsters an advantage similar to that which, in the past, was available to few.

As we have now seen, the qualities that permit individuals to solve life's problems may be learned in various ways: by parental plan, by early solitude, by early disadvantage, and, conversely, by early advantage. But what, exactly, *are* these special qualities that serve their possessors so well? In their book *Lessons from Childhood*, R.S. and C.M. Illingworth concluded, after studying the lives of 450 outstanding men and women, that high intelligence, perseverance, and the ability to get along with others were the qualities they most commonly possessed. The researchers found, too, that their 450 eminent people showed an unusually high level of originality and creativity.

High intelligence, perseverance, social desirability, and creativity are qualities that make *children*—no less than adults—eminent, and, possibly more important, permit youngsters to enjoy more fully the delights of childhood and youth. Let's consider, now, practical ways in which the first of these desirable qualities—high intelligence—can be developed.

4

Teaching a Newborn Child

Traditionally, the newborn infant has been regarded as a starting point in education or in conditioning, the embryo and fetus being thought to be free from external influence. But recent discoveries prove this assumption wrong. We now know that four weeks after conception, the embryo is already able to perform an impressive number of reflex actions and, three weeks later, is able to move its head, arms, and trunk easily. Presuming to teach a newborn child is, therefore, like starting a baseball game with the batter already on first base.

Beginning somewhere between the sixth and twelfth week of its existence, the embryo gradually becomes aware of sound: a developing sense that, in the ensuing months, will permit the unborn to distinguish between the sound of the mother's heartbeat and her stomach rumblings, the mother's voice and the voices of those she talks to (or listens to, as in the case of TV), and the sound of music. Recent experiments show that unborn children possess considerable musical discrimination. Vivaldi and Mozart are much appreciated, whereas Brahms, Beethoven, and all forms of rock music appear to be generally irritating. Moreover, fetuses not only listen to music, they sometimes respond by moving in tempo with the orchestra.

Facial expressions begin about the sixteenth week of pregnancy. The fetus has, by then, a discriminating taste and is able to discern any change in flavor of the amniotic fluid. And by this time, the fetus is sensitive to light. If the mother's stomach is exposed to a bright light, the fetus will startle and perhaps look away.

Any unhealthy habit possessed by the mother poses a potential danger to the embryo and fetus. Researchers have discovered that an excessive intake by the mother of caffeine, nicotine, or alcohol can cause irreversible damage to the unborn child, sometimes even killing it. Consider just the effect of nicotine. According to a study conducted by the School of Medicine, University of California at San Diego, nicotine decreases bloodflow to the uterus during pregnancy and can cause premature birth, stunted growth of the embryo, or hyperactivity in the born child – if, indeed, it survives. The U.S. Public Health Service estimates that about 4600 children are stillborn each year as a result of the mothers' smoking.

A post-natal activity that is apparently fashioned during the prenatal period is sleep. The fetus tends to sleep when the mother sleeps and, after birth, tends to perpetuate the mother's sleep pattern of the preceding months. We begin to see that what happens after birth is, in many ways, a mere continuation or an elaboration of what has already happened in the womb; and that the mind of the newborn child is anything but a *tabula rasa* – blank slate. Much scribbling has already taken place upon it, for better or worse, by the time the child is born. Education of the unborn is therefore not a science-fiction notion, but a reality; the mother's habits, predilections, nature, and environment weave a characteristic cloth that will not only distinguish her newborn, but confine him. As better ways are devised to detect, monitor, and assess the embryo's responses, we may find that everything the mother eats, drinks, breathes, hears, or otherwise senses tends to work a subtle influence on the unborn's eventual capabilities, favoring this or that personality trait, physical advantage, or learning aptitude.

But we may learn, too, that many supposed hurts inflicted before and during birth can be largely cancelled out after birth by love and wise management: a belief prompted by observing the great variation that can occur in children's natures depending upon who is caring for them. Some children, seen to be models of good behavior – happy, cooperative, and loveable – under the warm, but consistently firm, guidance of a professional caregiver, can sometimes become uncooperative, fretful complainers, yielding reluctantly only to bribe under the parents' inept management. If parents can work so great a deterioration in a wholesome child's nature by ineptness, then wisdom and love can conceivably work an equally striking improvement of the disadvantages arising from adverse experiences suffered in the womb or during birth.

Isn't this exactly what was seen in Chapter 2, when, by wise guidance, a mother raised her brain-damaged son's intelligence not merely to average, but higher than average?

The Newborn Child

Traditionally, parents have waited until children learned to talk before giving much thought to their education. We routinely defer instruction because of children's apparent all-round ineptitude. But physical ineptitude and intellectual ineptitude are different matters; and by ignoring this distinction we easily make a wrong judgment of the child's total capability. A baby's jerky head movements, his inability to control tongue, fingers, bladder – practically everything – can lead us to assume wrongly that the child's physical inabilities are matched by – or worse, are the result of – his intellectual inabilities: much in the way that the jerky, uncontrolled movements of a spastic easily invite a wrong judgment about the spastic's intelligence.

Viewed differently, then, the baby, struggling to learn the workings of an extremely complex machine – the human body – is really no clumsier than you or I would be if called upon to operate, without prior instruction, a crane, a bulldozer, or just the family car. Granted, the infant seems inept and incompetent when trying to learn how to energize this or that group of muscles and coordinate their combined tensions for a desired effect, but children's clumsy use of their bodies isn't reason to assume they have clumsy use of their brains. We don't know *what* the infant brain is capable of. Only now and then do researchers get some inkling. Dr. Lewis P. Lipsitt at Brown University found that even day-old infants are able to discriminate between a variety of sounds and smells. Dr. Lipsitt also found that the babies quickly became conditioned by those sounds and smells, and were soon able to respond appropriately: a response that was seen to be clearly intellectual rather than physical. Obviously, we have to be careful in presuming to know what the limits of early intellectual ability might be.

Dangerous "Experts"

One prominent researcher in the field of epistemology – the science that deals with how knowledge is acquired – has concluded from his lifelong experimentation with children that a five-month-old infant won't be able to retrieve a hidden object unless some part of it is left showing. Another internationally acclaimed authority on early childhood behavior states that, from his many years of observing and assessing children, babies won't be able to roll over unaided much before five or five and a half months. Yet Jason Kauppinen, whose education is described in Chapter 17, was able to locate a totally hidden object at age one month, and was able to roll over unaided at age three months. How was he able to do this? *His mother taught him how.*

The means of assessing children's potential abilities are still very primitive and often unreliable. In one much-used test of childhood understanding, a child is shown a tall, narrow container and a short, wide one. Both containers are capable of holding the same volume of liquid, which is demonstrated to the child by pouring the liquid back and forth between the vessels. Yet when the child is asked which vessel holds more, the child will invariably pick the taller vessel. He will, researchers have found, until he reaches the age of about eight.

What the researchers fail to realize is that they are merely engaging the youngster in a vocabulary test or, if you prefer, a game of words: a game in which the child can only lose because his understanding of words is primitive and imprecise in comparison with an adult's. "Which holds more?" The trick word here is *more*. To an adult, the word *more* has fairly precise limits, which children cannot know until they are taught.

In a child's limited experience, height is frequently a condition for *more*. For example, an ice-cream cone holding two scoops of ice cream contains more ice cream than one with a single scoop. And it is higher! And when a child builds a tower of blocks, more blocks go into the higher tower than a lower tower. Indeed, of the various types of mounds children encounter, be they mounds of earth, toys, or foods, the higher the mound, the more items are in it.

Children learn the meaning of *more* at a very early age, requesting, as they often do, more of this or that food, or imploring the parent to persist in some playful activity with them. However, children encounter the words *tall* and *height* (and their respective meanings) much later. Until a child learns at what point these words take over duties he thought were covered by the umbrella term *more*, the child will continue to think that anything *higher* is also *more*. In short, for a child, *more* has a quality of height built into it. But teach a child the meaning of *tall* or *height*, and the child will gain, as a bonus, a more precise understanding of the word *more*. If vocabulary enrichment of this sort takes place early, as was done with John Stuart Mill, Lord Kelvin, Norbert Wiener, and all the others, children will correctly assess that the taller vessel doesn't hold more, and they will do so long before the age of eight. Children's understanding of every scientific concept hinges on their understanding of words. Tragically, researchers fail to mention that their findings, surmises, and conclusions hold only so long as parents sit back and contribute no more to their youngsters' early education than the researchers and parents contributed to the children they studied.

Happy, Healthy Babies

The first condition for early learning isn't intellectual stimulation, but the absence of problems. Fretting, unhappy babies can't think about anything other than what is bothering them. If educating activities are to catch their interest, babies have to be healthy and happy.

Keeping babies healthy is, properly, the subject matter for an entire book, and the reader probably owns such a book already. By following the advice given in that book on matters of diet, medication, and hygiene, parents will have a potentially good pupil for the program to be described. But good food and good health don't guarantee that a baby will be *happy*; and without a contented and happy pupil, education can be both difficult and slow. Let's begin, therefore, by considering a few matters that help keep infants happy.

Newborn babies sleep most of the time, so a parent's first concern is to ensure that the infant sleeps peacefully. Babies sometimes cry even when placed in what would be for adults an ideal sleep-inducing situation: a dark, quiet room. Why? Because newborn children have never experienced quiet before. As we have learned, babies are accustomed, during their long occupancy of the womb, to hearing many of the sounds heard by the mother. And even when mothers themselves experience quiet, babies continue to hear the mothers' heartbeat: a sound that is found to soothe children even after they are born. Dr. Hajime Murooka, professor of gynecology at the Nippon Medical University, Tokyo, discovered that of 403 infants who stopped crying after hearing the amplified sound of a human heartbeat, 161 went straight to sleep in an average of forty-one seconds. Another study, in America, showed that infants not only cried less when exposed to the sound of a heartbeat, they gained weight.

A ticking clock has long been thought to calm a restive child. However, Dr. Murooka found the ticking of a metronome to be ineffective. Holding an infant close to the mother's heart, thought by some to have a soothing effect, was found to be only 40 per cent effective, in comparison with the 84 per cent effectiveness of the amplified heart sound.

Dr. Murooka has produced a record entitled *Lullaby of the Womb*. The record, which presents the sound of a human heartbeat as heard in the uterus of a woman eight months pregnant, quiets infants as if by magic. A second portion of the record diminishes children's reliance on the pacifying sound of a heartbeat by combining the heart sound with soothing classical music.

Side 2 of the record takes the baby another step away from dependency on the heart sound by presenting soothing music minus the heartbeat accompaniment: music that, incidentally, will soothe children of all ages, even adults.

The old-fashioned rocking cradle has long been known to pacify a fretful infant. But only recently has an acceptable reason been offered for its pacifying effect. The gentle rocking motion is now thought to soothe a baby because the motion approximates the semi-weightless movement the youngster enjoyed for so long in the amniotic fluid of the womb. A rocking cradle is, therefore, a better choice of bed for an infant than the common crib, particularly during the infant's first few months of life.

When the baby is awake, a pacifier or dummy nipple is often useful for keeping him in good spirits. Dentists say that pacifiers don't endanger correct teeth formation.

T.L.C.

An important condition for a baby's contentment is, of course, plenty of tender loving care. This raises the question of how often, and how quickly, parents should respond to a child's cry, and whether, in fact, there is a risk of spoiling a child by being too responsive.

A study conducted at Johns Hopkins University showed that prompt response to an infant's cry helped form a stronger bond between parent and child. And developmental psychologist Dr. Burton White believes that a child will not be spoiled during the first seven months no matter how promptly or repeatedly parents respond. Letting a baby "cry it out" is not seen to be either desirable or beneficial. (The entire question of affection and its great influence on child development is dealt with in Chapter 16.)

VISION

Once a child's contentment has been secured – or at least made more likely – the next requisite for early learning is that the baby be able to observe his surroundings easily. During the first few months, babies, even when lying on their backs, tend to face one way or the other. Babies' eyes have, at this stage, only a short depth of focus, but that isn't reason to obstruct their view. Indeed, a child would be disadvantaged under such conditions. In a study conducted at the Gesellschaft für Rationelle Psychologie, in Munich, thirty-eight children were raised in special Plexiglas cribs, which permitted unobstructed viewing in all directions. The children demonstrated remarkably quick mental development in comparison with others who had been raised in conventional cribs. For your baby, therefore, beds and travel conveyances having high sides are unsuitable. If the child's crib or cradle has bars, and therefore requires padding to protect the baby's head, wrap each bar individually with padding instead of surrounding the cradle with a high protective mat.

Newborn infants have limited control of their eye muscles. By studying infant eye movement with television monitoring cameras, researchers are able to determine how well babies can track objects with their eyes and focus on these objects. But this doesn't tell us how much infants are able to discern. To appreciate the difference between focusing and discerning, the reader need only fix his or her gaze on some object. This object will be seen sharply. Other objects situated within a 180-degree arc from side to side and about 160 degrees from top to bottom will also be seen, but not sharply. They will be merely discerned, those objects nearest the point of focus being more sharply discerned. If six-inch-high letters of the alphabet are positioned eighteen inches from our eyes and 20 degrees off the point of focus, the letters can easily be distinguished, one from the other, without shifting our gaze from the focal point.

We have no reason to believe that an infant's unfocused vision is any less discerning than an adult's unfocused vision. Indeed, this would

Figure 1: *A suspended tissue box makes an inexpensive mobile.*

explain how infants merely days old can be engaged in hand-eye coordination activities such as is described in Chapter 17.

MOBILES

A mobile is, as the name implies, something that moves. Almost anything suspended from the ceiling might serve as a mobile: a Christmas decoration, a soup ladle, even an empty detergent container. Turning slowly, as suspended objects will, mobiles can provide for your baby a continually fascinating center of interest. A mobile should be positioned where your child's head is turned most of the time. And if he has *two* favorite positions, you might hang up a second mobile for those occasions when the head is turned in the second direction.

A better type of mobile is one to which you can attach decorations. For example, an empty facial-tissue box can be decorated – each side differently – with felt-nib markers, pieces of foil, wrapping paper, pictures or patterns cut from magazines, bottle tops, buttons, ribbons, or almost anything colorful and contrasting in tone. Keep the mobile bright. If your pictures show real objects – say, a human face (and a large front view of a human face is, incidentally, recommended) – make sure the baby will see it right-way-up in his side-reclining position. If you construct several such mobiles, you will be able to change them every few days and increase your youngster's interest.

Alternatively, an aquarium might be positioned beside the crib at the baby's eye level to provide a constantly changing spectacle. Or, less costly, a large clear plastic bagful of water containing goldfish might be slung over the side of the crib.

47

A more important consideration at this time is to keep the *baby* mobile. Babies need to be handled and moved about frequently. By placing the youngster in a semi-reclining chair – with head support, of course – you will be able to take the child on your round of household duties.

A baby sling of the sort that gives head support is an even better type of carrier. The infant, when positioned at the front (almost back at home plate, as it were), enjoys the best of all possible worlds. The baby delights in the warmth of body contact with the mother, and the movement of the mother's body – the same movement the child experienced for so many months before birth – is completely natural and comforting to him.

A little-known benefit children gain by frequent movement is brain development. A child who is carried a great deal sees, in consequence, a moving world; and this condition has been found to exert a great influence on brain growth. Professor Boris Klosovskii, chief of neurosurgery at the Academy of Medical Sciences of the U.S.S.R., has performed experiments in movement with newly born puppies and kittens. One group of animals – the control group – was kept in a confined area. A second group of animals – the experimental group – was similarly confined but their enclosure was mounted on a slowly rotating turntable. This latter group saw, in consequence, a constantly moving world.

Beginning on the tenth day of the experiment (and ending on the nineteenth), Professor Klosovskii began sacrificing the animals in pairs, one control animal and one experimental animal, to note any difference in brain growth. The brain cells in the experimental animals – those that had been slowly rotated – were found to be from 22.8 to 35.0 per cent larger and more mature than those of the other group. (But note: the professor didn't plunk his animals in front of a television set. No experiments have been conducted to determine whether a small-sized two-dimensional *representation* of movement – as is provided by a TV screen – stimulates brain growth.)

A body sling is probably the best way to keep your youngster moving. And the final benefits in using the sling are yours: not only will you have a contented child, you will have both hands free for other activities.

CRIB TOYS

The best toys for use in the crib are those that can't roll or fall beyond the baby's reach. Toys that hang on strings from a bar across the top of the crib aren't really suitable because they bounce away and escape the child's unsure grasp. A good grasping array consists of toys that are semi-rigidly supported: toys that give slightly under the child's grasp and return to their original position when released.

Very little skill is needed to attach a toy to a string stretched from one side of the crib, at the top, to the other side at the top; then attach either the toy or the string, by means of a second string, to the baby's sleeve or sock. The child will soon learn to his delight that by moving a particular limb he can make the toy move. (There appear to have been no studies so far to determine how the choice of arm might dispose a child to eventual left- or right-handedness.)

The child will soon enjoy toys he can drop over the side of his crib and haul back up again by an attached string. If the objects rattle or make some sort of noise when they are dropped, all the better.

LANGUAGE

Children are able to understand the meaning of words long before they themselves can speak these words, though we don't know how early children can be taught to understand spoken words, nor how early they can be taught to talk. Note use of the word *taught*. The common misunderstanding is that both of these events — understanding speech and speaking — occur in their own good time, as if parents played no role in hastening or retarding their arrival.

You will recall, from Chapter 3, how Pastor Witte began his son's education, how he carried young Karl around the home naming the rooms and the various objects found in each. The same technique was used by the fathers of Lord Kelvin, Norbert Wiener, Adolph Berle, and William Sidis. In 1952, Aaron Stern used this same technique to educate his daughter Edith, a child who eventually entered college at twelve and became a mathematics instructor at Michigan State University at age fifteen. Like Pastor Witte, Aaron Stern openly declared his intention to raise a person of superior quality. In his book, *The Making of a Genius*, Stern writes, "I did not plan that Edith should be only a normal child; rather I publicly stated that I shall make her a superior human being, able to make a lasting contribution to the world. When I invited friends to see her I told them bluntly that she was destined to become 'a genius.'"

Aaron Stern began his daughter's intellectual growth by building her "listening" vocabulary. Conversation in the Stern home, as in the Witte home, was correct, slow, and spoken, when possible, while facing the child. Young Edith was taught the names of items around the home, and at five months of age, she could recognize 400 words: objects that she identified by gesture. By eleven months, Edith had been taught not only to speak, but to speak in simple sentence form. And by twenty-three months she had been taught to read.

Is it really so surprising that a child should quickly acquire a working knowledge of our language when, as we have seen from the findings at Brown University, infants can distinguish between various sounds on the first day of life? Children will understand 400 words at age five months, or no words at all, depending on what parents trouble to teach them. And children will be able to speak in sentence form, as Edith could, at age eleven months, or speak not at all, depending, again, on what contribution parents make to their children's early education. Furthermore, children will possess an IQ of 200, as Edith does today, or something less, depending, again, on what effort parents make to stimulate brain growth. *It is parents who largely establish the limits of their youngsters' capabilities.*

Your Language Program

Most parents won't want to go to the great lengths that Witte and Stern did to educate their children — nor need they do so to achieve striking results. Parents need merely capitalize more fully on those moments when they and their youngsters are together anyway.

Where should you start? With words. *Immerse* the baby in words. This is more easily accomplished if the child is carried around in a body sling. Talk, talk, talk to the child; the more the better. If you're not talkative by nature, *pretend* you are. Take the child on your round of household chores and chat with him. Give him a rundown on the weather, or news from around the neighborhood, or an update on the activities of your neighbors. Why not tell him the story of your life? If your child isn't transported around the home in a sling, then chatting to him is all the more important, for talking is a sort of touch beyond reach.

Sing to the child occasionally. If you don't know the words to a song, "la-la-la" will do nicely. And talk or sing to the infant while feeding him, burping him, bathing him, and while changing his diapers. The mother's voice, heard by the infant for so long in the womb, provides a natural reassuring sound for the baby. Chatting to a baby, therefore, helps to ensure his contentment.

THE LISTENING VOCABULARY

The most difficult word a child learns to recognize is the *first* one. Each word after that is easier. To understand the first word, a child must recognize that there is a relationship between voiced sounds and objects. Learning the first word can be made simple or difficult for the infant by the way the word is taught.

Begin by introducing your baby to the sounds of specific words: the names of objects he sees daily. The child's bath could serve as a good starting point. Say *bath* several times just before placing the infant in the water, and again several times while he is in it. Eventually, the child will associate the sound of the word *bath* with the pleasant experience of warm water, and he will show, by his enthusiasm, and perhaps by a glance at the bath, that he knows the word has some connection with bathing.

When teaching the child to recognize a word, don't obscure its sound by burying the word among other words: "Would Marigold like her bath now?" or "Isn't it nice to have a bath?" Neither of these sounds like *bath* at all. The child would have to be a wizard to isolate the sound of *bath* amid the jumble of other sounds. Similarly, don't teach "Winston's hat" or "That's a ball"; just teach *hat* and *ball*.

Continue with the names of other objects the child sees frequently: *diaper*, *spoon*, *sponge*, *powder*, and so on. Once a child's listening vocabulary is started (don't expect it to happen overnight, though), you will be able to enlarge his vocabulary easily if you observe a few simple rules:

1. Speak each word slowly, clearly, and loudly, while attracting the child's attention to the object with your hand, or while holding the object in your hand. Repeat the procedure a few times each day.
2. Teach a child only nouns; that is, the names of things he sees. Other parts of speech can be taught later when the child begins to form sentences.
3. Add new words one at a time and only when the child can easily identify all preceding words. Nothing slows learning as much as confusion (for adults and babies alike).
4. Avoid teaching, close together in time, objects of similar size or similar shape, or words having similar sounds: for example, *dog* and *doll*, or *doll* and *wall*.
5. Avoid teaching, close together in time, items situated near each other, or objects that are part of – or might be considered part of – some other item: for example, after teaching *hand*, let time elapse before teaching *fingers*. Similarly, let time elapse between teaching *wall* and *window*, the latter being, properly, a *part* of the wall.
6. Teach the names of only those objects the youngster sees often: objects that form part of the child's daily life.
7. Keep a list of the words you teach and review them often.

As children gain a listening vocabulary, parents' conversations and observations will begin to make more sense to them. Moreover, the exercise of learning – stimulating, as it does, neural growth in the brain – is therefore equipping the youngster with far more than language skill.

Your child can soon learn the pleasure of being read to. The fact that he won't understand what you are reading isn't important. Sit the youngster on your lap so he can see the text and the pictures while you read. Several benefits are gained by reading to a child. First, reading stories aloud permits parents to talk to their youngster without having to invent stories or conversation. Second, reading provides moments of warm, physical contact with the child. Furthermore, books become, in this way, pleasantly associated with parental attention and affection.

Lastly, the child will begin to see a relationship between your spoken words and the lines of small black symbols on the page: a connection that will more quickly become obvious to him if you run your finger along beneath the words being read; this, in turn, will familiarize the youngster with the practice of left-to-right reading – often a stumbling block when children begin learning to read.

Those books you read to your child at this time will probably become the first books he reads to himself (see Chapter 7), so select the books carefully. The print should be large, and there should be plenty of space between each line of text. Avoid books with wolves, witches, or other frightening villains. Though a child might be able to tolerate these grim characters while perched safely on your lap, he won't want to encounter them alone when he begins reading on his own.

Talking

A child's ability to speak, and to express his thoughts, comes as a great relief to parents. At last, the child can tell what ails him, can tell whether his stomach or head hurts, can tell whether he has been well treated by others in the parents' absence, and can describe other important matters. Speech is preceded by babbling, a babble that is often well-lubricated with saliva (deaf infants, however, don't babble; they merely make strange sounds). Encourage your infant to babble; babbling is the natural prelude to speech.

Developmental psychologists can predict, within rough limits, the age at which your child will be able to sit, crawl, walk with assistance, and, finally, to walk unaided. And there isn't much that parents can do to hasten these developments. Bone, muscle, and connective tissue must grow first; and parents have limited control over such growth. But when developmental psychologists predict the age at which a child will begin talking – and some *do* make such predictions – their guess is based on the premise that parents will not assist, encourage, or teach their youngster any more than parents have traditionally done.

You alone control the conditions that quicken or slow your child's ability to speak. The age at which he acquires this ability will depend on how much time you spend talking to him, building his listening vocabulary, and encouraging him to make pre-speech sounds (nonsense sound combinations that children manufacture before they speak proper words).

Your child will be able to understand many spoken words long before he acquires sufficient muscle skill to get his own lips and tongue around those words. To make talking simpler for your child, encourage him to speak just single-syllable words first: *ma, da, toe, soap, tub, hat,* and so on; then, gradually, introduce some two-syllable words: *baby, water.*

Children's first attempts at speech are, of course, amusing. *Water* becomes *wawa; juice* becomes *oos,* and so on. There is always a temptation to use the child's own simplified version of English when speaking to him. Resist the temptation. To ask a child if he would like some wawa is to present a distorted model for him to copy. When the child says *wawa*, treat his effort as a great accomplishment, while reinforcing the correct pronunciation of the word.

"Yes, good, good, Martin said *water*. Good boy, Martin. Well, let's get some *water* then. *Water*, yes, *water*. Here we are, Martin. *Water*."

"Oos."

"Oh, it's *juice* you want. My mistake. Good boy. Martin can say *juice*. Well now. *Juice*. Here we are, Martin. *Juice*. Drink your *juice*."

"Wawa."

The parents of Karl Witte and Edith Stern scrupulously avoided baby talk when teaching their children to speak: a condition that was commonly imposed in the early education of many eminent people. Terms such as *bow-wow, doggie, pussycat, tum-tum,* and *go bye-bye* can only hinder correct speech development.

The Playpen

When children begin crawling, at about eight months of age, many new learning opportunities become available to them – provided, of course, the youngsters aren't confined to a playpen. There are probably times when the use of a playpen makes sense, but playpens all too easily become infant jails. If you have a pet you wish to keep away from the baby, use of a playpen might be justified, although, in fairness to your heir, the animal and the child should take turns inside the playpen.

Children's safety is, naturally, of first importance. But instead of confining a youngster to a playpen, install protective devices around the home that shield him from danger while still allowing him to explore: a folding gate across any open stairwell, a self-closing mechanism on any door leading to a staircase; fittings – obtainable wherever items for infants are sold – to seal electrical outlets and to enclose any outlets to which appliances must remain plugged; and latches that prevent the opening of doors and drawers – though the child should be allowed to open cupboards that don't contain dangerous or breakable objects.

Look around the home and ask yourself what objects the child could tip over, capsize, break, or cause to fall on top of him. If you live higher than ground level, make the balcony childproof. Could the child squeeze between the balcony railings? Remember, most explanations of home accidents involving children begin with the words: "Who'd have thought he would...." It is a parent's duty to consider even the most improbable of accidents.

Babies musn't be scolded for being inquisitive or exploratory. To do so would stifle those very attributes that stimulate intellectual growth. If the crawling infant encounters something he could damage, or something that could harm him, then the parent hasn't properly childproofed the home. Granted, childproofing the home is an inconvenience, but a child must have certain freedom of movement as a right if he is to be considered anything more than a favored prisoner around the home.

Some authorities believe that learning to crawl plays an important role in the development of intelligence and that use of a wheeled walker can only thwart intellectual growth. Without doubt, a walker fills no traditional or natural role in human locomotion; and unquestionably, the less time babies spend in cribs, seats, walkers, and other devices, the more likely they are to practice crawling. Wise parents will therefore place their youngster on a blanket on the floor occasionally and encourage him to crawl.

Different babies move themselves along the floor in different ways. Various forms of crawling are thought to exert different influences on brain growth; the all-fours crawl (with opposite hands and knees moving forward at almost the same time) is considered superior to, say, shifting forward with the legs while in a sitting position.

When children eventually learn to climb, then walk, by clinging to furniture, a new range of potential dangers must be foreseen and guarded against. And, once toddling unaided, the highly mobile child has even greater opportunity to harm himself. The word *no* has its uses. Though *no*, unfortunately, offers a child no reason for halting an action (an explanation the child probably wouldn't understand anyway), *no* can stop an infant from touching certain objects that are difficult to shield from him (without building fences around the home): the record player, for example, particularly when it is in operation; the heating elements of the stove and their dials. *No* can also discourage a youngster from throwing toys or other objects, or floating them in the toilet bowl, from eating soap or toothpaste, and so on.

As soon as your child is able to understand simple explanations, he should, of course, be told the reason for not engaging in this or that activity. He must learn that certain items can harm him or can be easily broken by him. At that time, *no* should be accompanied by an explanation. By giving reasons for your restrictions, you encourage reasoning: a process that raises intelligence.

The Magic of Color

Color has been found to exert great influence on children's intellectual performance. A three-year study conducted at the Gesellschaft für Rationelle Psychologie, in Munich, showed that when children were tested in rooms painted their favorite color, or in colors they thought were beautiful—yellow, yellow-green, orange, or light blue—their average IQ score rose as much as 12 points; but when they were tested in rooms painted "ugly" colors – white, black, brown – their average IQ score dropped 14 points.

Children who played in the "beautiful" rooms with "beautifully" colored blocks and toys during an eighteen-month period scored 25 IQ points higher than children who had played in a conventional kindergarten setting. The researchers also found that "beautiful" settings increased children's general alertness and creativity. Another finding: in the orange room, friendliness and cooperation rose by 53 per cent, and irritability and hostility declined by 12 per cent.

If you aren't able to paint the walls of your youngster's room or play area with brilliant colors, attach large pieces of inexpensive cloth or cardboard to the walls. For example, six or eight large corrugated boxes might be opened out and flattened. These could then be painted – matt paint is best – with a color of your child's choice and attached to the wall. Or you might paint each flattened box a different color and overlap them slightly on the wall to give an abstract mural design. Covering large areas of the wall in this inexpensive way will produce the desired stimulating effect for your child.

Speaking in Sentences

As a child's speech vocabulary grows, he will begin to form two-word sentences such as *Too hot, More please, All gone.* Eventually, three-word sentences will follow: *Where Daddy go?, Dolly not here, Haven't got it;* gradually progressing to correct, simple sentences, such as *I like peanut butter, My daddy's a policeman, What's your name?*

As mentioned earlier, Edith Stern was able to speak in sentence form at eleven months of age. Any parent who puts a little heart into a program of early education might expect his child to be speaking in sentences by eighteen months of age, though some children will, of course, acquire this ability earlier, others later. Some youngsters experience great difficulty in learning to speak; and for reasons that aren't understood, they are usually boys. Albert Einstein, for example, was slow to talk. Einstein's speech was so backward at age four that his parents thought he might be mentally retarded. Even at age nine, he lacked skill in speaking. Unfortunately, we will never know whether – or how much – Einstein's speech problems might have been avoided by the procedures described here.

Encouraging a child to speak must always be a cheerful procedure; for what profit would there be if a youngster, in learning to speak, lost a care-free, smiling parent? A baby's first need is a warm, loving parent.

5

Convenience Education

Some parents have more time than others to devote to their children's education. Some mothers must place their baby, almost from birth, in the care of others on workdays. Other mothers can stay home for two, three, or more years with their child or children. To serve the greatest number of parents, we will put a hypothetical limit on the length of time a mother can stay home with her youngster. We'll assume, therefore, that you, the reader, have been staying home with your baby for a year and a half, but that now circumstances oblige you to return to your job. We will further assume that your youngster, now speaking in sentence form, will be spending the weekdays at a day-care center.

Choosing a suitable day-care center for your child justifies considerable thought. After all, the day-care environment can reinforce and supplement your home-education program, or can undermine it. (Choice of a suitable day-care center or nursery school is covered in Chapter 18.)

Filling Conversational Voids

As we saw in Chapter 3, some parents have gone to great lengths to give their children a superior education. But most parents today simply haven't time for an "immersion" training program. The program to be presented here gives children an education of great worth, yet does so with a minimum of parental time and effort. The program will also help parents cope more easily with three potentially trying situations they encounter with children: while eating, driving, and shopping.

Couples usually establish a mealtime routine long before their first child arrives and learns to talk. Perhaps they watch TV. Perhaps they discuss their health, state of the bank account, the car, the neighborhood, and other matters. The arrival of a third voice at the table—the child's— prompts, in many homes, little change in mealtime conversation. The child is largely ignored; the parents either talk around him, or talk not at all, and the child, thrilled at having finally acquired the ability to speak, is obliged to initiate conversation by whatever means he can.

The necessity of talking to a child at mealtimes can be avoided, of course, by switching on the TV set. But children need to talk if they are going to advance intellectually. Watching TV, therefore, can represent an educational step backward. But if parents *teach* during mealtimes by engaging children in educating activities, not only will youngsters learn, parents will establish a level of conversation they themselves will find at least tolerable, and possibly enjoyable. This doesn't mean that mealtimes need be given over entirely to a youngster's education, merely that brief educating activities at mealtimes can make the occasion more enjoyable for everyone.

Keeping a child occupied while driving can sometimes be difficult, too. But if the parent doesn't initiate some form of activity, the child will initiate his own. And if his creation takes the form of nonsense chatter or complaints, the parent will be less able to cope with the problems of driving: a hazardous situation, especially when driving conditions are bad. Engaging a youngster in educating activities while driving, therefore, can make a trip safer.

Shopping with a youngster is possibly less trying for parents than eating and driving, but here, too, educational pastimes can keep a child occupied, and an occupied child is less likely to be restless or demanding.

Parents can, of course, engage their youngster in educating activities any time they wish, but to serve the needs of the majority, we will assume that parents must, for one reason or another, limit their instruction to mealtimes, to moments when they are traveling with their child – by car, by bus, or simply when walking – and while shopping with their child. Even this three-terminal input, as it were, will provide an exceptionally rich educational program for your child. There is, however, still another possible input that offers interesting perquisites; and that is low-cost private tutors.

Educational Babysitters

Hiring tutors isn't new. Wealthy families have traditionally hired tutors to teach their children, if, indeed, they didn't own slaves, as the Romans did, to fill the role of teacher. Fortunately, neither wealth nor slaves are needed today to secure private tutors. Low-cost tutors are abundant, though I had to stumble on the source by fluke.

Several years ago I advertised for someone to tidy our apartment, but without success. Cleaning ladies being apparently rare, if not extinct, I finally arranged for a teenager to wash the dishes and tidy up. She did so, usually before supper, while I coached my daughters, just turned three and four, with their reading. However, after a few days of this arrangement – days of watching the dinnerware gradually being reduced to shards – the thought occurred to me that if the teenager coached the children, I could look after the household chores myself. So we switched jobs.

The new division of duties yielded an unexpected bonus. The children worked with the tutor in the bedroom, their voices muffled by the bedroom door: a pleasant turn that permitted me to prepare supper in relative peace. Those who have never prepared a meal while arbitrating claims and grievances, and hearing the past, present, and future concerns of two small, voluble gripers in loud, shrill voices can hardly guess the euphoria that relative silence brings.

Savoring this new, agreeable situation, I lost no time in launching a tutor hunt. As a result, no fewer than twenty-three girls, aged nine to sixteen, contributed to our educational program during the next six years. When the teaching time was eventually switched to after supper, the tutors began to fill the double role of tutor-nanny, engaging the children first in educational activities, then supervising their bath and toothbrushing (a dual service that may hold special appeal for other single parents).

In households where both parents work outside the home, the advantages of hiring tutors will be obvious. Even in homes where the mother spends all day at home with one or more youngsters, a temporary release from the children might be welcome. Moreover, children often show greater enthusiasm for learning when taught by an outsider. One mother attempted for years to teach her son to swim. When an outsider took on the task, the child was swimming in a month.

How can you find suitable tutors? A popular babysitter is a good bet. Girls who are in demand as babysitters have probably proved themselves to be reliable and responsible. They are also more likely to be relaxed and comfortable with children. Boys make good babysitters, too, though if your child is female, you may prefer to entrust her care to a girl rather than a boy. Children who do well in school are potentially good tutors. They may already have been called upon in school to help slower pupils, or they may have been "borrowed" by teachers of lower grades to help as teaching monitors. Ask youngsters in your neighborhood for the names of top students in their class, then speak to those children about your teaching needs. One suitable tutor will often lead you to another because the child's best friend is likely to have the same qualities you are looking for in a tutor.

What should these qualities be? John Locke's description of the ideal tutor, in 1693, provides a good reference point:

Seek out somebody that may know how discreetly to frame his manners: place him in hands where you may, as much as possible, secure his innocence, cherish and nurse up the good, and gently correct and weed out any bad inclinations, and settle in him good habits. This is the main point, and this being provided for, *learning* may be had into the bargain.*

My own children's tutors were chosen for their intelligence, their wholesome nature, and their good manners; they therefore taught a great deal just by their example. Though the tutors followed my teaching guidelines, they sometimes introduced ideas of their own. And they were encouraged to do so. One tutor composed a short play and coached the children in memorizing and speaking a few lines. The same tutor, a nine-year-old, taught them a folk dance and brought a polished stone to show them. Another tutor taught the children how to curtsy. Another taught them the rules for telling time by committing those rules to a song. The same tutor taught the children to read aloud with expression.

How much should you pay tutors? The law of supply and demand will influence the cost; but generally the rate will depend on the tutor's age. If a tutor is old enough to babysit, then he or she is accustomed to receiving a certain amount per hour for sitting and watching television, completing homework, or just lounging. So, for teaching, the tutor should get more than the going rate for babysitting. You might also want to pay a consideration for the distance he or she travels for each brief teaching session (which might run about forty-five minutes).

Children who are too young to babysit (perhaps younger than age twelve) will particularly welcome the opportunity to earn money; and they can be hired for the prevailing babysitting rate or possibly less. By finding suitable nine-, ten-, and eleven-year-olds (some of whom have a genius for charming younger children), parents can secure excellent tuition for their youngsters at low cost. Over the years I paid amounts that ranged from slightly less than the babysitting rate—for nine- and ten-year-olds—up to double the babysitting rate for the best of the older tutors.

More important than a tutor's age is his or her maturity. What degree of maturity will be needed to guide your child? That will depend on your youngster's age and temperament. Preschool-age children can usually be managed easily by a nine- or ten-year-old, but for *two* preschoolers, an older tutor will be needed. From my own experience, children who are six, seven, or eight years old are more effectively taught by youngsters who more nearly fill the image of an adult; say, age fifteen or sixteen.

How many tutors will you need? That depends on how many times a week you want your child taught by others. Much of the pleasure of teaching can be lost if a tutor teaches more than twice a week. Better,

---

Some Thoughts Concerning Education, John Locke (New York, 1964)

therefore, to have several tutors. Our own program, which sometimes ran seven sessions a week, provided work for as many as six tutors at a time.

Pick times for your child's instruction that suit both you and the tutors: after school, or after supper, and perhaps on Saturday and Sunday mornings. Instruction shouldn't be scheduled for any time your child would normally engage in some favorite activity, because this could arouse resentment for your teaching program.

If tutors are old enough to babysit too, parents will be able to run errands, shop, or visit a neighbor while their children are being taught. If your youngster attends school, and both you and your spouse work, the tutor, given a key to the home, could engage the child in educational pastimes after school until one parent arrives home.

All these activities—teaching while eating, while traveling, while shopping, and by young tutors—are what I call convenience education; educating, yes, but in a manner that makes life easier for parents.

Let's consider now what subjects your child should be taught. John Locke said: "When he can talk, 'tis time he should learn to read." Locke felt, however, that children should be taught to read in a fun-filled way: and that's the approach we will use.

6

Teaching Children to Read

In North America, reading instruction has traditionally taken place about four years after children learn to speak. But this delay is neither necessary nor desirable. As soon as children can understand the meaning of voiced words, they can be taught to interpret those same words in printed form. There are several good reasons for – and some little-guessed advantages gained by – teaching youngsters to read long before the age of six.

The first and most obvious advantage is the enjoyment reading adds to childhood. Children who can read signs, labels, and posters find greater pleasure in shopping excursions than children who can't read. Indeed, in an urban environment, surrounded as we are by print, the ability to read is more important than the ability to smell.

Another important benefit: children who can read books aren't dependent upon the presence and mood of an adult for the reading of their favorite stories. Nor are they wholly dependent upon TV viewing for their entertainment (which averages, according to an A.C. Nielsen survey, 23.5 hours a week for children younger than five). And the reading of bedtime stories becomes more enjoyable for youngsters when they can take turns with their parents in reading.

Another advantage, often overlooked, is that the world becomes a safer place for children who can interpret the meaning of FIRE ESCAPE, DANGER, BEWARE OF DOG, POISON, and similar warnings.

Early readers gain a valuable academic advantage, as well. Two studies, one in Oakland, California, one in New York, showed that children who could read before starting school remained ahead of the other children all the way up to Grade 6 (at which time the study ended). Not surprisingly, early readers usually excel in whatever field they choose. A study of 400 eminent men and women described in *Cradles of Eminence* led the researchers to report that, as children, the 400 showed their greatest superiority in reading ability, and that many of them were already reading by age four.

Teaching children to read permits youngsters to enlarge their vocabularies more easily; and as we will see in Chapter 9, size of vocabulary and intelligence are closely related. In a study of twelve children having IQs of 180 or higher, Dr. Leta Hollingworth found they had been taught to read at an average age of three; the latest age being four years, five months. And Lewis Terman and Melita Oden noted, in comparing eighty-one children who had IQs of 170 or higher, that their youngsters began reading between the ages of three and five.

Perhaps these children were able to read early simply because they were bright to begin with. Not so. *All* bright children don't read early. Yet *all* children, bright or not, learn to read early if their parents take the trouble to teach them. Moreover, learning to read has been found to stimulate neural growth in the brain. So greatly has reading ability been found to influence general intellectual ability, in fact, that mentally retarded children at the Institutes for the Achievement of Human Potential, in Philadelphia, when taught to read early, often reach a level of intelligence *higher* than that of normal children. How, then, might early reading ability affect *normal* children? It might just result in an intellect on the order of Lord Kelvin or Norbert Wiener. Farfetched? Consider the following case.

An Early Start

A few years ago, an associate, when told of the proven link between early reading ability and scholastic achievement, expressed astonishment, then related this story. His wife, who had never taught children before, began teaching their son, John, to read at the age of one year, nine months. The mother hadn't considered the boy's eventual school performance; she simply wanted the youngster to begin enjoying books early. The family was in the process of moving at the time and their books were in storage. Undaunted, the mother began teaching John from a liquor price list that happened to be handy, so the boy's reading began with *rum, port, vodka,* and similar beverages.

Young John soon graduated from liquids, and by the time he entered Grade 1, he had read about 250 books. The mother taught John no other academic subject during those preschool years, and during his school years she neither coached him nor offered him incentives for good performance. How *was* his performance? Pretty good. John won more than a dozen silver cups for high achievement. In primary school, he received the highest mark ever given for overall performance. And in college, he was awarded the highest mark ever given for a graduation thesis in honors economics.

Several universities – Yale, Northwestern, University of Toronto, University of Pennsylvania, University of Wisconsin, among them – courted the boy with offers of scholarships and bursaries to attract him for post-graduate studies. Today, John is a professor of economics at a major university. His father estimates that John received, over the years, about twenty-five thousand dollars in various educational grants.

But the most impressive part of the story was the look of surprise that preceded its telling. The parents had simply never connected, in their minds, the son's superb academic performance with his early reading ability. John's case seems to suggest that when children are taught to read early, and then encouraged to read, they become locked, as if on automatic pilot, to a flight path leading to academic excellence. If we want a second example of unplanned school success, we need only turn to John's younger sister, Kathryn, who was also taught to read early. Kathryn's IQ is in the genius range, and her school record was spectacular.

The final compelling reason for teaching preschoolers to read is that there isn't any valid reason for denying them so simple yet so valuable a skill, especially when there is no guarantee youngsters will be well taught when they eventually begin school. The child who can already read on entering Grade 1 is the only child in the class to whom literacy is assured if the teacher is burdened with a slow, faulty reading program; or if an otherwise good reading program is burdened with a slow, faulty teacher.

A number of strange ideas have gripped the educational community on the matter of reading, and the parent who isn't versed in the subject can be overwhelmed by seemingly impressive, but spurious, arguments. Let's look at a few popular misconceptions about reading that are held in high regard by some educators.

Reading Readiness

The notion that children must demonstrate certain types of behavior or possess certain skills before they can benefit from reading instruction is a popular idea based on a strange logic. Tests that supposedly indicate "reading readiness," or lack of it, merely indicate which children will probably be able to cope, and which children will not, when they are taught with a slow, complicated, and unsuitable reading program. Children who score low on such tests are said to be unready for reading, and their reading instruction is delayed when it should, instead, be simplified. In short, the philosophy behind reading readiness is that a delay in instruction is the best solution to an elementary teaching challenge. When a quick, uncomplicated, and completely suitable reading method is used for children's instruction, *all* children, even those who fail reading-readiness tests—even *infants!*—soon learn to read.

The senselessness of basing predictions on the results of reading-readiness tests is seen in the case of my youngest daughter, who at age two years, nine months, would have failed every reading-readiness test in existence. Yet she was reading two months later (described in *Teach Your Child to Read in 60 Days*). Two *years* later, in kindergarten, she failed a reading-readiness test, managing, in fact, to solve only one problem out of four though she was then reading at approximately a Grade 5 level. (Tested seven months later at the Special Education Branch of the Ottawa Board of Education with the Gray Oral Reading Test, the child, then entering Grade 1, was found to be reading at a Grade 6 level.)

How can a reading child fail a reading-readiness test? By inattention to detail. In one test, children are asked to detect small differences in illustrations. Drawings of a house, a gingerbread man, a rabbit, and a pig might be shown, one beneath the other down one side of a sheet of paper. Beside the house, and running across the page, would be three more houses. But some detail would be missing from each of these houses. One house might have a window and the chimney missing; another might have the door missing and have no smoke issuing from the chimney; the third might have two windows and a doorknob missing. Similarly, the gingerbread man, the rabbit, and the pig would each be accompanied by three similar figures with various parts missing. Children are asked to detect and draw in with a pencil the missing parts. To whatever extent children fail to notice the missing parts, so they are considered to be unready for reading.

Related to the "readiness" notion is the belief that children will teach themselves to read if they are really interested in reading, and cases have been reported of preschoolers supposedly having done so. But what is invariably meant is that parents have taught their youngsters to read *without intending to*. In other words, the parents didn't plan a program of instruction; they had no desire to teach; and they had no reason to believe – or even suspect – the activities they engaged in with their youngster, or questions they answered for the child, would result in the child's learning to read. But *intention* doesn't necessarily have anything to do with success in teaching (all teachers *intend* to teach, but not all succeed). Seated on the parent's knee, a child is usually able to view the text being read. If the parent moves a finger along beneath the words while reading and reads the same short story often, the child may eventually memorize the text and learn to identify each spoken word with the appropriate printed one. For some children, this small amount of guidance is apparently sufficient to give them a weak grasp of reading, a grasp the children can then strengthen by asking questions of the parent, or of a relative, or neighbor, or of an older child, perhaps in the course of playing school.

A California study of preschool readers found that though thirty-eight children had supposedly taught themselves to read, none had really done so; the children had, instead, picked up the clues to reading mainly by asking questions. But just because *some* children are able to figure out how to read with a minimum of unintended instruction isn't reason to expect *all* preschoolers to do the same.

The Sound of Print

We read partly with our eyes and partly with our ears. And once this fact is recognized, teaching children to read becomes a simple operation. Limericks provide irrefutable proof that our ears play a major role in reading. Consider one composed by George Vaill, retired secretary of Yale University.

> The bustard's an exquisite fowl
> With minimal reason to growl:
>   He escapes what would be
>   Illegitimacy
> By grace of a fortunate vowel.

Because we hear the rhyming and meter in our heads, limericks are just as enjoyable when we read them silently as when we read them aloud.

When reading, adults assign sounds to letters with great speed. The rules governing the sound of letters – singly or in combination – are sufficiently consistent that even misspelled words are identifiable so long as the substituted spelling is consistent with other letter-sound combinations. Prove it to yourself. What words are represented by *phyre, aiker, gnayl, lofe, kawmycks,* and *gnewed*?

The difference between skillful readers and poor readers is that skillful readers know the letter-sound code and can use it easily. The only time adults might ever notice their skill with the code is when they are obliged to give voice to names they have never seen or heard before – names such as Thredsborg, Crandelman, and Givsner. Readers of this book will be able to utter these sequences of printed letters because – and *only* because – they have a good understanding of the letter code. This same skill permits the literate person to give voice to words that he has never heard before: *disproportionableness*, and the jawbreaker *anti-interdenominationalistically*.

Teaching children to read, therefore, consists of little more than teaching them the letter-sound combinations, then encouraging youngsters to use this knowledge many times until they can decode words with speed and precision, as you and I do. By such exercise, children gain the equivalent of a "third ear," one that permits them to hear print.

Critics of the letter-sound system of reading claim that English pronunciation is too irregular to establish rules for letter sounds, often pointing to the various sounds that can be represented by the letters *ough*, as in *bough, bought, rough, cough, through.* But the consistency with which the *ough* combination of letters is seized upon to illustrate the inconsistency of our language is testimony itself to the absence of any other letter family having similarly erratic pronunciation.

Granted, there *are* irregularities in the English language, and assuredly, these irregularities could confuse a child if we thoughtlessly paraded all the variations and exceptions before the child's bewildered gaze. Who among us didn't mispronounce one or other of *viscount, yacht, island, magician,* or *epitome* the first time we encountered these words in print? But we muddled through, because about 85 per cent of our language is entirely consistent with letter-sound rules we have all learned — learned, it should be noted, *not* by reciting rules, but by actually using the language. Of these rules, some are easier than others to learn. By introducing the easier letter-sound combinations to children first and forgetting about the exceptions, we can quickly give youngsters an understanding of the mechanics of reading. And when children see the magical effect produced by letters, and when they gain rudimentary skill in interpreting letter-sound values, we can gradually begin to introduce the variations and exceptions.

Of the several ways children might be taught to read, most are either a letter-sound (or phonic) method, or a whole-word (or look-say) method, or a mixture of the two called "language experience": a method that can vary greatly from classroom to classroom. The phonic method, when correctly used, has no equal for speed and ease of learning. *All* children learn to read well by the phonic method. When, however, the phonic code is ineptly taught — as it is in many classrooms — the results can be as bad as when the other methods are used. The Reading Reform Foundation has coined the term "phony phonics" to describe the practice of inept letter-code instruction.

The next chapter presents a step-by-step reading program that may take two, three, or more months to complete. Most of the other chapters in the book contain at least some material that suits non-readers equally well as it suits readers — including, strangely enough, Chapter 8, "Encouraging the Habit of Reading." Parents who don't intend to teach their child to read immediately, or whose child can already read, may proceed with that material.

7

How To Teach Your Child To Read

Before starting to teach your child to read, study this entire chapter. Some matters mentioned later in the chapter will apply equally well to the beginning of your reading program.

In some homes, the parents alone will teach reading. In other homes, tutors will help. And in some homes, tutors may run the entire program. In the instruction that follows, the parent is seen as the sole teacher. Other parents, who will be depending on the help of tutors, can interpret the text accordingly, guiding their tutors, and providing them with the lettered material – or, indeed, simply handing tutors this book, supplying them with the basic materials, and letting the tutors look after the lettering themselves.

A Two-thousand-year-old Error

Though children are commonly taught the alphabet – and, indeed, even taught a song to make memorizing it easier – knowing the names of the letters (ay, bee, see) only serves to confuse children when they begin learning to read. This teaching error, which dates back to Greek and Roman days, has caused the unjust punishment of an incalculable number of children. Through the ages, schoolchildren were exhaustively drilled for a year or so in reciting the alphabet. Then, when they still proved unable to read, they were flogged for being obstinate by teachers who were themselves ignorant of the fact that there is little connection between the *names* of the letters and the ability to read. Today, children's television programs and schoolteachers alike naively perpetuate the teaching blunder.

To read, children need first know how to speak, and second how to use the letter code. Learning the letter-sound code and knowing how to use it is easier for children if they are first taught to distinguish between the sounds heard in speech. Adults sometimes aren't aware that almost all spoken words are made up of more than one sound. For example, the word *cat* is a combination of three sounds: the throat-clearing sound of the *c* (a sort of "kuh" sound, but without grunt or voice given to the "uh" part), the voiced sound of *a*, and finally, the tongue-palate sound of *t* (simply the sound of air escaping with no voiced accompaniment).

Communicating with a Child

Another error we easily make when instructing a child is to use words the child doesn't understand. For example, the question "Can you think of another word that begins with the sound 'kuh'?" is meaningless to a child who doesn't understand the meaning of *another*, *word*, *begins*, or *sound*. The question might as well be asked in Gaelic.

Be extremely careful, therefore, to avoid using words that will confuse your child. Scrutinize the instructions that follow for words your child may not understand, and either teach him these words or substitute ones he knows.

Speech Sounds and Letter Sounds

Traditionally, the first letter children have been taught is the letter A. There is, however, no inherent "firstness" to A. Our purpose is better served here if the letter C is the first one taught. Show your child the letter C on page 69 and tell him this shape tells us to make the throat-clearing sound (but not necessarily using the words *shape* or *sound* in your instruction), a sort of "kuh" sound, but without grunt or voice being given to the "uh" part. Just say, "This tells us to say 'kuh,' Edwina." Encourage the child to produce this sound while tracing her finger around the shape of the letter a few times. Never refer to the letter by its name (which sounds like "see"). Refer to it merely by the "kuh" sound. If your child is already familiar with this figure – perhaps from watching television – and has already learned to call it by name ("see"), then you will have to explain that the *names* of the shapes and their *sounds* are two different things (and you may now be obliged to teach the words *name, sound*, and *different*). Explain that though one animal is named a cat, it doesn't say "cat," but "meow." Similarly, though certain shapes have been given the names "ay," "bee," "see," "dee," and so on, the shapes "say" other sounds when they are used in words (and you may now have to teach *word*).

Generally, the easiest single sound for children to distinguish or isolate in a spoken word is the beginning sound of the word. Quiz your youngster on words that start with C. "What sound does *car* begin with, Dexter?" He isn't likely to know, so make the sound for him, pointing out, in turn, that the large C tells us to make that same sound. Have your child repeat the sound. "What sound does *cow* start with?" He probably won't know, so make the sound for him and have him repeat it. "Nice going; you're doing fine. What sound does *cat* begin with?" Again, he probably won't

68

CAT
PNE
UIO

Figure 2: *The letters here and on the following two pages are used to help children learn letters in preparation for reading.*

SBH

MG

LRD

FKW

VJX

YZQ

know, so tell him and perhaps go back to *car*. But now slowly *stutter* the beginning sound to help him: "What sound does *c-c-c-car* start with?" He might be able to isolate the sound, but don't count on it. Have him produce the stuttered version of the word. Proceed similarly with *cow, cat, crib, cuddle, caterpillar, candy,* and the names of any relatives, friends, or neighbors whose names begin with the hard C sound.

Make a duplicate of the letter C using a wide felt-tip pen or brush and clip it to the sun visor of your car. At mealtimes, prop up, or fix to the wall, the large C, and draw the child's attention to items that begin with the C sound. "What sound does *c-c-c-cup* begin with, Dexter? And what about *c-c-c-can*?" Bring items to the table that complement your exercises in sound isolation: a camera, a candle, a can-opener. Or simply introduce appropriate words: *cowboy, carpet, curtain*, and so forth.

Identification of C might even become a mealtime game. Ask the youngster to try to find Cs on packages, cartons, and cans (a suitable game, too, when shopping at the supermarket); or bring a newspaper to the table and let him locate Cs in the headlines.

You may be surprised at the difficulty a child can have in detecting the beginning sound of words. The problems children face when learning to read are more clearly seen if we imagine ourselves suddenly thrust into a society that uses sound symbols different from our own. Told that the symbol ✛ represents the hard C sound, we wouldn't have much difficulty spotting two such symbols in a sign at the supermarket (Fig. 3)—a simple task because we have, in the past, compared *billions* of symbols. (You will, in fact, make about 500,000 such comparisons while reading

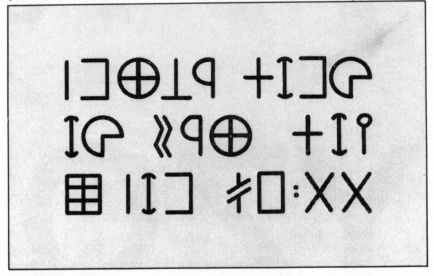

Figure 3: *Can you read this? Imagine how hard reading is for a child.*

72

this book). The child who has singled out the shape of C and associated a sound with it only one or two hundred times must be excused for not possessing anywhere near your skill or mine in comparing shapes. We must therefore demonstrate monumental patience, exercise prodigious restraint, and lavish infinite praise and affection when teaching youngsters to read. (Incidentally, the sign says: FRESH CORN ON THE COB 6 FOR $1.00).

Encourage your child, and be patient. Never show concern or disappointment (even though you might sometimes feel it) when he fumbles words. Instead, express delight and be quick to compliment your youngster when he succeeds in isolating a sound. And if you occasionally seem to "jump out of your skin" with surprise and delight, he'll think the exercise is lots of fun.

Your child should develop three distinct and separate skills before a second letter is introduced:

1. he should be able to easily produce the correct sound for C when he encounters it;
2. he should be able to detect the C sound in spoken words beginning with that sound;
3. he should be able to pick out Cs in print.

These skills may take your child a week or two to acquire, depending on how much time you spend encouraging him to try.

When your child can easily locate Cs in print, can sound them correctly, and can identify spoken words that begin with the C sound, show him the letter A on page 69 and have him trace around its shape several times with his finger while making the A sound (as heard in *rat*, not *rate*).

Make a duplicate of the letter A, clip it to the sun visor in the car and, while driving, quiz your youngster from a list of simple words he knows – or can easily be taught – that begin with this sound: *accident, ambulance, alligator, ant, apple, apartment, animal, ankle, astronaut,* and *axe*. These same words will serve for your mealtime quizzes, too. "What sound does *a-a-a-apple* begin with, Aurora?"

Engage the child in the same activities for A that you engaged her in for C. Be sure not to teach the child the lower-case or "small" a at this time, nor refer to the already learned letter C. When, and only when, the child can associate the correct sound with the symbol A, and can detect the A sound at the beginning of words, and can pick out the As in print, is she ready for the next step.

Having learned two letters now, the child is apt to confuse them, so she needs practice in distinguishing between the two. A game fills this purpose admirably while serving a second important need: that of entertaining the child until she can read books. Then the books themselves will entertain her.

The Egg Carton Game

Games suitable for young children generally combine a minimum of logic with a maximum of repetition and nonsense. The following game fills that description. All you need are a hundred blank business cards (obtainable at any stationers – or use the backs of any old business cards you may have), two dozen pennies (or marbles or poker chips if you prefer), an egg carton, six small pieces of differently colored paper, six bottle caps, glue, and a wide felt-tip marker.

Cut three business cards in half. To each half, stick a small piece of colored paper – a different color on each card – as shown in Figure 5. Place the cards in a soup bowl, face down. Stick a small square of each of these same six colors inside the lid of the egg carton, as has been done in Figure 4.

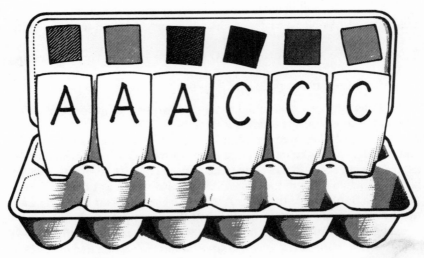

Figure 4: *The Egg Carton game.*

Figure 5: *Cards with different colors.*　　**Figure 6:** *The letters on larger cards.*

Print the letter C on three business cards as shown in Figure 6, and the letter A on three others. Bend the cards slightly at their bottoms and insert them in the back row of the egg carton, as in Figure 4.

Because the counters – which can be coins, marbles, or poker chips – are to be handled in the presence of food, they might be cleaned in bleach before beginning the game. In the course of the game, the counters will be deposited in the various cups of the egg carton. Children like things that rattle or clatter, so place a bottle cap – metal-side-up – in the bottom of each cup of the carton. Now each coin, when deposited, will issue a reassuring click.

Before showing the child the game, review the letters C and A separately. That done, place something – a jar, perhaps – behind the egg carton to hold the lid in an upright position.

The play begins thus: The child takes a card from the soup bowl, finds its matching color inside the lid of the egg carton, deposits a counter in the *front* cup that lines up with that color, and sounds the letter printed on the card in the rear cup. The card he drew is placed to one side. The child then draws another card from the bowl, finds its matching color in the lid of the egg carton, deposits a counter in the appropriate front cup, and sounds the letter in the rear cup.

The game continues in this way until a counter has been placed in each of the six front cups. The child then puts the six colored cards back in the bowl, face down, and, drawing them again one by one, now places counters in the *back* cups, each time sounding the appropriate letter. This time, though, the youngster removes the letter card from the rear cup when he deposits the counter. When all six cards have been removed, the game is over.

It will be obvious to the reader that the child could just as easily have placed counters in the twelve cups without drawing any colored cards. True. The point is, however, that the procedure *looks* important to the child – important "business," as it were – and makes him feel important, too, because he is creating his own chance order of events.

The parent now accepts the six cards from the child as payment for a treat, which may take the form of six raisins, or six peanuts, grapes, cherries, or what have you – but always some food item the child wouldn't normally have expected as part of the meal. Or the six cards might be accepted as payment for some treat to be eaten after supper. Or the item "earned" might be something other than food: a paper figure or doll from a press-out book.

Instead of using colors to distinguish the cards in the soup bowl and on the lid of the egg carton, you might match heads of comic characters, or photos of members of the family, or symbols (if you want to simultaneously teach the child to identify and name stars, circles, squares, rectangles, ovals, and triangles).

The Question of Rewards

The use of rewards is sometimes questioned, so a word on this practice might be in order. Some people believe that giving youngsters rewards is unnecessary, perhaps even degrading, as if one were training an animal. Whether rewards are degrading must remain a matter of opinion. But the *necessity* of rewards is a different matter. Those parents who are fortunate enough to have teaching experience, or who have a knack for fascinating children and turning their attention this way or that, may not need to use rewards. From my own observation, though, rewards are indispensible in the education of children by parents who are pinched for time and lack special skill.

There are, unquestionably, teaching situations where extrinsic or external rewards are neither necessary nor desirable; where, in fact, payment of a reward would condition the learner to devalue the intrinsic pleasure of the activity. But there are, with equal certainty, other situations where quick, pleasant learning will not be achieved without the use of extrinsic reward; particularly in the acquisition of "tool" skills such as reading, writing, and arithmetic. With each, the pupil is required to pass through an initial period when there is little inherent pleasure in the activity. Reading, when it is well taught, has probably the shortest such period.

Those who have given some thought to the matter acknowledge the value of extrinsic rewards in three situations: to engage children in activities that would not normally interest them; to provide children with enough basic skill in a complex subject so they can begin to enjoy the intrinsic satisfactions (as in reading instruction); and to engage children in an activity they have previously avoided. (See "How to Turn Play Into Work," *Psychology Today*, September, 1974, pp. 49–54.)

The questions of *whether* the use of rewards is justified, and if so, for how long it is justified, and what form the rewards should take, will, sensibly, depend on the subject being taught, the circumstances under which the subject is being taught, the skill of the teacher, and the age and temperament of the pupil. No general rule is possible.

Educators argue less about *whether* rewards should be paid than about what *sort* should be paid. Concern is rarely voiced if the reward takes the form of praise or compliment. But very young children are stomach-oriented. And they can't chew compliments. Parents will therefore wisely pay in whatever currency their child values. A point sometimes missed is the fact that reliance on compliments alone as a reward can pose a hazard. The child who continually hears "Clever boy!" or "Clever girl!" is apt to succumb to the belief that he or she really is quite special; whereas the youngster who merely gets a raisin to munch on is spared the ego-building influence of compliment.

The use of rewards here plays an important role while children are gaining skill with the brute mechanics of reading. Gradually, as reading becomes easier and children begin to enjoy the material they read, rewards are discontinued and the content of each book becomes its own reward. (Indeed, when, eight months after the commencement of our own reading program, my daughters were reading fifteen to twenty simple books a week, the reading of those books at bedtime became itself a reward that was conditional upon brushing their teeth.)

The Dunce Puppet

The Reading Game or School Game – whichever you choose to call it for your child – becomes more entertaining and exciting if you introduce a puppet to the game. Children love to crow over the mistakes of an apparently silly person (hence the great popularity of Laurel and Hardy). By giving voice to the puppet and letting him have a turn at the game, he can be made to perform all sorts of outrageous errors that will keep the child amused. If, in addition, the puppet is made to fill the role of braggart, presuming to know everything while actually knowing very little, your youngster will become emotionally caught up in the Reading Game, and he'll clamor to play the game as soon as he sits at the table. The puppet can, thereafter, be made to fill the role of pupil, so that your child – now a teacher – may teach the puppet to read. By the use of rewards and the puppet, the reading program can become so delightful

Figure 7: *The dunce puppet is a useful and entertaining teaching tool.*

for your youngster that playing the game may be made a reward itself, one that is dependent upon some other condition: "Well, eat just that spoonful of spinach, Timothy, then we'll get on with the School Game."

Some parents ask, "How do you work the puppet?" It takes just a little nerve and a little practice. If you have a hand puppet that permits you to open and close the mouth, fine. You'll find, though, that the natural tendency is to close your hand (and the puppet's mouth) when it should be opening. Practice reversing this natural inclination until you can do it easily. Even a puppet with a fixed mouth – or just a teddy bear or some other stuffed animal – can fascinate a child. Children tend to see what they want to (adults, too, perhaps?), so you need only provide a silly voice and sputter out a line of chatter to hold the child's attention. Make sure you look at the puppet when it is "talking," thus directing your child's eyes to the puppet and adding to the impression that it is the puppet speaking, not you.

When your child can easily distinguish between A and C, and can make the appropriate sound for each, the letter T can be brought into the game. Several days before your youngster is to be shown T – or any other new letter – engage him in the exercise of detecting that sound at the beginning of words; in this case words such as *truck, tire, train, taxi, tap, table, television, toy,* and *tongue.* Show your youngster the T on page 69 and have him trace its shape with his finger while making the appropriate sound – sounded not as "tee," but as a voiceless rush of air as the tongue leaves the roof of the mouth. And help him find Ts in the newspaper headlines. Finally, print T on two business cards and substitute these in the game for one A and one C. The six cards in the game will now be two As, two Cs, and two Ts.

When the material used in the egg-carton game is well known to the youngster and you no longer need to watch and correct him, the game might be taken along in the car. With the game positioned on the child's lap, perhaps on a kitchen tray, he will be able to play a couple of games while you drive.

Reading Words

When your youngster can quickly and easily distinguish between the letters C, A, and T, he is then ready to read his first word, *cat.* Print CAT on two cards, and use these cards in the game along with one A, one C, and two Ts.

Don't expect your youngster to immediately see that the blended sounds of C, A, and T compose the stretched-out name of a four-footed creature. Even though the parent points out this obvious (obvious to an adult, that is) fact, the child may fail to see the connection. Don't make a big issue of his puzzlement. The information will eventually click into place on its own.

A child will need plenty of practice in the ritual of left-to-right information gathering before he can easily identify the sound symbols in CAT in a left-to-right order, and not in a right-to-left order. To a child, there is no logic in a one-way-only direction for reading, so don't expect your youngster to become accustomed to left-to-right decoding until he has practiced the procedure a few hundred times. Even then he may have occasional lapses and read backwards. Such errors are completely normal.

One technique that encourages and facilitates left-to-right reading is to cut out and glue the head of some comic character on the left side of the card (Fig. 8). Asked what the funny figure is saying, the child is likely to begin sounding letters nearest the comic head first.

Figure 8: *Cartoon characters placed on the top left corner of cards help children remember to read from left to right.*

Make certain the child sounds each letter in CAT before speaking the entire word. At this stage, we are not so much interested in his learning to read a particular word as in his learning a sounding-out procedure that will soon permit him to figure out, by himself, words he has never seen in print before. Don't, therefore, discourage the child from sounding each letter in a word before reading the entire word. His voiced procedure, then, would be "Kuh, a, tuh – cat," but with the *uh* in "kuh" and the *uh* in "tuh" representing only an escape of air and no voiced sound.

An important rule to observe is to never introduce new material to the game so long as your child is unsure of material already presented. So important is this rule, and so susceptible is the rule to parental oversight, that it deserves repeating: *Never introduce new material to the game so long as your child is unsure of material already presented.*

When your child is easily able to deal with the letters C, A, and T, and with the word CAT, introduce the letter P, sounded not as "pea," but simply as an unvoiced expulsion of air as the lips part. The steps to follow with the letter P are those already used for the letters C, A, and T, and are the same steps to be used for introducing each successive letter.

1. Help the child detect the sound of the letter in words beginning with that letter.
2. Have him trace with his finger the shape of the appropriate letter (on pages 69 to 71) while making the correct sound.
3. Help him to find the letter in printed text – newspaper headlines, perhaps – and sound it properly.

How many times will the child have to play the game to learn the material well? There's no knowing. Children progress at different speeds. Proceed *slowly.* Many parents make the mistake of introducing new letters and words too quickly. *Don't rush.* Just because the child seems to know the material well today doesn't mean he will know it well tomorrow, and if his lapse of memory is coupled with the presentation of new material, his confusion is increased. Give extra time to any material that seems to confuse your youngster.

Children, like adults, don't enjoy activities that make them look dumb. If your youngster's enthusiasm seems to drop, it might be because he is unsure of the material. In this case, hold off. Buoy up the child's self-confidence by bringing back into the game material he knows well. You aren't likely to bore the youngster with old material. Children rarely become bored with being *correct*, especially when it wins them rewards and fun with the silly puppet.

After learning the letter P, your child will be able to read two new words: *cap* and *tap.* But don't – now, or at any time – introduce *two* new items to the game at the same time. This second important rule will help ensure your child's quick progress. If your child doesn't know that a cap is a type of hat, show him one, or show him a picture of someone wearing a cap. Similarly, if there are any other words in Figure 9 that your child doesn't know – for example *wig, van, vessel, fizz* – explain their meaning to him long before they are included in the game.

Print CAP on two cards and let your youngster play the game with these plus two CAT cards and two T cards. When, after several games, he is completely at ease with this material, print TAP on two cards and substitute these for the two T cards.

Figure 9 shows the letters and words that have been learned to this point (down to position 4), and the order in which new letters and new words should be included in the game.

	NEW LETTERS	NEW WORDS		NEW LETTERS	NEW WORDS
1	C		14	G	GUM PIG
2	A		15	L	LEG PAL
3	T	CAT	16	R	RUG CRIB
4	P	CAP TAP	17	D	DROP GLAD
			18	F	FROG PUFF
5	N	CAN PAN	19	K	KISS SINK
6	E	PEN NET	20	W	WING WIG
7	U	CUP NUT	21	V	VAN VESSEL
8	I	TIN PIN	22	J	JUG JUMP
9	O	TOP POT	23	X	FOX FIX
10	S	SIT NUTS	24	Y	YES YOU
11	B	BAT TUB	25	Z	ZOO FIZZ
12	H	HOT HEN	26	QU	QUICK QUEEN
13	M	MOP MAN	27	TH	THIS THAT

Figure 9: *The letters and words at position 4 are those learned up to this point. New letters and words should be added in the order shown.*

Row A, on page 82, shows the six cards as they will now appear in the game. In Row B, two cards – Pair 1 – have been replaced with two new cards bearing N. In Row C, these have been replaced. In Row D, and in

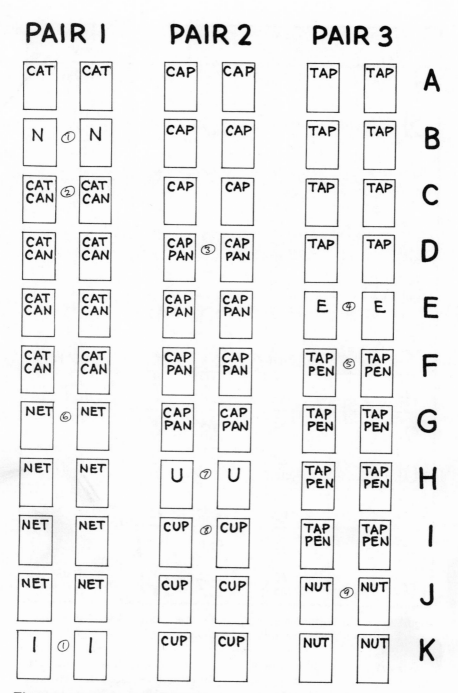

Figure 10: *In each row (A-K), new words or letters are introduced. Row K corresponds to position 8 in Figure 9.*

each successive row through to Row K, two more cards have been replaced.

Row K shows the appearance of cards in the game as the material at position 8 on Figure 9 is about to be introduced. The small encircled numbers on page 82 show the order in which the pairs of cards are changed. Follow this same progression, 1 through 9, when introducing the rest of the material in Figure 9. Teach your child to sound each new letter in the same way it is sounded in the new words that accompany it. Notice that the following letters are *not* accompanied by a voiced sound: S, H, F, K, X ("X" at the end of a word has the sound of "KS"). Be careful not to add a grunted "uh" on the end when sounding N, M, L, R, W, V, Y. And, finally, stop the voiced sound quickly as soon as the tongue or lips make their movement in the letters B, G, D, J. Giving a sound tail to, say, B – as in "buh-h-h" – provides the child with a poor understanding of the B sound.

The four remaining vowels are pure voiced sounds. E is given the sound heard in *pen*, but drawn out: eh-h-h. U is sounded as in *cup*: uh-h-h. I as heard in *tin*, and O as in *hot*, are similarly drawn out.

If, in the course of learning the material down to position 27 on Figure 9, the child prefers to occasionally read words without sounding the individual letters, fine, but *don't* coach him to do so.

If the child wonders why two Ss or two Fs or two Zs are used (in *kiss, vessel, puff,* and *fizz*) when just one of each would seem enough, simply tell him that's the way it is. You will, however, need to point out that two Es and two Os (as in *queen* and *zoo*) combine to form a new sound. Explain the CK combination in *quick* briefly. Just say that the C sound sometimes takes the form of CK. The child need not sound the individual letters in *you*, one of the irregular words in our language.

When cards bearing two words have been removed from the game, they should periodically be brought back into the game for review. Children have a short memory for newly learned material.

How quickly will your youngster learn the material down to Row 27? That depends mainly on how often he plays the game and how well you first teach the letter sounds. If the child plays one or two games at supper time, and a few games each week with tutors, his speed of progress may surprise you. The accelerator is repetition. The more often the child plays the game, the more quickly he will progress.

Your youngster may at some time surprise you by claiming never to have seen a word before, even after having previously read the word dozens of times. Or he may suddenly begin having difficulty reading a word after having read it correctly a hundred or so times. You may also be amazed to find your child reading, without apparent concern, upside-down, or even sideways. The truth is that children sometimes possess astonishing skill for reading in an unconventional manner, and so they see little reason for not doing so. Such deviations are, within limits, completely normal. But if your youngster's progress ever stops, or if he seems to have continuing difficulty in isolating speech sounds, you might have his hearing tested. Or if the youngster has continuing difficulty in distinguishing between smaller versions of letters, you might have his vision tested.

Reading Bingo

When your child has learned the material on Figure 9 down as far as the word BAT (Row 11), you will then be able to engage him in a new educating pastime while driving. Letter the sixteen words he can now read in a grid (Fig. 11) and play Reading Bingo. Prop a list of the sixteen words on top of the dashboard and call them off at random. With the grid set on a tray on his lap, and with a small bowl of peanuts (split in two to prevent rolling) or raisins, the child places an edible item on each word you call out. When he forms a line in any direction, he eats the markers; either those in the winning line or all the markers on the grid. You can alter the winning pattern to any one you choose: the child might be

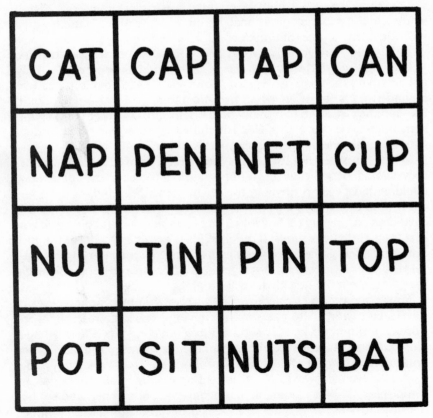

Figure 11: *The Reading Bingo game.*

obliged to fill *two* lines, or perhaps the four corner squares.

Your child's reading ability at this point may be limited to sounding out individual letters—a small step short of proper reading. To help him locate the correct square for any given word on the bingo grid, sound out the letters before you voice the word: to illustrate, "N-n-n, eh-h-h, tuh—net." And, to be certain the child is placing markers in the correct squares (without taking your eyes off the road), have him sound out the letters of each word he places a marker on.

This game can easily be played in the home before supper, thus serving to keep the youngster occupied while the meal is being prepared.

As each new word is learned, it can be lettered on a piece of paper and glued atop the word the child knows best on the grid.

As new letters are learned, many more words *could* be included in the game than those few shown in Figure 9. But adding words to the program might slow a child's progress. Our purpose here is to quickly give the youngster use of the letter code: a skill that will then permit him to pry open the contents of unknown words much in the way that a can-opener would let him discover the contents of unlabeled cans of food. As the child gains skill in using the letter code, he will gradually stop sounding individual letters in a word before reading it. He will instead begin to sound, mentally, the letter sounds he has been sounding orally.

When the child has learned the material down to Row 27, you can begin to teach him the lower-case or "small" letters. The method to be used here reduces confusion to a minimum: of particular concern are the lower-case letters *p*, *q*, *b*, and *d*, which have always puzzled children. Begin by helping the child read the top sentence on page 86.

The use here of an alphabet with serifs (small feet and hats on the letters) will serve to familiarize your child with this typographical detail and will also reduce his confusion between the capital **I** (which appears as I when it hasn't serifs) and the lower case **l** (which appears as I without serifs). You will need to explain that O and W sometimes combine to give us the sound in *brown* (sometimes they don't, as in *show*). The youngster may be surprised to find a different sound being given to O in *over*. Just explain that the letter sometimes stands for this sound, too. The ER combination in *over* should receive just a brief explanation, as should the pronunciation of E in *the*.

That's the Way It Is

Parents shouldn't feel personally accountable for the irregularities in our language. Those irregularities that can be explained easily should be explained; those that can't should be treated with a matter-of-fact "That's the way it is." Keep rules to a minimum, and leave yourself a loophole by saying this letter or that letter "usually," or "often," or "sometimes" sounds in such-and-such a way (depending on which of these words is

A QUICK BROWN FOX JUMPS OVER THE LAZY DOG

b– 1 A QUICK bROWN FOX JUMPS OVER THE LAZY DOG

e– 2 A QUICK bROWN FOX JUMPS OVeR THe LAZY DOG

a– 3 a QUICK bROWN FOX JUMPS OVeR THe LaZY DOG

n– 4 a QUICK bROWn FOX JUMPS OVeR THe LaZY DOG

r– 5 a QUICK brOWn FOX JUMPS over THe LaZY DOG

g– 6 a QUICK brOWn FOX JUMPS over THe Lazy Dog

i– 7 a QUiCK brown FOX JUMPS over THe Lazy Dog

f– 8 a QUiCK brown fox JUMPS over THe Lazy Dog

j– 9 a QUiCK brown fox jUMPS over THe Lazy Dog

q–10 a quiCK brown fox jUMPS over THe Lazy Dog

m–11 a quiCK brown fox jumPS over THe Lazy Dog

t–12 a quick brown fox jumPS over tHe Lazy Dog

l–13 a quick brown fox jumps over tHe lazy Dog

d–14 a quick brown fox jumps over tHe lazy dog

h–15 a quick brown fox jumps over the lazy dog

suitable—and is *understood* by your child). The statement, for example, that the letters *C* and *H* *always* represent the sound heard in *church* is proved wrong in the word *school*. Rules such as "*C* before an *E, I,* or *Y,* has a soft sound, and *G* before an *E, I,* or *Y may* have a soft sound" (if you happen to know such rules) make reading instruction unnecessarily difficult and dull for children.

When your child can read the "quick brown fox" sentence easily, explain to him that there is another way the B sound can be shown. Show your youngster the lower-case b in the second line on page 86, then let him read Sentence 1 a couple of times. The next day, explain that the letter E can appear differently. Show him this new letter form and let him read Sentence 2 a few times. Continue, in this way, explaining a new letter form each day and letting him read the next sentence.

Motivation

If a child loses interest in the reading program, the parent has probably tried to advance too quickly, or has failed to make the program a fun-filled procedure with occasional laughs for the youngster. A parent might then be tempted to coax the youngster to engage in the exercise. Better, though, to take a break from the program or turn it over to one or more tutors.

Edible rewards, though holding little attraction for children during a mealtime reading session, can be a great help to the tutors at other times, bearing in mind, of course, that a child's basic nutritional requirement must never be conditional upon engaging in an educational activity. If tutors teach before supper, the treats will have to be kept small so they don't upset the child's appetite. Junk foods—candy, potato chips, popcorn, corn puffs, sugared cereals, and similar fare—aren't recommended before a meal. If the child's appetite is going to be diminished by pre-supper treats, let them be wholesome foods: peanuts, circles of banana topped with a small dab of peanut butter, or small sections of other fruits.

If tutors teach after supper, sweet foods, and perhaps even some junk food, might be included in the treats before toothbrushing. In our home, the children, at age five and six, would work diligently for a tutor for forty minutes non-stop to collect a prized plateful of treats each: three potato chips, seven corn puffs, two grapes, three animal crackers, a tiny square of cheese, twelve peanuts, one coconut covered date, and four small cereal wafers.

The suitability of this or that food item as a reward will be determined by circumstances. A youngster who eats candy and pastry every day may not be too excited about getting a few peanuts. Also, a five-year-old has different reward preferences than a two-year-old.

A youngster of four or five may welcome a store-in-the-home arrangement that proved popular with other children of that age. Take the youngster out shopping and buy a few small items he would like to work for: gummed stickers of birds or animals, press-out books of dolls and doll clothes, a water-gun, plastic jewelry, model cars, and other items. These objects might then be displayed prominently in the dining area or even attached with clothespins to a line strung up expressly for that purpose. Each time the reading game is played, the child is credited with a certain amount of money toward the purchase of a particular item. The youngster might, in fact, get to keep the twelve pennies used in the egg-carton game as savings toward the desired item. You will find that when a child finally earns a desired toy, he appreciates the item far more than if it had simply been given to him as a gift.

Reading Books

Your child, knowing the upper- and lower-case letters, and having a good basic understanding of the letter-sound code, can now begin learning how other letter combinations – *or, ur, sh, ph,* and so on – are sounded: information that can be gained while reading simple books. A child's first books should be purchased, rather than borrowed, for two reasons: first, parents will then be able to turn the books into reading-instruction texts by adding words to each page, and second, a youngster will enjoy reading these same books months, perhaps even years, later.

Buy books for your child that have the following features: large print, only one or two sentences per page, and plenty of space for you to print in words of your own.

The exact reading procedure to follow will vary with the books selected; but for purposes of illustration, let's suppose the first page of book one contains the sentence: "Two children named Harvey and Gertrude lived near a large forest." If the child doesn't know the meaning of *forest*, explain to him what a forest is, finding somewhere a picture of a forest if an illustration isn't shown in the book. Next, explain, word by word, any new letter combinations in the sentence. The word *two* can't be explained logically. Just tell the child it's a word that doesn't sound the way it looks, and let the matter go at that. In *children*, your youngster meets the CH combination for the first time. Teach the child a couple of words that contain this same combination – perhaps *cheese* and *lunch* – and print these words on the page of the book. In words such as *named*, where the letter A is pronounced differently from the way the child has learned to sound it, simply point out the change needed without getting involved with rules of pronunciation (E at the end of a word...). And when a letter is not pronounced (as in the case of E in *named*), mention this too. "In this word, Chester, we say *ay* instead of *a*, and we don't sound the *eh-h*." In *Harvey*, the youngster encounters the AR combination, so the words *car* and *farm* could be printed in.

Continuing in this way, a simple reading book can be turned into a valuable textbook for the child. As you progress through its pages, you will have less need to insert words because there will be fewer letter combinations your child hasn't already encountered. Include in the egg-carton game those words your child has difficulty with. When he stumbles over a word, don't read it for him. Instead, encourage him to sound out the letters and identify the word for himself. If the youngster guesses at a word, point out to him that he is merely guessing. Make a few wild guesses yourself and have a laugh. Then help him to sound out the letters. Sometimes you may be surprised at the number of words your youngster manages to puzzle out without your help. For example, in sounding the letters of *was*, an unknown word *wass* (rhyming with *pass*) would seem to be indicated; but the child will then alter the sound and, after reading the word a few times, will automatically correct the sound. Children have been seen to puzzle out, without help, the words *someone, nose, ear, water,* and others. You may find your youngster doing the same.

A common mistake parents make when their children begin reading is to try to hurry them into thicker books. Resist the urge. Choose for your child simple books with no more than a couple of hundred words.

Don't discourage your youngster from reading aloud. Only by hearing him read can you tell if he is having problems with his reading. Similarly, don't discourage a child from running his finger along beneath words. He'll discontinue this practice on his own when he no longer finds it reassuring.

When your youngster has read his first dozen books or so, he will be ready for the final procedure that turns a beginning reader into a lover of books, and that is the subject of the next chapter.

8

Encouraging the Habit of Reading

Teaching your child to read doesn't guarantee that he will become a skillful reader. Nor does it guarantee that reading will ever play an important part in your youngster's life. For example, a child who has been taught to read, but who is then allowed to watch unlimited television, may not turn to books very often for entertainment. And the child who reads seldom is unlikely to read skillfully; and lacking ease in reading, he will tend to avoid reading all the more. In this way, a pattern is established that thwarts any improvement in reading.

The question of television and its role in children's education is considered in Chapter 14. For the moment, while we are concerned with improving children's reading, TV will be considered, at worst, a negative influence and, at best, a slow teaching ally. The effectiveness of the procedures described in this chapter will, therefore, be lessened by the amount of TV your child watches.

Let's consider first a child who has been properly taught the letter code and has used his new knowledge repeatedly. We might call this child a beginning reader. Our goal now is to encourage the youngster to use his reading ability and form the *habit* of reading.

The child in question might be a two-year-old who is now reading simple books, or he might be a teenager who rarely reads, one who may, in fact, read little better than the two-year-old. The teaching challenge in each case is different, and each challenge must be dealt with separately. Let's begin with the preschooler.

Words, Words, Words

If a child is to enjoy books, he must first be able to understand the words he encounters in books. Children will understand in printed form only those words they understand in spoken form. The sentence, "They jumped into the canoe and paddled away to the island," is meaningless in either spoken or printed form to a child who doesn't know what a canoe is, or a paddle, or an island, and who doesn't understand the concept of *into*. Obviously, therefore, to enjoy children's books a child must first understand the words he is going to encounter in them. (General vocabulary growth, of great importance for understanding the world at large, is dealt with in the next chapter.)

Seeing a new word several times, as well as hearing it, helps children to learn words quickly; therefore, display each new word your youngster learns where he will see it often. Print a list, in large letters, of the new words and attach the list to the refrigerator or to the wall in the dining area. If the lists are attached in a way that permits their easy removal (as by magnets to the refrigerator), the lists can be taken along with you and clamped to the sun visor while driving.

How quickly will your child's vocabulary grow? That depends on your method of instruction. Attempting to teach a child many words in a short space of time will generally prove to be slow and ineffectual. The child will merely confuse words or forget them. The following method will increase your child's vocabulary at a good rate while minimizing confusion and forgetfulness.

Teach your child a new word before breakfast — perhaps while dressing him. Use the word several times in sentences, and have the child speak the word a few times. During breakfast, refresh the child's memory of the word and introduce him to a second new word — again, having the child repeat the word a few times. Review the two words while driving or walking with the youngster to the day-care center (if you work outside the home), and introduce the child to a third new word. Review the words on the way home from the center in the afternoon. Then, later, either during supper or when the tutor is in charge — review the three words along with all the other words the child has learned during the past five or six days. This means that about eighteen words would be reviewed at some time during the day.

The seventh day after a word is introduced it might be omitted from the suppertime reviews, *but only for a few days*. Then, once again, include the word in the suppertime review, to be then omitted from the review for a slightly longer period; only to be reintroduced yet again to refresh the child's memory. By this method of periodic review, spaced by increasingly longer periods of omission, the child won't forget the words you teach him, nor will he be confused. And three words a day — twenty-one words a week — is excellent progress. You may, in fact, choose to teach just two new words a day — still a good advance.

What words should you begin teaching your youngster? That depends on what words he already knows. If your child benefited from the early instruction prescribed in Chapter 4, he will already have a larger-than-average vocabulary. But let's suppose your child wasn't taught early, and that his or her vocabulary is about the same as that of most eighteen-month-old youngsters.

An important first source of words is the child's body. Does he know the names given to the various parts of the body? Find out. Ask him if he knows what we call this or that body part.

If the child knows the body parts by name, what items does he see or handle daily that he perhaps can't name? Pronounce each new word slowly, distinctly, and repeatedly, asking the child to repeat the word after you each time. Does your youngster know the names of every item on the supper table: the cutlery, the various vessels and receptacles? If so, look around the kitchen; or fetch from the kitchen to the dining area those common objects he might not know the name of: toaster, egg cup, saucepan, ladle, strainer. Though parents can't take along a table in the car for the daily run to the day-care center (if *table* is one of the three words for the day), they *can* take along smaller items for the child to name during the trip.

Parents tend to forget what words children know or don't know. The habit of not naming simple objects for children until a year or so after they first see those objects prompts in parents a practice of chronic deferral. And the child, on reaching the point at which his development is actually being inhibited by this deferral of knowledge, emits no beep to let parents know the moment is at hand for them to produce the long-stored nugget of information.

Laughs are Important

Don't forget to be silly. The teaching of new words each day—and particularly the review of previously learned words—shouldn't be a dreary procedure. How about testing the puppet's memory on some of the words? Have the puppet make some stunningly ridiculous responses. (Use of the puppet is described on page 77.)

And employ surprise! Some item hidden beneath the child's overturned cup or bowl at breakfast is sure to delight him: an eraser, a thimble, a clothespin, a thumbtack, a cork. Show the youngster how the object works and add its name to your word list.

Why not add a touch of showmanship to your program? "Well, Begonia, just wait until you see what's under your cereal bowl this morning. No, I can't tell you because then it wouldn't be a surprise, would it? But just wait 'til you see it!" Such a procedure might speed the dressing operation or brighten your daughter's early-morning spirits if she tends to be grumpy. An elastic band or a paper clip may not seem very exciting to you; but to a child seeing them for the first time (or, rather, hearing the item named for the first time and seeing how it works) such objects are fascinating.

Don't forget to teach words that tell what objects are made of – *wood, metal, plastic, rubber, paper, leather, cloth, glass* – and show two or three objects made of each.

One of the new words each day might be some object seen while walking or driving with the youngster, or merely something seen from your window. Does the child know *cloud, apartment building, sign, grass, roof, tree*?

Make use of objects seen in newspapers and periodicals. "Look, Eduardo, see this bunch of flowers the lady's holding? It's called a bouquet." Cut out the photo, print *bouquet* on it and begin a word file for periodic review at mealtimes and when the tutors are teaching. Equip the tutors with old mail-order catalogs and other books containing many pictures, and have the tutors print in for the child the names of the objects shown.

The Importance of Concepts

Of great importance for the understanding of printed information is an understanding of relative position: *in, out, between, under, over*, and so on. A child having many times witnessed people walking between things – between buildings, between animals, or between other people – without ever hearing or understanding the meaning of the word *between*, is not hampered in understanding action seen on television by his ignorance of the word. But when reading a book, a child can't properly understand what is taking place in the sentence, "The wolf jumped between the rabbits," unless he knows the meaning of *between*.

The following device will permit you to teach your youngster words dealing with position and movement. Construct the simple castle (Fig.

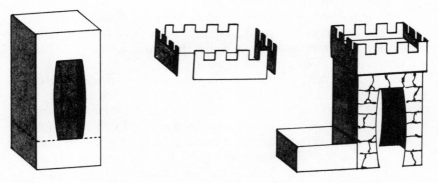

Figure 12: *A castle constructed from a tissue box helps teach concepts.*

94

12) by cutting an empty facial-tissue box along the dotted lines in the manner shown. The opening from which tissues were formerly withdrawn becomes a large door. Cut a similar door in the back of the box (the former bottom) so that a small figure can be made to march in the front door and out the back door. Turrets can be cut, as shown, from four strips of cardboard – corrugated cardboard is best because it gives the projecting effect shown – and glued around the top of the castle. The small part you cut from the bottom of the tissue box is then glued to the side of the castle. This is the moat. If your youngster can't understand what a moat is, make it a swimming pool, perhaps with an alligator or two to add excitement.

By positioning and moving small figures or soldiers around the castle, you can explain the meaning of *top, bottom, on, over, between, apart, together, next to, around, near, far from, up, against, inside, outside, under, down, front, side, rear* (or *back*), *in front of, beside, behind,* and so on. A small car might be driven through the castle to explain *forward, backward* – and even *sideways.* But remember, concepts of position are easy to confuse, so don't teach your child more than one concept each day, and review them regularly.

While driving or walking with your youngster, make a game of identifying words of position or placement: "Look, Hyacinth, the airplane is *over* the houses. Can you see anything else that is *over* the houses? The clouds? Right! Can you see anything that is *over* our head? Trees? Right! See this? It's called an awning. What's going *under* the awning? We are. Right! Can you see anything else that is *under* something else?"

Since a child is less likely to confuse words representing items that differ greatly in position or use, divide your sources of words, and introduce just one a day from each source. For example, one of the three words a child learns each day might be an item seen inside the home or a pictured item; the second word might be something seen outside the home; and the third word might be a "language" word (perhaps a preposition or adjective).

ADJECTIVES

Adjectives are both abundant and valuable.

big – little	large – small	hot – cold	tall – short
long – short	hard – soft	smooth – rough	open – closed
high – low	fat – thin	strong – weak	heavy – light
thick – thin	dry – wet	full – empty	clean – dirty
fast – slow			

Though these adjectives are presented in pairs, don't teach them in pairs. Teaching a child, close together in time, two bits of information that are related invites confusion. If you are teaching *wet*, then compare it to *not wet* instead of to *dry*. When, a week or so later, the child is thoroughly familiar with the term *wet* and what condition it stands for, you can then introduce the special word we have for the non-wet condition.

Does your youngster know the principal colors yet? These, too, are adjectives. Cut different colors from magazines, glue them to a sheet of paper, and print the appropriate name beside each. Teach just one color a day and review it often. "This is *yellow*, Baldwin. Can you see anything in the kitchen that's also yellow? Banana. Right!" Encourage the child to use each new word himself. The more associations or links that are formed with the word in the child's mind – by hearing it, by seeing it in print, and by speaking it – the more easily he will remember it. "What's this color again? Yellow. Right! And what color's the banana? Yes, of course. Yellow!"

An effective way to teach the names of colors, while heightening the child's ability to distinguish between them, is to give the youngster a swatch of material or piece of paper in a particular color and have him locate items around the home bearing that same color.

When your child is acquainted with all these terms and feels confident in using them (which may take a month or two), begin introducing the notion of degree: *high, higher, highest; hot, hotter, hottest;* continuing in this way with all the adjectives listed above. The pair *dry – wet* might be omitted from this exercise, as would *open – closed.*

Adjectives of quantity are important, too. Counting is dealt with in Chapter 11, and parents should read that chapter before attempting to teach their youngster to count. For the moment, children can be taught the idea of *one* and *two*. But don't teach merely the words *one* and *two*. Instead show the child the difference between one spoon and two spoons, one fork and two forks, one cup and two cups, and so on.

Other simple concepts of quantity can be taught with a number of pennies, marbles, or poker chips: *some, many, all, none, most, more, less* (*less* if quantity, *fewer* if in the number of items). "Here, I'll give you *some* marbles, Lucretia, and I'll take *some* myself. Now I'll put *one* marble here for teddy bear. I won't give him *some* marbles because he has no fingers to hold them – right? Here, I'll give you *more* marbles. Perhaps I'll take *more* for myself."

As each new word is introduced, be sure to add it to your list so the child can immediately see its printed form. You will, at that time, be able to explain briefly any irregularity in letter-sound relationship that arises – as, for example, in *couple, some, none, rough, through,* and so on. Make a brief note of any difficulty your child experiences and mention it to the tutors. They can then give extra time to the problem.

Reading Comprehension

As was mentioned earlier, a child will be able to understand in printed form only those words he understands in spoken form. But understanding whole *groups* of words that describe a particular situation, or a way of thinking, poses a different problem.

A person being taught to drive a car must remember many things. He must not only remember to push down on the clutch instead of the brake when changing gear, he must also remember which gear he's in and the correct position of the next gear he wants. Then there's the accelerator to worry about – don't race the engine. And other cars, pedestrians, traffic signs, and lights must be watched and considered.

If, after completing a spine-tingling drive around the block, the sweating learner were asked by his instructor if he'd noticed the large beautiful dog tied up under the apple tree beside the white cottage, the instructor would be thought mad. The beginning driver can't divide his attention between driving and admiring the scenery. He's happy just to get around the block without an accident. Only the skillful driver can give attention to the scenery.

Similarly, the beginning reader, concentrating as he is on reading from left to right, then remembering to drop one line lower – careful, not *two* lines – and to begin reading from left to right again; all the while applying a particular letter-sound rule to this word, but a different, perhaps conflicting, rule to some other word, can become so absorbed with the mechanics of reading that he fails to notice the "scenery": the fact that the story is about a dog tied up under an apple tree beside a white cottage.

We might now understand why parents of beginning readers sometimes say: "Yes, he can read, but he doesn't seem to understand, or even remember, what he reads." Of *course* the child doesn't. The youngster is probably too taken up with the task of processing or deciphering a train of individual words to be able to sweep them quickly together to form a vivid mental image of what the author pictured in his own mind. If a child reads so slowly that, by the time he has worked his way laboriously through to the end of a sentence, he has forgotten how the sentence began, the youngster can't, of course, properly understand what he reads.

When a child's reading becomes quick and sure, he will then – like the skillful driver – be better able to notice the scenery. Comprehension in reading, therefore, is dependent not only upon skillful use of the letter code and possession of a working vocabulary, but upon the speed and ease (speedreading not intended) with which a person can process lines of text. *Facility* in reading is, therefore, a condition for understanding the material read. And because the speed with which a child reads is largely dependent upon how *much* he reads, the child needs to be encouraged to read often. Let's consider ways to increase a child's reading.

Blueprint for a Bibliophile

There is one surefire way to turn a child away from reading: oblige the youngster to read books he finds difficult. Preschoolers, even when they are reading at a Grade 3 or 4 level, still prefer to read very simple books, books found in the Grade 1 and 2 section of the library. Parents will wisely resist the urge to lure youngsters into reading advanced material. By reading easy books, children grow to love books. Better that children read twenty simple books of their own choosing each week than four difficult books of their parents' choosing.

Someone has said there are three ways to get something done: do it yourself, hire someone to do it, or forbid your children to do it. There is no denying that children's interest in any venture soars when apparent limits or restraints are placed on it. This holds for reading, too. One tactic that increased my own children's interest in reading when they had just turned three and four was for me to seem unenthusiastic about letting them read in bed each night—a pedagogical put-on, if you will. After reading each thin book they would ask permission to leave their beds for another. A flimsy objection was promptly fabricated to apparently deter further reading: the lateness of the hour, or the fact that they'd already read one or two books. But, of course, "reluctant" approval was then given for a third, fourth, and even a fifth book.

The reader may perceive a risk in letting children think they can alter a parental preference, but a risk will exist only in homes where parents are habitually undecided or are generally weak in their resolve. In our home, the children knew that extended reading was the only activity open to negotiation.

And during the day, on weekends, ways could always be found to place some small, easily surmountable obstacle in the path of their reading, thereby raising reading to the level of a reward. An objection might be raised that they weren't dressed yet, or that their clothes were scattered on the floor, or that their toys were disorderly; this, prompting a small amount of industry on their part which, in turn, won them the right to read.

When your child has read a few hundred books (not necessarily *different* books, for some might have been read several times), and his vocabulary has grown, he will begin to show interest in longer books. Such books will increase his vocabulary even more. When my two were four and five, the elder child asked if the dinosaurs in museums were kept in cages. I replied that all the museum had were old bones, whereupon the younger child announced that they were called fossils: a word she had learned by reading a simple book at the day-care center.

We will presume your child watches TV occasionally. The subjects he watches on TV might serve to stimulate his interest in books dealing with those same subjects; for example, undersea exploration, wildlife, UFOs, space travel. You may be surprised at the selection of simple books available at the public library that deal with many fascinating scientific subjects. Ask the librarian to explain how the children's section is set out, then spend some time acquainting yourself with the contents of the various shelves.

Series Books

Despite what has been said about the delights of scientific enquiry, parents shouldn't overlook the importance of reading for entertainment. Our purpose in teaching children to read shouldn't be to fill their life with science and technology. Fiction has a role to play, too. Ask the librarian which fictional works are popular with children at your youngster's reading level. Series books (sets of books having the same heroes or heroines) are a good choice. They wouldn't have grown into a series if the author hadn't proved that he was able to fascinate children. Perhaps you, yourself, enjoyed the adventures of Nancy Drew, the Hardy boys, the Bobbsey twins or Enid Blyton's books from England.

But don't expect your youngster to graduate to the series books quickly. Thick books (and series books tend to be thick) can discourage children if they aren't reading quickly and effortlessly. A child may read for two or three years before he will tackle books of 25,000 words in length, and another year or two may pass before he wants to read books of 60,000 words or more.

The series books aren't always available at public libraries, so you may have to buy your own. One way to keep costs down is to buy secondhand books. Used hardbound books can be purchased for as little as twenty-five cents each. Children love to read the same book many times, so, by purchasing books instead of borrowing them, you can offer your youngster a handy, constantly tempting source of entertainment (and a welcome alternative source of entertainment to television).

The Schoolchild

If your child is already in school but hasn't yet learned to use the letter code easily, begin the reading program described in Chapter 7. How will you know if your youngster can use the code easily? See if he can read the text on page 100, taken from *Adventures with Mac* by Dulce Gould.

A child who has been correctly taught the letter code (not all schoolteachers teach it correctly) and has practiced using the code will find the text easy to read. Youngsters age two to five at the Early Learning Centre, in Don Mills, Ontario, read this text after a few months of instruction. Yet, at Overland Public School, situated next door, children aren't

"Look, Tim," said Pinky, "a rat."

"A rat with a sack," said Tim slowly. "Where has he come from and where is he going?"

The rat stepped quickly along the path He did not stop to look.

He did not stop to sniff.

Down the path he went, quickly and softly.

---

expected to read this same book until they reach Grade 4.

Will your home reading program conflict with what is being taught at your local school? That depends on *what* is being taught there. In many classrooms, slow and faulty reading programs are used. The most famous reading program of all time, featuring characters named Dick and Jane (a program that, incidentally, was finally removed from the market after having created an incalculable number of functional illiterates and unenthusiastic readers), advised Grades 1, 2 and 3 teachers thus in the teacher's guidebook:

> Avoid having the children pronounce the phonetic [letter-sound] elements separately. Blending is done mentally, not vocally. Words should be pronounced as wholes in order that the appropriate sound and the natural blend of the elements will be produced clearly but not distorted.

It's true: some children *can* learn to read even when they must adhere to this phonics-hobbling rule. But not *all* children can! And because many youngsters are not able to puzzle out letter blendings by the prescribed "in the head" manner, they progress slowly and haltingly, grow discouraged, and lose interest in reading as each month, each term, each

---

Reprinted from *Adventures with Mac* (copyright 1967) by permission of Holt, Rinehart and Winston of Canada, Ltd.

year passes. They turn, instead, to the no-hassle entertainment offered on television.

If your child can read the text on page 100, fine. Your job will then be to improve his reading by methods presented here and in the previous chapter.

Will your child's teacher mind? His teacher should be delighted. After all, you will be demonstrating the very initiative and support that educational journals deplore the lack of by parents. And, looking at it another way, every child who can read well at the end of Grade 1 or 2 — whether taught by the teacher or the parent — is scored as a success by the teacher and by the school.

If your child is eight years of age or older and can't read the text on page 100 easily, the youngster has a reading problem; the older your child the more serious the problem. In addition, the unskilled reader is often burdened with more than an ignorance of the letter code: he may also be burdened with some mistaken ideas about himself, suspecting perhaps that he is backward, or that he suffers a learning disability, or that learning to read requires some magical ability he obviously lacks. Possessing any of these ideas, a child is as good as hypnotized into thinking he can't become a skillful reader. And no one on Earth who is convinced he *can't* perform a specific task can possibly do it. Studies show that people unconsciously make events occur to support and perpetuate their convictions.

If your child has, for one or more reasons, convinced himself that he just isn't cut out for reading, a convincing case will have to be presented to make him see that he is an unfortunate victim of faulty teaching. And considerable enticement may be required — especially if the child is a teenager — to make him *want* to try again to learn and use the letter code easily.

One way around the problem is to explain to the child the steps described in the preceding chapter, then let him teach a preschooler to read. If you don't have a preschool-age child, perhaps a neighbor or relative has. You might then agree to pay your youngster for his teaching time, if the neighbor or relative will merely provide the pupil for your child to teach.

By playing the egg-carton game with a preschooler, a teenager will gain skill in using the letter code as his young pupil does. And not only will the teenager learn to read, he will gain a great feeling of accomplishment by teaching another to read. Naturally, you will have to read the instructions in Chapter 7 for your child before each lesson so he will know what to teach next. Adult illiterates can learn to read in this same way, by being taught how to teach a preschooler to read, then being given the opportunity to do so.

The Reluctant Reader

A reluctant reader is a youngster who can use the letter code reasonably well, but who reads seldom, and usually slowly—each condition being partly due to the other. Our goal is to motivate the child to read more often. We can do this in several ways. But first let's consider the child's dependence on electronic equipment for entertainment. Any child who spends a couple of hours a day watching television or listening to music hasn't much time left for reading; at least, not if he also spends time outdoors. One solution to the problem is to limit electronic entertainment or keep it in some way proportional to the amount of time spent reading. For example, one minute of television viewing might be permitted for each minute spent reading. Does it work? In one reported case, a child thus contracted became so engrossed in his book that he forgot to turn on the TV set at the appointed time. Ways to control TV viewing and encourage reading are described in Chapter 14.

Read to your child at bedtime. Eight- and nine-year-olds—and sometimes even ten- and eleven-year-olds—still enjoy being read to. But to promote reading skill let your child take turns with you in reading.

Parents might promise to buy any record or tape cassette the child wants, or buy any other desired object—or simply pay cash—for book reviews. The child merely chooses a book on any subject that interests him, reads it, and gives the parent a comment on the book, perhaps describing what he thought were its good and bad points.

Bribery? Not at all; merely fair payment for effort, in this case *academic* effort instead of muscular effort. And another important purpose is served here. Children appreciate the value of money more, and they gain a greater feeling of personal worth, when they earn their spending money. Some parents, realizing that a free handout of cash each week instills no sense of self-reliance in children—and can even be demeaning—put a price on various household chores; or, more commonly, the child is simply expected to take care of certain household duties whether the relationship between the duties and the allowance is ever spelled out. Many children wash dishes, take out the garbage, mow the lawn, or look after other chores. But what is wrong with expecting children to perform *academic* chores for their allowance, especially when the improved reading skill that results from the arrangement will benefit children far more than delivering papers or washing dishes ever will? When, with such a program, a child's reading improves, six, eight, or ten months later, payment can begin for some other academic activity, the child then being so habituated to reading that he reads books without having to be urged or paid.

THE COMIC KINGDOM

Children love comic books, but because the violence in some comic books is excessive, they are sometimes thought to be beneath mention as literature. Perhaps rightly. However, the literary worth of comic books isn't our concern here. We're interested in skillful reading, not aesthetics, and to whatever extent comic books can prompt youngsters to use their reading ability, comic books will be considered valuable.

Comic books were found to be the salvation for illiterates at a high school near Toronto. Teenagers reading at a Grade 2 or 3 level were bused from forty miles around to begin their long climb to literacy by reading comic books. Anguish over a child's low-level literary preferences is senseless if the child refuses to read anything better. In order to *improve* a child's choice of literature, we must first get him *started* reading.

Wily librarians in one English town entice children into their libraries by means of "comic boxes": boxes into which children can deposit their old comic books in exchange for others. The librarians have found that many children go from the comic boxes to books on the shelves.

Not *all* comic books are unsavory. By skimming through books before purchasing them, you can weed out undesirable ones. The yellow pages of your telephone book may list, under Book Dealers, stores that feature new and used comic books. In one, you may find the Marvel Classic Comics, a series of comic books depicting classical tales: *Dr. Jekyll and Mr. Hyde*, *The Invisible Man*, *Tom Sawyer*, *The Iliad*, and *The Odyssey*, among them. After reading the comic version of such works, your youngster may be tempted to read the original.

One comic-book series that features good artwork, quality paper and binding, and has a low level of violence is *Tintin*, a series that delighted children in France for years before it was translated into English. Another notable series is *Asterix*, the story of a mythical Gaulish tribe that outwitted the Roman invaders. Though seemingly dull in subject matter, the stories are both clever and funny.

MAGAZINES AND NEWSPAPERS

Children's magazines contain some of the best material being written today for youngsters. Indeed, it's a matter of survival that they do so. Children won't tolerate dull writing. By subscribing to children's magazines you automatically enlist the help of top-flight writers and editors to fasten your youngster's thoughts on reading. Issues of popular children's magazines – *Highlights for Children*, *National Geographic World*, *Children's Digest*, *Jack and Jill*, *Owl*, *Ranger Rick*, to name a few – can sometimes be found at the public library. Borrow a few issues; see which of them catches your child's interest, then subscribe to one or more.

For teenagers, there are *Hot Rod*, *Popular Mechanics*, *Mechanix Illustrated*, *Superteen*, *Seventeen*, and several more magazines with *teen* in their titles that deal with topics of particular interest to this age group. All are available at any well-stocked newsstand. You might agree to purchase any periodical your child agrees to read.

Newspaper reports can contribute greatly to your reading program. Each time you see a report that would interest your child, tell him just enough about the report to rouse his curiosity. He will then be tempted to read the entire article himself. Youngsters are particularly interested in news stories about children, animals, and mysterious events.

Sometimes a news story will spark a child's curiosity sufficiently to send him to the encyclopedia in search of more information. No family should be without an encyclopedia, nor need they be. How to find inexpensive sets is revealed in the *Encyclopedia Buying Guide*, kept in the reference section of your local public library. If you can't afford a new encyclopedia, you can buy a used set at a secondhand bookstore, sometimes for a fraction of its original cost. Most of the matters that interest children change little over a ten-year period, so don't think you have to buy a recent edition.

An encyclopedia may be produced in more than one binding with a considerable savings for the less expensive type. The Encyclopedia Britannica, for example, has three such bindings, though only two of them are generally known. Salespeople tend to keep the information to themselves because of the loss they suffer in commission on the cheaper versions.

The greatest single source of fascinating reading is the public library, which offers books on a variety of intriguing subjects: space exploration, mysteries of the sea, strange creatures, unusual people, and so on. Ask the librarian to suggest some books that fit this description. You may have to fill out a book-request card and wait your turn for the more popular books.

Mealtime etiquette might be bent in the interests of literacy; any of the books or publications that have been mentioned could be propped up and read aloud at suppertime by parent and child taking turns. Bookstands that hold books upright for easy reading can be bought at most stationery stores. An encyclopedia affords you almost limitless fascinating reading. Let your youngster name a topic he'd like to know more about; how honey, or peanut butter, or ice cream is made; or details about elephants, tigers, crocodiles; then bring the appropriate volume of your encyclopedia to the supper table for shared reading.

Each of the ideas that have been described will encourage your child to read more, will improve his reading ability, and will, in consequence, work to improve both his immediate and eventual performance in school. And you may discover a bonus. You may find, as I did, that by playing a role in your youngster's education, you begin to fill gaps in your own.

9

Vocabulary Growth

The size of a child's vocabulary influences his intellectual standing and educational progress more than any other body of knowledge he possesses. Though other matters will be considered in the remaining chapters, a parent who does no more than teach a child to read (Chapter 7), lead a child to a love of reading (Chapter 8), and extend a child's speech vocabulary by the methods described in this chapter will ensure the child a brilliant mind and predispose him to academic success.

Why is the size and quality of a child's vocabulary so important? Because words are the working tools of thought. A child who has collected only a small set of these tools can neither understand other people's thoughts properly, nor easily express his own. Isn't the same true for adults? Any adult limited to a small vocabulary – say the vocabulary of a twelve-year-old – is ill equipped to comprehend and discuss subjects at an advanced level. Knowledge of words, therefore, permits children to "plug into" our society, permits them to make fuller use of their brains and their imaginations.

Psychologists have found that the range of a child's vocabulary is one of the stablest indicators of the youngster's intellectual development from year to year. Children's IQ tests are divided into several parts, one of which measures the size and quality of vocabulary. Researchers have discovered that children's score on the *vocabulary* portion of IQ tests is just about the same as their score for the whole test. In other words, for children at least, large vocabulary and high IQ are pretty much one and the same.

Should we really be surprised by this finding? Isn't this exactly what the fathers of Bentham, Mill, and Witte believed, and proved, more than a hundred years ago? The intriguing part is this: enlarging children's vocabularies is *easy*. No expensive equipment is needed, no special training. Almost any parent can enlarge a child's vocabulary simply by engaging the youngster in vocabulary-building activities.

When my own children were found to have some intellectual advantage, the surprising part for me (after the initial surprise at the results of the test) was in learning that their high scores were almost totally dependent upon their knowing words the tutors and I had taught them. Had we *not* taught these words to the children, or had we taught the words *poorly*, the children wouldn't have known or remembered the meanings of those words, and their scores on the test would have been low. Looking at the IQ test in a slightly different way, then, I realized that the test was virtually an evaluation of how well the tutors and I had performed as teachers.

But doesn't this hold, in fact, for most tests given to children? For example, the mark that a schoolchild gets on a test is often, in reality, simply an assessment of how well the teacher has done his job. This might explain why inflated marks are a general practice in many classrooms.

Whereas teaching a child to read is a relatively short, simple task, enlarging a child's vocabulary is a task that can span years. Accordingly, the material presented in this chapter isn't to be completed before children begin spelling, printing, and writing (dealt with next chapter), but is to be learned along with those skills. If your child has, at this point, learned the words presented in Chapter 8 (the simpler adjectives, prepositions, and the names of commonly seen objects), he may now begin learning more advanced words: words that will raise him to the "gifted" level. Some procedures used here are merely extensions of methods that have already been described in Chapter 8. Let's start with those.

Wall-to-wall Pictures

Clip photos from picture magazines and attach to them slips of paper bearing the names of various objects seen in the photo (as has been done in Figure 13). Old *National Geographic*s are a particularly good source of pictures for this method of vocabulary expansion. Each picture will usually permit you to introduce several new words. For example, a photo

Figure 13: *Pictures with labels attached aid vocabulary growth.*

of a square-rigged schooner might permit you to teach the words *ship, sail, mast, wave, horizon, porthole, cabin, deck*, and other nautical terms.

Each picture, with its several word slips in place, might then be affixed to a wall for review after toothbrushing and before the reading of bedtime stories. In fact, the various walls around the home—in the kitchen or dining area, in the child's bedroom, the bathroom, the foyer—might be turned into "pages" of an immense vocabulary book. The youngster reads each word slip, locates the object in the picture and, if appropriate, describes its purpose. Review of the pictures can take the form of a game, each wall of pictures being considered a different "island" for your child to visit in his search for some treasure. The treasure might be paper clips that have been attached to certain of the word slips beforehand. The youngster might receive a small treat for discovering and bringing back the paper clips from an explorative journey around the home. For preschoolers, valentines from a large bookful of press-out cards have proved to be a great hit.

A hint of adventure will be added if the child straps on a rocket pistol or hitches up a sword for a daily tour of the islands with her tutors. Or she might be a doctor visiting the islands to take care of the sick people and animals. Let your child suggest how she would like this or that exercise to be run. Such ideas may not be earthshaking (in your opinion), but they'll be *hers,* and for that reason, they will captivate her.

Pictures might also be fastened to card stock and propped up for review at mealtimes, or pinned to a low string line in the dining area for easy viewing. Or pictures might be glued in a large scrapbook to make a picture dictionary: a book you may ultimately want to keep as a souvenir of a particularly interesting period in your child's development.

If your tutors are able to print neatly, you might simply provide them with old magazines, paper, glue, and a felt-tip pen, and let them select and mount suitable pictures. Old picture magazines can be bought cheaply at used-book stores.

Pictures selected for vocabulary growth should show, whenever possible, the object's function and its size in relation to people. A child might think a canoe to be the size of an ocean liner unless someone were shown in or beside it. And a picture of a wheelbarrow would mean little to a child unless someone were shown using it.

Mealtime Show and Tell

What items does your child see at, or near, the supper table whose names are still not known to him? Does he know the words *wire, electrical plug, electrical outlet, paint, wallpaper, keyhole, faucet* (or *tap*), *thermometer, hinge, pattern, shape, grain* (of wood)? Look around your home for other items. Print their names on word slips. Introduce your youngster to each item, its name, and the word slip, and review the word frequently.

Items that can't be seen at or near the dining table might be brought *to* the table. An assortment of objects kept in a bowl near the table could be removed for periodic review: a nut, bolt, screw, washer, carpet tack, nail, screwdriver, needle, cork, candle, magnet, a piece of sandpaper, string, or thread. Look in cupboards and drawers to see what small items might be brought to the table, named, and explained. Even a handful of coins will permit you to teach the words *dull, shiny, round, circular, copper, silver, nickel, click* (together), *roll* (on edge), *metal.*

Words from Reading

Children enjoy hearing (and reading) stories that excite wonder, astonishment, or humor. Such stories can be used to teach new words in an entertaining manner; and a way, too, that makes remembering them easier. Newspapers are a good source. Consider the following report.

NEW YORK – More than 500 items, including broken thermometers, can openers, keys, bolts, chains and 300 coins were removed from the stomach of a 155-pound man here Tuesday. Doctors, who took two hours to retrieve the material, said the peculiar eating habits of the patient, mentally ill and unidentified, did not hurt his esophagus or intestinal tract.

Depending on which words the child already knows, he might be taught *items, bolts, removed, retrieve, material, peculiar, patient, mentally ill, unidentified* (and *identified*), *esophagus, intestinal* (and *intestine*). Such a story could be glued into a scrapbook entitled Newspaper Report Book for periodic rereading.

Take turns with your child in reading aloud from books at supper time, adding to your lists each new word your youngster doesn't know. In one home, the person having the least amount of food left on his or her plate reads an entry in a children's encyclopedia until someone else catches up. A book on natural history sometimes replaces the encyclopedia and yields not only words, but fascinating details on natural phenomena: how the immense tsunami waves are created; how quicksand pits are formed (and how to get out of one); why one type of wave (a bore) flows upstream instead of down, and other matters of interest to children and parents alike.

Food packages, wrappers, and labels are a source of useful words: *ingredients, recipe, nourishing, flavor, servings, mixture, product, contents, directions, teaspoonful.*

The famous McGuffey readers are credited with having raised the vocabulary of the children of immigrant Americans to a highly literate level. The books gave them, in fact, a level of speech that is normally associated with affluent homes and scholarly parents. The McGuffey readers, first published in 1836 and still used today in some schools, contain words not found in the average child's vocabulary: words that are then explained at the end of each entry. For example, an essay on the elephant in the fourth reader is followed by a definition of those words used that might be unknown to a nine-year-old: *quadruped, pendulous, commerce, proboscis, stratagem, docile, asylum, unwieldy, tacitly, epidemic, nabob.* The sixth reader contains some of the best English prose ever written. The McGuffey readers, rich with the themes of honesty, kindliness, consideration, respect for others, and other virtues, are ideally suited for use in your program of vocabulary growth. In fact, by having the child read aloud from these books, you or the tutors could make the readings serve as an exercise in diction; every final *d*, *t*, and *ing* to be clearly enunciated.

Words While Driving

Your child may now know the names of the more common objects seen while driving, such as *car, truck, building.* Find out what words he *doesn't* know: perhaps *bridge, motorcycle, taxi* (or *cab*), *license plate.* Gradually progress to less common words: *pedestrian, motorist, intersection, speedometer, high rise, skyscraper, underpass, boulevard, tarpaulin* (on trucks).

A known word might lead to the introduction of an unknown word. "See that, Wesley, that's called a bridge. You already knew it? Well, it's made of metal. You knew that too! Well, do you know where metal comes from? From a large hole that people dig in the ground. The large hole can go down into the ground for a mile or more. It's called a mine, and the people who dig it are called miners. They dig the hole so they can bring up a special sort of rock that contains the metal. And this type of rock is called ore." By such means the child will have learned *mine, miner,* and *ore.* You will naturally have to refresh his memory of the words a few times. If you are teaching a child to spell at this time in preparation for printing (described next chapter), you can also spell each new word for him.

Another way to find new words while driving is by topic. Take *speech* for example. What words do we normally connect with speech? *Talk, whisper, shout, holler, call, tattle, gossip.* Take another topic, music: *whistle, song, sing, singer, tune, melody, solo, duet, trio, quartet,* plus, perhaps, the names of musical instruments your child has seen, or instruments he hears on the car radio. See how many words your youngster can think of unaided, then hint at others before finally adding those words he doesn't know yet.

Sentence Lists

Another way to teach children new words is to compose sentences employing those words. These sentences are then written or typed on cards. The child reads the sentences aloud once or twice a day for a number of days. Over a period of a year, my own children (then five and six) read 1,500 sentences composed for this purpose, beginning with fairly simple ones containing just one word they didn't know.

When something *improves*, it gets better.
Daily means every day.
When something is *ordinary*, there is nothing special about it.
The sides of the door are *parallel*.

The children read each sentence a dozen or more times during a period of months. As their vocabulary grew, less common words were introduced to the exercise. One TV program they were permitted to watch, "Batman," featured an astonishingly rich vocabulary (to titillate adult viewers). Less obscure parts of the dialog were noted on a pad kept handy for that purpose and these were included in the children's sentence lists; hence:

"Let's ponder the crook's motive," said Batman. *Ponder* means to think about something. The *motive* is the reason a person does something.
Batman said of the Joker: "His insane conceit may betray him." When someone has an extremely high opinion of his or her own ability, appearance, or worth, we say that person is *conceited*.

Eventually, the plots of TV movies were employed as vehicles for expanding the children's vocabularies. Typed comments on situations the children had seen in the movies served to maintain their interest in the exercise. For example, the film *Manhunt* was used as the means of introducing the following italicized words:

Thorndyke *eluded* his *captors* by following the *bed of a stream*. This *foiled* the dogs that were *tracking* his *scent*.

And for the film, *Prisoner of Shark Island:*

Dr. Samuel A. Mudd *set* the broken leg of John Wilkes Booth, the man who *assassinated* Lincoln. He was *accused* of *complicity* in a *plot* to kill Lincoln, had to *stand trial*, and was *convicted*.

For *Scott of the Antarctic:*

Scott's *adventure provided* a *series* of *unbearable hardships* for himself and his men.

One can't predict which words taught in this way will lodge in a child's mind. Those words youngsters find no use for are simply forgotten. (Quizzed four years later, the children knew all the words in the preceding sentences except *complicity*).

Voice-over Television

Television can be made a vehicle for vocabulary expansion. Consider the picture tube as you would the page of a picture book, and use the gaps between narration to teach words that are relevant to the picture being shown. "That's called a *seaplane*, Zinnia, and those two long things underneath it are called *pontoons*. That large sailboat it's flying over is called a *yacht*." If you have remote control over the sound, you'll be able to edit the program and fit in your comments (or "educational commercials") more easily. Keep a pad and pen handy to jot down any new words for review at a later time. Programs such as "Stationary Ark" and "Ark on the Move" provide not only a model of good English usage but a constant supply of valuable, if seldom heard, words. *Gregarious*, *agile*, *ingratiating*, *nocturnal*, and *diurnal* were used in just one program about lemurs.

Encourage your child to ask the meaning of words he hears in conversations and on TV. But be careful that while explaining the meaning of a word you don't use other words the child doesn't know. If there isn't time to fill his request immediately, make a note of the word and discuss it later.

Use of the Dictionary

The dictionary will eventually contribute greatly to your child's education. Methods of teaching the use of the dictionary are described in Chapter 12. Our purpose here is merely to acquaint children with the basic role of a dictionary while using it for vocabulary growth in a simplified way.

An intermediate dictionary will be needed: one that is between a children's and an adult's dictionary. The dictionary you select should contain at least 20,000 or 30,000 entries and perhaps 1,000 good-quality photos or drawings. For the moment, we are primarily concerned with the illustrations.*

Leaf through the section containing words beginning with the letter *A*, and mark an X opposite any pictured item that the youngster already

---

*The *Xerox Intermediate Dictionary* (New York, 1973), with 34,000 entries and 1,400 illustrations, meets these conditions.

knows by name. Also, mark an X beside any pictured item that is beyond your youngster's present vocabulary needs; for example, *acropolis, acute angle*, and *apogee*, if pictured, are of little value to most children younger than nine or ten.

In the following exercise—one well-suited to the tutor's management—the child merely reads aloud dictionary entries for those pictures that are *not* marked with an X. Four such entries might be read each day, with a review of earlier entries.

A simple game can be made of the procedure by placing one, two, three, four, five, or six dots beside the various pictures. The child then rolls a die to determine which entry to read. Or, by marking the pictures appropriately with symbols or colors, a different sort of die (obtainable at educational-toy stores) might be used; for example, one having the cyphers 1 to 6 on the six faces, or having different colors, or different geometric shapes.

Tutors should show the youngster how to use the pronunciation code and encourage the child to do so. When the child completes the entries in the *A* section, mark the illustrations in the *B* section.

After your vocabulary program has been in progress for a year or so, the "Word Power" feature of *Reader's Digest* could be included in your program. Even then, however, the more obscure words should be crossed out. Have the child read just the answer page, not the quiz page.

Conversations with your youngster can be a highly effective means of increasing his vocabulary. When chatting, don't limit yourself to words the youngster knows. Use words he *doesn't* know, then explain the meaning. For example, if the child expresses awe at a high-priced car, instead of saying, "It costs a lot of money," say, "It's an expensive car, Olaf. *Expensive* means it costs more than most other cars. Look, there's another *expensive* car over there." Find occasion to use any new word two or three times and encourage the child to use the word himself.

There are, of course, other ways to enrich your child's vocabulary—by visiting museums and other centers of learning, and by the program of "educational opportunism" dealt with later—but procedures of this sort fall outside the basic convenience educational program. Chapter 15 explains how parents can supplement the basic program.

10

Spelling, Printing, and Writing

The activities described in this chapter are intended primarily for children who can read; however, even non-readers can benefit from and enjoy some of the activities.

Spelling, printing, and writing exercises aren't as inherently entertaining for children as reading is. But children's interest can be maintained if parents make the exercises fun and limit the amount of time children spend at them. Accordingly, parents should present the material in the next chapter, Chapter 11, along with the material in this chapter. Each day, a child would then engage in fifteen minutes of vocabulary growth, fifteen minutes of spelling, printing (and, eventually, writing), and fifteen minutes of the material presented in Chapter 11.

Spelling

At one time, children were taught to spell while they were being taught to read: a teaching error that created confusion in children's minds between letter sounds and letter names. However, once youngsters have learned to read skillfully, they are no longer likely to be confused by the fact that letters have names as well as sounds, or that most of these names don't sound the same way the letters sound when used in words (A, E, I, O, and U, when used in their "long" or "hard" sound form, being the principal exceptions). But, to be safe, begin with the consonants: skip A, and begin with B. Tell your child that B — and, of course, its lower-case form, b — is called "bee"; then have the child pick out and name some upper- and lower-case Bs in a newspaper text.

Next, teach the child the name for C ("see"), and let him pick out and name upper- and lower-case Cs and Bs. Continue in this way through the alphabet — D ("dee"), F ("eff"), and so on — leaving A, E, I, O, and U until the last.

To give your youngster practice in distinguishing between letter sounds and their names, play "I Spy," a game you probably already know, while driving, walking, or eating. In this game, one player announces, "I spy with my little eye something that starts with ..." and he names a letter. The other players then look around and name various items they can see that start with the required letter. If one guesser manages to name whatever item the other player had in mind, the guesser wins, and it is then his turn to "spy" something. If the guesser fails, though, his opponent takes another turn.

When, after a week or two, a child has learned the names of the letters and can work his way along a line of text – in either capitals or lower-case letters – naming each letter easily, he will be ready to play other spelling games.

Holding a Pencil

A child must learn another skill before he can begin printing. He must learn to hold and manipulate a pencil. This extremely difficult task may require several months of practice. In preparation for printing, show the youngster how to hold a pencil while he is learning the letter names. Encourage him, when he is scribbling or coloring, to hold the pencil or crayon in a way that will eventually be suitable for writing.

A child can be encouraged to manipulate a pencil in several entertaining ways. First, buy a quantity of tracing paper or onion-skin paper, then tell your youngster you are going to show him how to print, or make print pictures. Place the thin paper over a word in a newspaper headline or an advertisement and trace around the letters with a pencil or pen. When the child sees how words can be "lifted" off the page in this way, he'll be eager to do the same. Tape the thin paper in such a way that it will stay in position until the "picture" is finished.

You might print, in letters large enough for tracing, words that hold special fascination for your youngster; chief among them being his name. A child's age will determine what other words he would like to trace; perhaps *bomb, jet, doll, doctor*. Ask him.

Treat your child's tracings as works of art and post them prominently on a wall or door. As the child's tracing improves, he might be encouraged to trace two, three, or more words on a single sheet of paper; then two or more of these sheets could be fastened together with staples to form his first "book."

Children can also be encouraged to trace cartoon characters from comic strips. It matters little, really, whether children trace letters or comics, because both exercises develop skill in manipulating a pencil.

Carbon paper can provide another fascinating exercise for a child. Simply show the youngster how carbon paper works and let him trace figures or designs from publications onto paper. Carbon paper introduces an element of surprise because children can't examine their carbon duplicates until the drawings are completed.

Show your child how spectacles, mustaches, and beards can be drawn on the faces of models in newspaper and magazine advertisements. An old mail-order catalog will provide dozens of faces suitable for alteration. Perhaps hats and jewelry can be added to the figures, too, and patterns can be added to any unpatterned clothing worn.

Supply your child with blank paper and show him how to draw funny faces. Those shown in Figure 14 are all simple to draw. If paper is scarce

Figure 14: *Drawing funny faces encourages children to use a pencil.*

around your home, use the backs of circulars that arrive at the door or in the mail. Or you might purchase, at a toy store, a drawing pad that can be repeatedly erased by lifting the front plastic sheet away from the black waxed backing.

Devices that permit youngsters to draw patterns—a spirograph or stencils—prompt considerable manipulation of a pencil or crayon. Another way to encourage use of a pencil is to play ticktacktoe with your child.

When playing ticktacktoe, be sure to let the child draw the grids. This will give him even more exercise with the pencil. Let your child win most

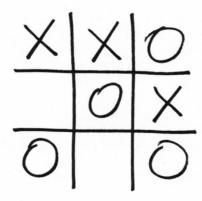

Figure 15: *A completed game of ticktacktoe showing a win for the Os.*

of the time and he'll be eager to play five or six games with you during supper, and perhaps five or six more with the tutor later. If the child begins to suspect you are letting him win deliberately, have him play the game against the puppet (described in Chapter 7). The puppet, being a dull fellow, will, of course, make all sorts of blunders in playing the game.

Spelling Games

Spelling games can provide entertaining moments while you are driving or walking with your child. Begin with simple words: "Know how to spell *dog*, Marco?" He probably won't, so spell it for him. "Bet you can spell it now, eh?" Let him spell it. "Any other word—perhaps special words—you'd like me to spell?" Fill his requests, then see if he can still spell *dog*. Repetition is, in this case, the key to quick learning. And don't forget to let him perform later for your spouse: "Marco can spell *dog* now, dear. You don't think so? Okay, Marco, let Daddy hear it."

Over a period of weeks, gradually advance from the short, simple words—*car*, *cat*, *sky*, *road*—to longer, more difficult words: *bicycle*, *crane*, *bridge*, *avenue*, *people*, *building*. The child will probably need reminding for a couple of days before he can remember how to spell the trickier words.

Play a sign game with your youngster. While driving, direct his attention to some word that can be seen on a sign—perhaps the word *new*—and ask him if he can spell it. Of course he can! He spells the word simply by naming the letters on the sign. When the sign is lost from view, ask him if he can still spell *new*. Then ask him five minutes later if he can still spell the word. And finally ask him half an hour later. One small point: pick signs that are far enough away to give your child time to locate the word and spell it before the sign passes from view.

The sign game can be altered slightly for play at mealtimes using food labels, wrappers, and packages. For example, point to the word *cereal* on the packet and ask the child if he can spell it. When the youngster has named the letters, put the packet where he can't see the word and ask him if he can still spell *cereal*; then repeat your requests later, with gradually lengthening lapses.

While eating, make a point of spelling, for the child, the names of items within view: *fork*, *cup*, *spoon*, and print them so he can see the words. Over a period of weeks, introduce longer words: *curtain*, *ceiling*, *refrigerator*.

Soon, the child will discover that the letter-code knowledge that permits him to look at a word—say, *caramel*—and puzzle out how its sound can be used in a reverse manner, when printing or writing, to determine how the word is spelled. He will begin to see that the *sound* of a word conveys clues to what letters need be strung together to form that sound. Moreover, as the youngster's spelling improves, he will start to take pride in this ability, and will begin to pay closer attention to the spelling of words he sees around him and in books. You may, as a result, soon find your child's spelling skill progressing at a surprising rate.

A month or so after beginning the spelling and pencil-holding pastimes, a child will be ready to combine these skills in printing. Encourage the child now to *copy* words rather than merely trace them. No more tracing paper or onion-skin paper for the moment. Show the youngster how he can lift words from a page simply by looking at the words and copying them on his own paper. When the child is able to copy words easily, he will be ready for the last step to skillful printing.

Lists, Lists, Lists

A child's main need now will be to get plenty of practice in printing. One exercise your youngster will enjoy is the printing of lists. Show him how he can print various lists, helping him, when necessary, with spelling. Here are a few suggested lists that interest most youngsters.

Some Ways I Would Like to Travel
Flowers I Like
Wild Animals I Like
Tame Animals I Like
Toys I Like
Things I Like to Do
Things I Like to Eat
Things I Would Like to See
Birds I Like

As each list (containing ten or twelve items) is finished, post it conspicuously or give it a colorful cover (to form a one-page book), whichever the child prefers. Purchase some colorful peel-off animal stickers at the stationery store and attach one to each list as a sort of seal of approval.

Another valuable exercise: have your youngster print your shopping lists for you, helping him with the spelling. When you go shopping, be sure the child takes a pad and pencil along, and spell the names of those items that interest him. His printed list of items he likes at the supermarket or department store will be sure to win compliments from Daddy, Aunt Agnes, Grandma, and others.

On another occasion, you might appeal to his generosity, and help him compose a list for Daddy, or some other relative, called, "Things I Would Like To Buy for You." What a hit the list will be with the appropriate recipient!

Encourage your youngster to begin listing the titles of books he reads; a job he will be able to handle all by himself simply by copying the spelling from the cover of each book. Post the list prominently so he can add new titles as he finishes each book.

Just a Reminder

Explain to your child that a memorandum, or memo, is a note we make for ourselves so we won't forget to do something. Encourage him to make memos for tasks that must be done on the morrow: WATER THE DAN-DELIONS, FEED THE GOLDFISH, GET FLEA POWDER FOR SCAMP, and so on. By leaving these brief notes for himself in a place where he will be sure to see them the next day, the child will develop a sense of system and responsibility.

To increase the amount your child prints, you might reward him for printing in a way that invites still more printing. For example, children love to print the names of items on self-adhering labels and attach them to the appropriate objects: *door, wall, chair, table,* and so on. Therefore, gummed labels can be made a reward for some other printing. The "other" printing might itself be a particularly valuable exercise. For example, the child might be asked to find in his dictionary four words that interest him. He would then print the four words in a lined exercise book, which might be called a Dictionary Book. For entering the four words in his book, the child might receive four stickers on which he could then print the names of any four items around the home (receiving help, of course, with the spelling), then attach the stickers to those items. The four words the child printed in his Dictionary Book could be discussed at supper time, thereby reinforcing whatever understanding he had already formed of the words.

When you write friends or relatives, ask your youngster to print a brief message for enclosure in your letter. If the season is right, brief letters might be prepared for Santa Claus. And how about notes for the Tooth Fairy, either in preparation for teeth that will eventually be falling out or just as a sort of dental report? And there is, of course, occasional opportunity for printing a thank-you note, either for a gift or for some form of help received.

Encourage your youngster to print and post signs, beginning, perhaps, with the door of his bedroom: GUTHRIE'S ROOM, WELCOME, PLEASE KNOCK, THANK YOU. Perhaps you would like some signs for your own bedroom. Or your youngster might print – and post prominently – signs for the kitchen: BEWARE OF STOVE, KNIVES ARE DANGEROUS, and for elsewhere in the interests of safety, cleanliness, or tidiness: DON'T LITTER, WIPE YOUR FEET. And perhaps one for the supper table: WASH YOUR HANDS.

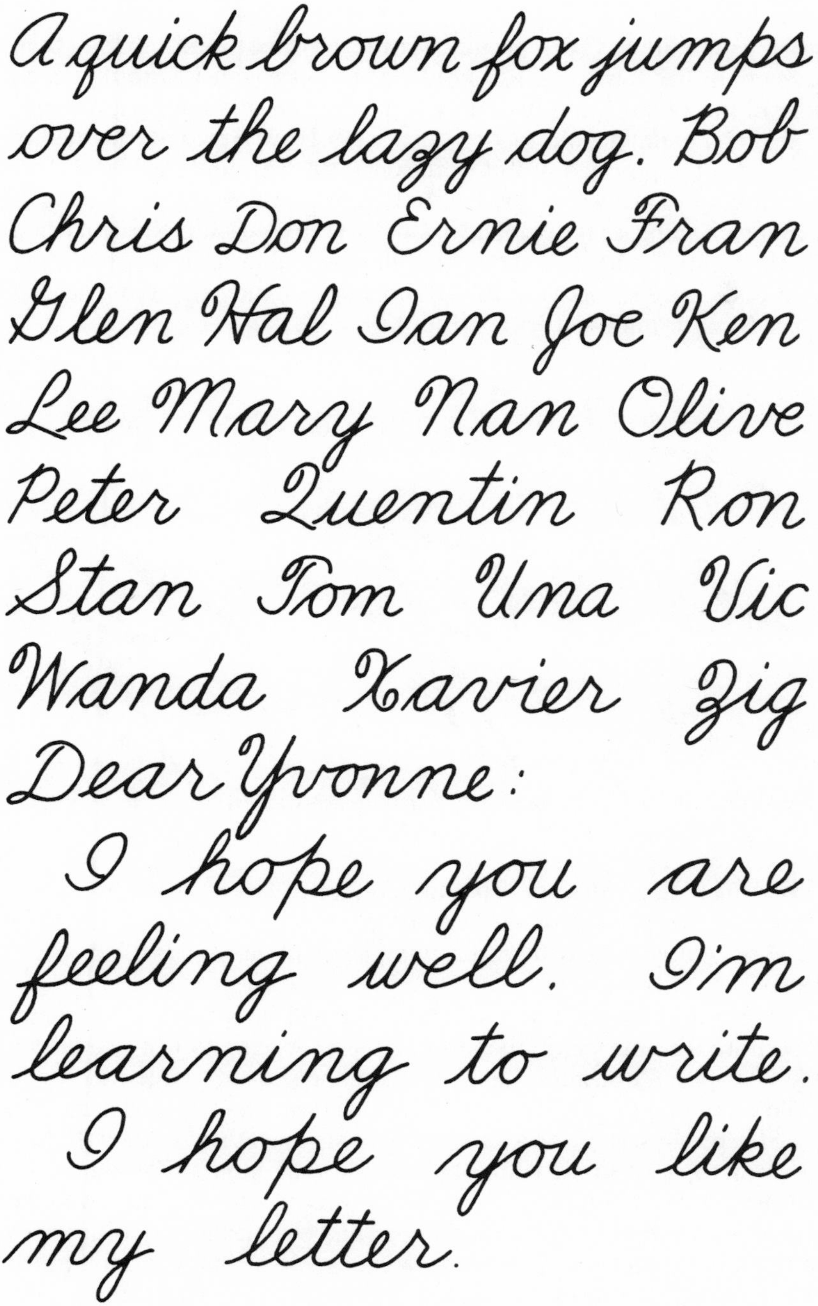

A quick brown fox jumps over the lazy dog. Bob Chris Don Ernie Fran Glen Hal Ian Joe Ken Lee Mary Nan Olive Peter Quentin Ron Stan Tom Una Vic Wanda Xavier Zig Dear Yvonne:

I hope you are feeling well. I'm learning to write. I hope you like my letter.

Figure 16: *A writing sample for handwriting practice.*

Writing

When your child has been printing for two or three months, he will then be ready to begin writing. But now the youngster must learn that each letter of the alphabet has two more forms: upper- and lower-case script.

Begin by making a photocopy of page 119. Place a piece of onion-skin paper over the photocopy and let the child trace around the letters. You will have to explain that writing, unlike printing, is usually produced without stopping; that we don't "draw" letters as is usually the case when printing. You will have to show your child where to begin when writing some of the letters, and what special succession of movements are needed to produce certain other letters (Fig. 17).

Figure 17: *Children may need help learning the succession of movements necessary to form some of the letters.*

Writing with a ballpoint pen is difficult for children because the point tends to slither around under their loose guidance. Therefore, purchase for your youngster a pen with a fine plastic point, or have him use a pencil.

Tracing around the script on page 119 will be a slow and difficult procedure for your child; therefore, limit his tracing to just two lines a day. On special occasions he might trace the short message which you could then send to a friend or relative. On completion of such a tracing, write the person's name on a separate piece of paper, then position the thin paper on top of it so the youngster can add that name to the salutation.

When your child has traced script for a month or two, put away the thin paper. Give him instead lined paper, and encourage the youngster to copy, rather than trace, the script. Don't expect his copy to look much like the specimen script, though. He'll probably manage only a wild approximation. But, of course, give him praise, praise, and more praise for doing so well. And your praise needn't be empty, either. If you can

120

actually read what he has written, the child will be doing wonderfully well. Remember, some adults, after writing for many years, still write poorly; sometimes their writing isn't even legible.

Your child's writing may, in fact, never look like the specimen script. That isn't important. Children quickly impose their own characteristic variations on the writing of this or that letter.

When your child begins to write more easily, encourage him to write short stories; just a dozen words or so at first. A five-year-old youngster hit on the idea of clipping photos from a news magazine, then using them to illustrate her story based on the pictures. One such story featured a picture of a man fleeing across a street. A second picture in the story showed a man adjusting a FOR SALE sign in front of a house. Her story: *Once upon a time a man was walking across the street and he found a house with a sign and the sign said for sale so he went inside to see if there was someone in the house and there was no one so he lived in it. the ind.* The fact that one man pictured was black, the other white, didn't seem to matter; which seemed a nice touch.

The Encyclopedia Quiz Game

Here's a writing exercise your youngster will love because it makes him look very-smart, and makes you look, well, less smart. First, give him a lined exercise book, perhaps imprinted with the impressive title, The Encyclopedia Quiz-Kid's Book. Next, show the child how to compose interesting questions from encyclopedia entries. For example, on leafing through the encyclopedia (finding entries by alphabetical order, an advanced matter, is dealt with in Chapter 12), he might chance upon the entry for *ostrich*. On reading about ostriches, he would discover that these immense birds lay eggs six inches (or fifteen centimeters) long, and three pounds (or over one kilogram) in weight. (It is presumed here that the child will have advanced sufficiently with the material in Chapter 11 to appreciate these measurements).

Show the child how he could then write in his quiz book the sentences:

How long is an ostrich egg? Six inches.

How heavy is an ostrich egg? Three pounds.

Then, flipping through another volume, he might find the entry on elephants; and, on reading about elephants, might then compose a couple more questions and answers:

How many kinds of elephants are there? Two, the African and Indian elephants.

Do female elephants have tusks? Only the African elephants.

When your youngster sees he has the means of teaching *you*, he'll be delighted to compose four such questions each day for supper-time quizzing.

Another obvious benefit to the encyclopedia quiz is that it leads children to self-education, which is, properly, the goal of any instructional program, whether the instruction is given at home or in school.

Discipline

Theoretically, discipline shouldn't be a matter for consideration in a book given to education at home; and parents may, if they wish, keep their children's educational exercises and discipline separate. However, I chose to combine the two, and found advantages in doing so.

Tired of disciplining the children, then age six and seven, by forbidding them this or that liberty, or entertainment, I decided to harness the children's misconduct and forgetfulness for the advancement of their education. And so, the traditional school punishment of writing "lines" was introduced. Thereafter, instead of missing a particular TV program they favored – a disagreeable sentence to mete out and enforce – the children were allowed to watch the program but were obliged to write in an exercise book a certain number of times the sentence: *A quick brown fox jumps over the lazy dog.*

After four months of this, the children's writing improved wonderfully, but their neglectfulness didn't; so the lines took the form of comments on specific offences; for example, *I must not leave my shoes lying untidily in the bathroom for three days*, or *I must stop pouting when I'm asked to do something.* The lines were also used as a vehicle for vocabulary growth: *I must dress with greater expedition.*

One child had a flair for forgetting, and when she had filled an exercise book of lines and started a second, I began to get the uneasy feeling that the campaign couldn't be won. The remindful value of the lines being apparently negligible, the children were obliged to copy, instead of reminders, a certain number of lines from their encyclopedia into their exercise books.

The practice of giving educational assignments as punishment, mentioned here and elsewhere in the book, may rest uncomfortably in some readers' minds. The whole question of disciplining children is one that has, unfortunately, not been set down in bronze so that parents might know the unquestionably correct action for children's every breach of conduct. Theorists on the disciplining of children are numerous and often contradictory. They are, too, sometimes childless or failures themselves as parents; and parents who sit on the firing line, trying to puzzle out what form of retributive action might help prevent some undesirable act being repeated for the hundredth time, look despairingly for direction from on high. Giving children academic tasks to perform instead of banishing them to their rooms, or forbidding or withholding some desired pleasure – or, heaven help us, clouting them – may not be a perfect solution to the problem of chastisement, but it is one that at least equips children with skills that will serve them well throughout their lives.

122

Pen Pals

When your youngster can write, you might arrange for him to write to other youngsters. Lasting friendships have been formed through correspondence, sometimes between people who never actually met face to face. Correspondents, or pen pals, aren't difficult to find. You need only write to the Board of Education in any English-speaking city or town and ask if someone would please pass your letter along to the principal of an elementary school. You might explain in your note that, though your child is only five, six, or seven, he can write and would like to find a child of similar age who could correspond with him. Enclose a letter of salutation from your child, one that includes a little information and invites a response.

The British Isles are a good source of young correspondents because children there begin Grade 1 at age five instead of six, so seven-year-olds, and sometimes even six-year-olds, are often able to write letters.

Unsure about what sort of response to expect from school boards, I sent exploratory notes, along with letters of salutation from my daughters, to towns in England, Wales, Scotland, Ireland, Mauritius, Jersey, New Zealand, the Hebrides, the Seychelles, the Bahama Islands, and the Tonga Islands. Fortunately perhaps, the timing was wrong; and with the summer holidays about to start, some of our letters might have been pigeonholed, then forgotten. In any case, the children had plenty of practice in writing salutational letters, and they did, in fact, end up with pen pals in England, Wales and Scotland.

Parents will be spared the constant need to supervise their children's correspondence if they help youngsters organize their letter writing. Children tend to forget to answer letters. And even when they do answer them, they sometimes forget they've done so. Prepare a chart, as shown in Figure 18, for your child. List pen pals across the top, and dates of arrivals and responses down the side. When a letter arrives, your youngster should insert the date of its arrival; and when the letter is answered, that date, too, should be inserted.

Children frequently can't think of what to say in their letters. Furthermore, they often can't remember whether they've already told someone a particular piece of information (admittedly difficult if a child is corresponding with more than one pen pal). Make a News Events chart (Fig. 19). The child should enter items of interest in a few words as they occur: FELL OFF MY BIKE, FOUND A DOLLAR, AM LEARNING TO SWIM, HAVE A WART, and so on. When a news item is mentioned to a pen pal, the child places a tick mark beneath that pen pal's name and opposite the appropriate item.

One of the first things a pen pal will ask is his correspondent's birthday. This date should be noted beside the pen pal's name so that a birthday card can be bought, or drawn, by your child in good time for mailing.

	Adolf LaRocque Jan.10	Giuseppi McNab Mar.20	Igor Armstrong Nov.2	Menachin Murphy Apr.23
Received	June 4	June 20	July 8	Aug. 10
Sent	June 20	June 30	July 18	
Received	July 7			
Sent	July 8			
Received				
Sent				
Received				

Figure 18: *Penpals' names and birthdates and a record of letters.*

NEWS EVENTS	Adolf	Giuseppi	Igor	Menachin
We made ice cream	✔	✔	✔	
learning to play ping-pong	✔	✔	✔	
had hiccups for ½ hour	✔	✔	✔	
beer tastes terrible	✔		✔	
am growing chives	✔		✔	
have measles			✔	
don't watch much TV				

Figure 19: *A News Events chart.*

Your youngster will need help in composing his first letters, so you will have to guide him and offer suggestions. If pressed for time, you might simply compose a letter – either handwritten or typewritten – for your child to copy, mentioning in the letter that "Daddy is helping me write this." Though the youngster is merely copying your letter, he will nevertheless see how thoughts are put on paper, and he will gradually be able to take over more of the composing.

You may find that even when you have composed letters for copying, the child will, in his own copy, introduce so many errors and crossings out that the copy will be unsuitable for mailing. Letter writing might then be made part of the child's academic curriculum, continuing for a few minutes each day until a reasonably neat copy is produced.

You may also find that the child is still writing some letters of the alphabet poorly. Have him practice those letters for a couple of minutes each day.

Finally, you will find that, generally, children like to receive letters much more than they like to write them. You may have to introduce the rule, as I did, that no newly arrived letter may be opened while there is still some letter unanswered: a villainous rule that, nevertheless, works in the pen pals' best interests.

Paying Bills

A well-educated six- or seven-year-old, now able to write, will be able to pay the monthly bills for you, learning, in the process, elements of business practice. The following notice, affixed to the wall, was found to provide adequate guidance for paying bills.

Invoice Processing Procedure

1. Make out check for the correct amount as per specimen. (A check for the telephone company for a given amount, dated and signed, was affixed to the notice.)
2. Address an envelope if an envelope doesn't accompany the bill.
3. Stick a stamp on the envelope.
4. Record letter in the Mailing Book.
5. Present check for my signature, along with envelope.

This job paid ten cents (in 1976). The children made quite a few mistakes at first, but eventually became skillful.

The various activities described in this chapter can give your child an advancement more valuable than the sum of the individual abilities; they can give him an ease and confidence in using words.

11

Counting, Measuring, and Computing

The fact that there are 40,000 muscles in an elephant's trunk or that the world's smallest mammal (the fat-tailed shrew) is just an inch and a half long would hardly astonish a child who didn't know how much 40,000 is or what an inch is. Let's consider, therefore, those quantities and measurements that permit children to better understand the world around them.

Counting

Some primitive peoples have only three numbers or categories in their counting vocabulary: *one*, *two*, and *many*. The idea apparently never occurred to them that single increases above *two* could be created and given names; and that if these names – equivalents of our *three, four, five*, and so on – were committed to memory, people would then be able to carry around in their head a "ruler made of words" with which they could measure, and keep a mental record of various quantities. The word-ruler that civilized peoples carry around in their head has virtually no limit to its measuring ability, except, of course, for the length of time needed to count as high as one wishes.

When we teach children to count, we begin with the first short length of the word ruler, from one to ten. But when children recite "One, two, three, four, five, six, seven, eight, nine, ten," they are not necessarily counting. This recitation of sounds has no meaning for a child who doesn't understand the relationship that exists between these sounds and the observable increments they represent (and this is the reason that, on page 96, the words *one* and *two* were taught in combination with objects: one spoon, two spoons, and so on).

We will presume that, at this point, your child has learned to count two objects. Let's extend his ability further: one spoon, two spoons, and now *three* spoons. Don't push ahead too quickly with *four, five*, and *six*, though. Remember, these are new words to the child, and he can easily confuse one word for another. Wait until the youngster has used the word *three* a couple of dozen times for the counting of similar objects – three plates, three pots, three jars, and so on – before introducing another new word, and another new idea, *four*.

By teaching your child just one new counting word a day, he will be able to count to 100 in less than half that number of days; the reason being that when the child counts to twenty and learns how easy it is to count from twenty to twenty-nine, he will do so. At that point, stop. Don't introduce the word *thirty* for two or three days, else the youngster may begin confusing it with *twenty*.

While learning to count to 100, your child should count only objects he sees, rather than recite numbers. When he has learned to count to ten, you may find yourself running short of spoons and knives for him to count, so change to marbles or pennies. And now the child can stop naming each item counted. That is to say, he need only count "One, two, three," instead of "One penny, two pennies, three pennies." When your youngster reaches twenty, you may want to switch the counting to some commodity you have in greater quantity: pieces of uncooked macaroni, dried beans, or other foodstuffs.

When the child learns *thirty*, he will then be easily able to count from thirty to thirty-nine. Again, don't teach the youngster *forty* until two or three days have passed and he has *twenty* and *thirty* well memorized and clear in his mind. Continue in this manner, gradually introducing the new words *fifty*, *sixty*, and so on up to 100.

When the child reaches 100, he will still need much practice in counting to 100 before he can count quickly and correctly. Counting to 100 makes a good game while driving or walking; one player voicing the odd numbers while the other fills in the even numbers. Counting the even numbers is more difficult for children than counting the odd numbers because youngsters must initiate each new tens group: twenty, thirty, forty, and so on. Let your child count the odd numbers, then, when he gains skill and confidence, let him count the even numbers. For another eventual variation, each player might count two or three numbers in succession. While driving, look for things to count: mailboxes, fire hydrants, trucks, or anything else that is plentiful.

To encourage counting, you might provide something the youngster can earn each time he reaches 100. At age four and five, my own children were allowed to remove a card from a large book of press-out valentines each time they counted to 100. In a week they had reduced the book to a skeleton of paper remnants and were counting quickly and accurately.

When your youngster can count to 100 easily, encourage him to count to 1,000, counting a little each day, beginning where he left off the previous day.

On reaching 1,000, a child will still have only a rough idea of what this quantity means. He needs to *see* a thousand objects to understand the immensity of that number. Place a spoonful of uncooked grain – rice or barley, for example – on a dinner plate and let the child separate 100 grains (more easily accomplished if he makes ten groups of ten grains each). This done, put the unused grains back in the packet and group the 100 in the center of the plate.

"Let's suppose, Althea, that we're up in a helicopter in the Arctic Circle, and we're looking down on a herd of reindeer. Each grain of rice here is a reindeer. This is just a small herd, of course. Only a hundred animals. Let's see what a herd of 200 reindeer would look like." Pour the 100 grains onto a piece of creased paper, then pour the grains into a kitchen measuring spoon. Depending on the size of grain used, you might find that the 100 grains barely measure a level half teaspoonful. Pour the grains back onto the plate; measure from the packet of rice another level half teaspoonful and add them to the plate. "Well, there's what 200 reindeer would look like. Quite a few, right? Let's have a look at 300." By successively adding half teaspoons of rice, you will be able to show the child what 300 items look like, 400, 500, and so on up to 1,000.

"Hey, that's a lot of reindeer. But do you know that some northern people have as many as 10,000 or 12,000 reindeer in their herds? Let's see what a herd that large would look like." By pouring the 1,000 grains onto paper, then into a measuring spoon, you may find they compose a heaping tablespoon. The dinner plate will be too small for larger measurements, so use a table top now or a large piece of paper spread on the floor. By adding successive heaping tablespoons of grain, you can show the child what 2,000 objects look like, 3,000, 4,000, and so on up to 10,000.

To give a youngster some understanding of the quantity one million, buy some metric graph paper squared in millimeters. Several sheets glued edge to edge to form a square one meter by one meter, would contain a million tiny squares.

Estimating

A child's understanding of quantity and groups can be sharpened by playing a game of estimating quantities at mealtimes. The ability to estimate quantities accurately is usually acquired only over a period of years. Adults might estimate that there are about ten radishes in a bundle, or twenty people waiting for a bus, or fifty dandelions growing on a lawn, and they might not be far wrong in their estimates. It is probably the lack of this ability that prompts children to use the term *zillion* to describe any number of objects that exceeds their estimating ability.

A good start in teaching children to estimate quantity is to show them how to associate numbers with groups of dots. For this, dice work well.

Begin with just one die, parent and child taking turns to see who can roll the "greatest number of dots." Following each roll, don't tell the child what number has been rolled; let him count the dots and find out. After a few days of this, he will, of course, sort out in his mind the patterns of dots, and know, without counting, how many dots are showing.

When the child has learned the dot patterns and can recognize them easily, add a second die. Now both dice should be rolled each time. Being unable to add yet, the child will need be shown how to continue counting from the dots on one die to the dots on the other. The purpose, at this moment, isn't to teach adding; nor should the child be expected to eventually recognize that, say, six dots and six dots, for example, always add up to twelve (though he *may* do so). The goal here is merely to help the child gradually see that it takes "quite a few" dots to make twelve: an association between number and cluster that will permit the child to look at a cluster of peas or people and estimate that there are "about twelve."

The child's estimating ability can be extended beyond twelve in an entertaining way at mealtimes. While the child closes his eyes, the parent places a number of small items – say, dried beans – on a plate. The child opens his eyes and when he has studied the beans for a second or two, the parent covers them with a lid. The youngster estimates the number of beans, marks that number down, then counts the beans to see how close his estimate was. The amount by which he was wrong becomes his score. Then it is the child's turn to place a number of beans on the plate for the parent to estimate.

Play the game for ten minutes. The player with the lowest score wins. If the parent starts with a handicap, he will be able to try hard to win instead of purposely erring in the child's favor. Continue playing from day to day until the child develops a good sense of group size.

Understanding the meaning of *number* in both its spoken and visual form now, the child is ready to learn the terms we use for measurement; words that will add great worth to his understanding of number. Begin with distance.

Distance

Begin teaching your child short distances. Show him a ruler; tell him, and show him, what an inch or a centimeter is, and explain that rulers help us to understand what other people mean. For example, when Uncle Ben tells us over the phone that he caught a fish eleven inches or twenty-eight centimeters long, we need only get out our ruler to determine exactly how long the fish was.

Your youngster will enjoy measuring items on the supper table. Make a list of the objects he measures, marking down whatever measurement he gives you. Rather than becoming involved in fractions, show the child how to measure to the nearest inch or centimeter. If he doesn't know the meaning of *height*, *width*, *length*, and *thickness*, this is a good time to teach him those terms. Have him measure the height of a ketchup bottle, the length of a spoon, the distance across a cup (no need to mention *diameter* at this moment), and dimensions of other items at hand.

Eventually, you will be able to make a game of estimating distances, taking turns quizzing each other on how long or how tall this or that object is, then measuring the object to see how close the estimate was.

When your child gains skill in estimating short distances, explain that there are twelve inches in a foot or 100 centimeters in a meter, and have him measure longer distances: an exercise that might be made easier if you give him a yardstick or a meter stick to use. You might mention that detectives are very observant of distances and dimensions, often having to measure this or that object, then send the youngster off with a pad, pencil, and yardstick to measure anything he pleases around the home. Or, even better, accompany him.

Your youngster will quickly learn what a mile or kilometer is if you determine, by referring to the odometer in your car, some landmark a mile or a kilometer from your home. If the object is situated on a route you often drive with the child, his repeated passing of the one-mile or one-kilometer point will quickly give him an understanding of that distance. Other points might be established at distances of two, three, and four miles or kilometers, and so on, from your home.

Another way to teach your youngster the meaning of *mile* or *kilometer* is to walk the distance. The scale on a city map will let you find an intersection of streets a mile or kilometer away from your home. Perhaps your child can count the number of steps he must take to get there.

Time

The purpose here isn't to teach a child how to tell the time (though this exercise will prepare your youngster for eventually acquiring that skill), but merely to teach him the units of time measurement and to help him estimate the passage of time. The measurement of time can be made a mealtime game. First, teach your child how long a second is. Show him how to measure the passage of seconds by counting elephants: "One elephant, two elephants, three elephants," and so on. (The length of time it takes a child to count each elephant is about one second.)

To the glass front of an electric clock (one that has a sweep second hand) attach a ring of paper bearing the numbers 5 to 60 in increments of five, blocking out, thereby, the numbers 1 to 12 (Fig. 20). Show the child how, by waiting until the sweep hand is at 60, he can measure any number of seconds up to 60. When the child can easily measure the passing of seconds in this way, have a time quiz.

130

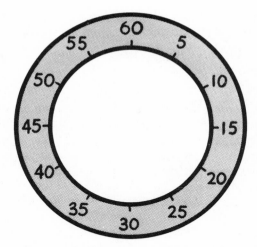

Figure 20: *A ring of numbers placed over the figures of a clock can aid teaching the passage of seconds.*

The clock is placed in such a position that only one player can see its face. That player then asks the other to estimate the passing of a certain number of seconds, and tells him when to start (when the sweep hand is at the 60). Once started, the other player announces when he thinks the required number of seconds has passed.

The measurement of minutes doesn't lend itself nearly so well to mealtime games, though it has been used to stimulate appetites when excessive dawdling occurred over some food item. The announcement that some particular food had better be eaten in the next five minutes can give children an understanding of that time span as effectively as a game would.

Both driving and walking provide opportunities for estimating, and measuring, the passage of minutes. How long will it take to travel to Aunt Olga's, or walk to the store? You and your child can each estimate the time needed, then keep track of the number of minutes that actually pass.

To give children an understanding of what an hour is, set an alarm clock to ring in an hour's time. If you are taking a long trip with your youngster, estimating when the alarm clock is about to ring can provide an educating diversion.

The length of a day will, of course, already be known to your child. But does he know there are seven days in a week? Can he name them? Hang a calendar near the supper table to provide ready reference for dates. Choose one that has a large square for each day, and encourage the youngster to draw a simple picture of the weather—a sun, a cloud, raindrops, snowflakes—in the square for each day. The child will quickly gain a good understanding of the days and weeks. "Remember when it rained last Wednesday, Bascombe?" And he'll be able to verify this by his calendar drawing. When the child has learned the days of the week, teach him the months of the year.

Weight

Guessing, or estimating, weight provides much entertainment at fairs and exhibitions. It can provide entertainment at mealtimes, too. Begin by teaching your child what an ounce or a gram is. Kitchen scales are usually too insensitive to accurately indicate ounces or grams; you might therefore purchase an inexpensive letter scale for this purpose.

Make a chart on which the child can keep track of everything he measures. How much does a pen weigh? A spoon? The saltshaker? Scissors?

When the child has gained an understanding of weight measurement, bring an assortment of objects to the supper table and play a weighing game with him. An item is chosen; each player handles the object, feels its weight, and marks his estimate on a piece of paper. The item is then weighed, and congratulations given.

Teach your child that there are sixteen ounces in a pound, or 1,000 grams in a kilogram, then continue the game with heavier objects, using the kitchen scale to verify their weight. If you own a bathroom scale, you might weigh some heavier objects so your child can extend his knowledge of weight. If an object won't fit on the scale, stand on the scale holding the object (if practical), then subtract your weight from the total to find the weight of the object. How much does a kitchen chair weigh? A bicycle? The cat? The dog?

Finally, the child should be taught to understand the meaning of a ton, or tonne in metric. Explain that small cars weigh about a ton, that rhinoceroses weigh two or three tons, and that a large elephant might weigh about five tons.

Liquid Measure

Teach your child that there are two pints in a quart, and four quarts in a gallon. If you buy milk only in quarts, divide a quart in half to let the youngster see how much a pint is. What part of a pint does he normally drink in his cup or mug? Measure the amount in a measuring cup.

Sometime when you are walking past a service station with the youngster, show him a 50-gallon drum, used in many garages as garbage containers. How many cups of milk would a 50-gallon drum hold? *Not* a zillion.

Teaching the child that there are 20 fluid ounces in a pint or 1,000 milliliters in a liter will let you compare, during mealtime, the contents of various cans, jars, and bottles.

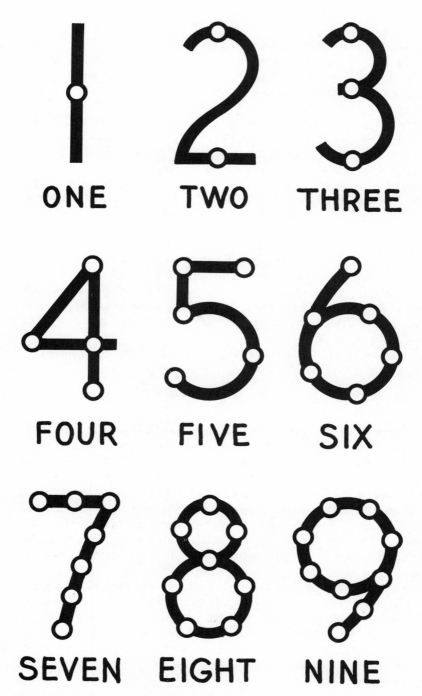

Figure 21: *The total of the circles in each numeral equals its value.*

Computing

Computing, here, will deal only with simple day-to-day calculating needs: adding, subtracting, multiplying, and dividing. The child knows, at this point, that the sounds of "one," "two," and "three" represent visible increases. What he needs to know now is the shorthand we use to compute quickly.

Explain to the child that instead of writing words for numbers, we use signs for them, a sort of code: "Yes, Pierre, just like spies have." Show the youngster that, in our mathematical code, "one" appears as 1. "This is to fool the Plug-uglies, a fierce tribe of mathematics-hating monsters who eat numbers on sight" (if you want to continue the spoof for his pleasure). Show him that "two" appears as 2. The numbers on page 133 will help the child sort out and remember the signs we use for numbers one to nine. Each number has the word for that number beneath it and each contains the same number of circles that the number represents. The child can always count the circles or read the word if he wants to assure himself at any time that everything is correct. Make a copy of page 133 and purchase a supply of onion-skin paper or other thin paper. Position a sheet of paper over the numbers, securing it at the edges with masking tape, and show the child how to trace each number, drawing through the middle of each circle.

When the youngster can remember the various number symbols and can make them easily, he is ready to begin adding.

Adding

Set this book, open at page 133, on a book-stand so the child can refer to the numbers whenever he wants to. Explain that there are two other secret symbols used in the mathematical code: +, which means "and," and =, which means "is the same as." Balance a ruler on your finger and explain to the child that "is the same as" works like the point of balance on your finger, and that whatever goes on one side must always be balanced on the other. Place two pennies side by side at one end of the ruler, and at the other end, place one penny on top of another. Point out to the child that though the pennies are arranged differently, the ruler still balances at the same point when it is placed on your finger again.

Bring a few dried beans or pieces of macaroni to the table. Place one bean in front of the child. "If I add another bean to that one, Solomon, how many would there be?" Add the second bean. The child will, of course, say "two." Show the youngster how this event or transaction would be described in code ($1 + 1 = 2$). Let him see that the coded message or statement is consistent with the number of dots shown on the special numbers; and that the dots on each side of the "is-the-same-as" sign balance just as the coins on the ruler balanced. Turn the coded message around $(2 = 1 + 1)$ and let the child see that the statement still makes sense, and that both sides still balance.

"All right, we have two beans. What if I add another bean? How many would there be now?" Add the bean. The child will see that there are now three. Once again, show the child how this transaction would be expressed $(2 + 1 = 3)$ and show him that this coded statement is consistent with the dots on the special numbers. Finally, let the youngster see that $1 + 2 = 3$.

This will seem very simple to you, but be careful: it isn't simple for your child. His mind must get a purchase on the new information in his own way and in his own good time. When, after a few days or weeks, this information has dropped into place in your youngster's frame of logic, advance again slowly.

Now, you might take a different approach. Place four beans on the table and mark down "= 4." Give the child another four beans and ask him ways they might be separated. If he separates his beans into two groups of two, mark his grouping "$2 + 2 = 4$," and show him that this statement is consistent with the dots on the special numbers. If he divides his beans into groups of one and three, mark that grouping, "$1 + 3 = 4$."

Continue in this way, from day to day, using more beans and new numbers. You may find that the adding your child learns one day may be forgotten the next. Children don't realize that the information $1 + 1 = 2$, or $1 + 2 = 3$, is something to be remembered for future use when those numbers are encountered again; therefore, an important part of the child's daily exercise should consist of repeating the sums he has already dealt with. When the child has progressed up to number 6, for example, his daily adding, perhaps under the tutor's guidance, would be:

$1 + 1 =$	$1 + 2 =$	$2 + 1 =$	$3 + 1 =$	$1 + 3 =$
$2 + 2 =$	$1 + 4 =$	$4 + 1 =$	$2 + 3 =$	$3 + 2 =$
$1 + 5 =$	$5 + 1 =$	$2 + 4 =$	$4 + 2 =$	$3 + 3 =$

When the child can add $5 + 4$ and $4 + 5$, show him the shorter way that sums can be shown, in which the numbers are placed one above the other. Show the plus sign in each case so the child won't be confused later when he deals with subtraction and multiplication. Here are the problems the youngster will now have covered, shown in the new form. The child may need help working with these until be becomes accustomed to the new presentation.

$$
\begin{array}{cccccccccccccccccc}
1 & 1 & 2 & 1 & 3 & 2 & 3 & 2 & 4 & 1 & 1 & 5 & 2 & 4 & 3 & 6 & 1 \\
+1 & +2 & +1 & +3 & +1 & +2 & +2 & +3 & +1 & +4 & +5 & +1 & +4 & +2 & +3 & +1 & +6
\end{array}
$$

$$
\begin{array}{cccccccccccccccccc}
2 & 5 & 4 & 3 & 1 & 7 & 2 & 6 & 5 & 3 & 4 & 8 & 1 & 2 & 7 & 5 & 4 \\
+5 & +2 & +3 & +4 & +7 & +1 & +6 & +2 & +3 & +5 & +4 & +1 & +8 & +7 & +2 & +4 & +5
\end{array}
$$

$$
\begin{array}{cc}
3 & 6 \\
+6 & +3
\end{array}
$$

Writing out this many sums for the child each day could become burdensome. You might therefore have photocopies made, the child filling in a new sheet each day. Or give the child a sheet of onion-skin paper to place on top of the sums. His answers would then be marked on the onion-skin.

You may find your child counting on his fingers as an aid to adding. (One of my daughters did. In fact, the manipulation of her fingers eventually became so quick that their movement resembled the conversation of a mute.) Or you may find the child making dots beside each number and counting the dots (as my other daughter did). Don't discourage either of these practices. Children drop these aids voluntarily when they gain skill and confidence in adding.

There are different theories about what children should be told when they encounter the number ten; one belief being that they should be taught the one is in the tens column, and that there is nothing in the units column. This information is perfectly true, but, like the workings of an automobile transmission, it can be very confusing for a child. Better to simply say that the combination of 1 and 0 stands for ten, and drop the matter.

Mental adding can now be made a pastime while driving or walking. But keep the sums easy until the child gains confidence. "How much is one and two, Flavius?" Let him quiz *you* occasionally. This will still provide good practice for the youngster because he will have to verify the accuracy of your answers. What if you give him a wrong answer? Try it and see.

If you enlarge the size of sums, and give the child daily practice in adding, the child will soon be adding well: a skill that, despite the availability of low-cost pocket calculators, remains of great value.

My own children were adding skillfully at ages six and seven. They gained their skill partly from the sums in their regular curriculum of home activities, and partly from a special sort of supplemental program that had, years earlier, improved my own adding ability.

Extracurricular Math

Back in the 1940s, one innovative high-school teacher gave detentions that were either long or short depending on one's ability to add quickly and correctly. He would chalk up an immense adding problem eight or nine figures wide and a dozen or so figures high. As each offender (his detention periods always had good turnouts) arrived at the correct answer, he was free to leave.

This early experience prompted me to let the children's misdemeanors sponsor a program of extracurricular adding; and one child, who had a knack for getting into hot water, was soon speeding in the direction of adding supremacy. (In fact, she became pretty good at subtracting, multiplying, and division, too.)

Of the ways that children may be punished, computing assignments are possibly the least damaging to the parent-child relationship. Unfortunately, though, the effectiveness of computing as a punishment gradually diminishes; for, as children gain skill in computing, so they begin to take pride in their uncommon ability, and almost welcome each opportunity to demonstrate their skill.

Subtraction

Subtraction is simply the reverse of adding. Follow the same simple steps, in reverse, that you used to teach adding. Introduce the symbol for subtraction (–), and explain that this means "take away." "Here are two beans, Emerald. Now if I take one of them away, how many would be left? Right! One." Show the child this transaction in coded form (2 – 1 = 1). Continue in this way, progressing gradually to more beans and larger numbers; and make subtraction a game in the car.

You will eventually have to explain "borrowing" from the left-hand column. Show the child how, for example, in the problem below, the 7 is reduced to a 6, and the 3 becomes 13.

$$
\begin{array}{r} 7\,3 \\ -\,2\,6 \\ \hline \end{array}
\qquad
\begin{array}{r} 6 \\ \not{7}\,13 \\ -\,2\,6 \\ \hline \end{array}
\qquad
\begin{array}{r} 6 \\ \not{7}\,13 \\ -\,2\,6 \\ \hline 4\,7 \end{array}
$$

Multiplication

The idea of multiplication can be taught in a simple way. "Look, Sheldon: suppose we went to the store and bought a loaf of bread. Then, when we got home, I decided that one loaf wasn't enough, so we went back and bought another loaf. How many loaves would we have now? Two? Correct!" Show the child how these purchases might be written down (A in Fig. 22); which, unfortunately, has the same form as an adding problem. Introduce the multiplication sign to your child. In fact, you might write it in a different color or circle it to draw it to the child's attention.

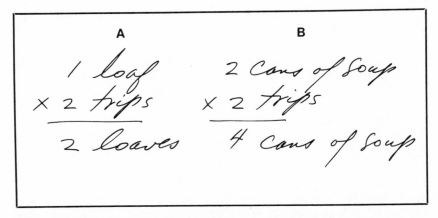

Figure 22: *Multiplication can be taught by imagining trips to the store.*

"And suppose we made a trip to the store and bought two cans of soup, but then I decided we needed two more; so, we went back again and bought two more cans. How many cans of soup would we have?" (shown at B). Continue in this way, proposing, each time, two trips for the imaginary purchase of three quarts of milk, four grapefruit, five lemons, six bananas, and so on, up to ten items.

Don't forget the important contribution a puppet can make to your mathematics instruction by offering ridiculous answers or demanding absurd food items such as rubber-band sandwiches, chocolate-covered Ping-Pong balls, Kentucky-fried dew worms, and so on.

Teach the three-times table by engaging in three imaginary trips to the store. The youngster will soon see that multiplication is similar to adding, and that three times two is really two plus two plus two.

Show the child that the purchases made on the various shopping trips can be entered on a chart (A in Fig. 23). Make up a blank grid similar to that shown at B and, as the child gains skill with the two-times and three-times tables, let him, as a daily exercise, place a piece of onion-skin paper over the blank grid and fill in the answers he now knows.

Division

Fortunately, division problems don't look like addition, subtraction, or multiplication problems. Place four beans on the table and ask your youngster to make two groups of the beans, having the same number of beans in each group. You might have to help him. Then show the child how this separation is described in coded form (A in Fig. 24), and how the answer would then appear (B).

Now ask the youngster to divide six beans into two equal groups. When he has done so, show him how the problem would be written

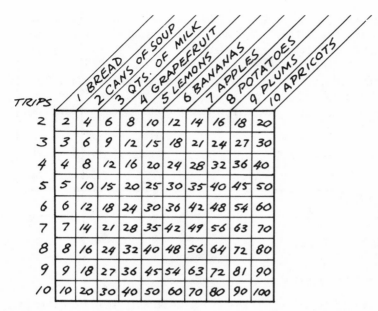

TRIPS	1 BREAD	2 CANS OF SOUP	3 QTS. OF MILK	4 GRAPEFRUIT	5 LEMONS	6 BANANAS	7 APPLES	8 POTATOES	9 PLUMS	10 APRICOTS
2	2	4	6	8	10	12	14	16	18	20
3	3	6	9	12	15	18	21	24	27	30
4	4	8	12	16	20	24	28	32	36	40
5	5	10	15	20	25	30	35	40	45	50
6	6	12	18	24	30	36	42	48	54	60
7	7	14	21	28	35	42	49	56	63	70
8	8	16	24	32	40	48	56	64	72	80
9	9	18	27	36	45	54	63	72	81	90
10	10	20	30	40	50	60	70	80	90	100

Figure 23: *A: A multiplication chart based on trips to the store.*

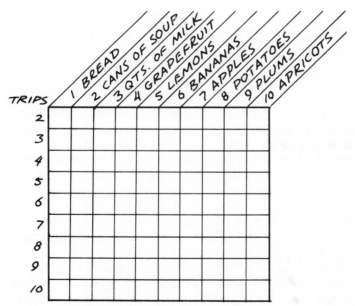

B: The same chart left blank to be filled in by a child.

down, and what the answer would be. You might draw the child's attention to the fact that division is the reverse of multiplication; that the number we need at the top is the one that, when multiplied by the number on the left, gives us the number on the right.

When the child gains skill at short division, teach him – or have tutors teach him – long division. The teaching of long division, of decimals, percentages, fractions, and other mathematical skills can easily be handled

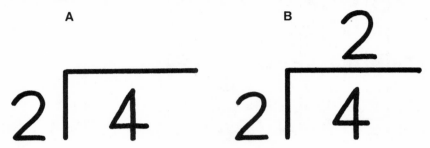

Figure 24: *A division problem, and its solution.*

by the tutors if you provide them with a textbook. *Arithmetic Made Simple* by Sperling and Levison, an inexpensive paperback book, will permit the tutors to style a mathematics program to your wishes. Have the child taught angles and degrees, and he will be better able to understand latitude and longitude, dealt with next chapter.

When your child has learned long division and decimals, he will be able to engage in comparison pricing.

Comparison Pricing

Unfortunately, children have few opportunities to make use of their computing ability. One practical use, comparison pricing, requires considerable effort, but it's worth working at.

Comparison pricing means calculating the unit cost of a commodity to find out which quantity of the commodity is cheapest. Some retailers use tricky pricing methods to make unwary shoppers pay more for their purchases. For example, knowing that many shoppers reach instinctively for the large-sized package believing that larger packages are most economical in the long run, merchants sometimes raise the unit price in the large packages higher than that in smaller packages.

Take an example. Suppose dry dog food costs 95¢ for a five-pound bag, $1.70 for a ten-pound bag, and $5.13 for a twenty-five-pound bag. Which bag has the cheapest unit price? To find out, determine the cost of *one* pound of food in each of the bags. At A, the price of the five-pound bag (95¢) divided by the number of pounds (five) tells us that one pound

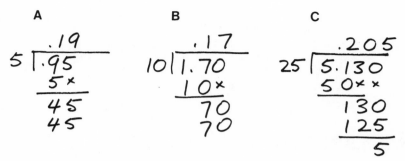

Figure 25: *Comparison shopping uses division.*

of food in that particular bag costs 19¢. The cost of one pound of food in the ten-pound bag, at B, is 17¢. And the cost of one pound in the twenty-five pound bag, at C, is about 20½¢. In this case the best purchase is the ten-pound bag, not the largest bag.

When only two sizes are being compared, a quicker choice can be made by finding the unit cost in the smaller container, then multiplying this amount by the number of units in the larger container. To illustrate: a two-pound bag of some commodity costs 56¢. The five-pound bag costs $1.25. The cost of one pound in the small bag is 56¢ divided by 2, or 28¢. If the price per pound were equal in both sizes, the large container *should* cost 28 × 5, or $1.40. But it costs just $1.25; so there is a saving in the larger bag.

Teach your child, also, how to compute change from a purchase; first by using coins. For example: suppose 25¢ is offered to pay for a 17¢ item. Show the child that we begin counting at the price of the purchase, and add coins up to the amount given: seventeen plus three pennies makes twenty, plus five cents makes twenty-five.

Next, increase the amount tendered to 50¢, then a dollar. Equipped with sufficient notes and coins, the tutor might engage the youngster in a game of store, buying and selling various toys and bric-a-brac, thereby requiring the exchange of money and the computing of change.

12

Advanced Knowledge and Skills

When a child asks where pomegranates grow, or the distance to the moon, or what worms eat, the response, "I don't know," is an educational dead-end unless it is followed by "Let's find out." The child who can read, but who hasn't yet learned how indexing works, might be told which volume of the encyclopedia to fetch. The parent can then locate the appropriate entry for him and have the child read it aloud.

How much better, though, if the child is able to locate information in the encyclopedia without parental help. The purpose in this chapter is to equip children with advanced knowledge and skills that will extend their information-gathering power and will fit them better for a continuing—lifelong!—program of self-education.

Indexing

A major advance is achieved when a child learns to understand the process we call *indexing*. Prepare nine cards with a word printed on each: *ant, arm, ash, bat, big, bus, cat, cot,* and *cup.* Turn them face down and mix them up. Print a letter on each of three other cards: A on one, B on a second, C on a third, and place them side by side to form the headings for three columns. Your child turns over one of the nine word cards and positions it near the card bearing its beginning letter. He turns over another and positions it appropriately, continuing in this manner until all nine cards have been correctly positioned, three beneath each letter.

Now take the three cards, *ant, arm,* and *ash.* Tell your child to notice the second letter in each word and to tell you when he hears one of these letters, an N, an R, and an S. Then recite the alphabet slowly. When you get to N, your child *may* notice that N occurs in the second position in *ant.* (Then again, he may not. This is a difficult challenge.) If he doesn't notice, draw his attention to the N, and position the card so it will be topmost in the word column beneath the letter A. Continue reciting the alphabet to R, at which point, the R in *arm* would be indicated. Again, your child may not notice this. In fact, he may still not be clear what is expected of him. Position the word *arm* beneath *ant*, and continue your recitation to S for *ash*; place it, in turn, beneath *ant*.

Mix the three cards and repeat the whole operation. Your child will gradually learn to ignore the first letter in each word and pay close attention to the second letter. When he is eventually able to indicate the appropriate card for you as you recite the alphabet, put *arm*, *ant*, and *ash* aside, take *bat*, *big*, and *bus*, and repeat the whole procedure. When your child learns how to sort *bat*, *big*, and *bus*, repeat the whole procedure using *cat*, *cot*, and *cup*.

Your youngster will begin to see that, by this new method of sorting words, there is a "firstness," a "secondness," and a "thirdness" to each set of three words that is intimately tied in with the sequence of the alphabet. When, after a week or so of practice, the child is brimming with confidence, add to the exercise nine more cards bearing the words *and*, *art*, *ask*, *bag*, *bit*, *bus*, *can*, *cob*, and *cut*.

Repeat the same sorting operation ignoring, for the moment, the third letter in each word, and when your child is able to position the cards correctly, six beneath each of the three letters, show him that *ant* and *and* have, by our sorting method, a first and second quality about them that is determined by their third letter and its position in the alphabet. Then show and explain the precise order for each of the six words in the three columns. When, eventually, your child has this procedure clear in his head, show him how the information can be used to play a game – Bargain Hunting. For this, you will need a mail-order catalog.

First, establish certain pages in the book as "bargain" pages – perhaps those pages that have a number divisible by five: 5, 10, 15, and so on. To begin the game, the first player might say "Towels," then locate towels in the index. If towels are shown on a bargain page, he gains a point or a treat; perhaps just a cornflake. The other player then names some item and checks the index to see if it is on a bargain page. The game continues in this way. If the child is encouraged to check in the catalog not only his guesses but those of the other player, too, he will soon become skillful in using the index.

Another good exercise in indexing is provided by encouraging a youngster to locate the names of friends and relatives in the telephone directory.

Learning to find words in a dictionary is a great academic advance for children. Encourage the child at every opportunity to find words in the dictionary on his own. Unaided, a child may take, at first, four, five, or more minutes to locate each word. This is hard work for a youngster, so some form of treat should be provided to keep his interest alive.

Once skillful at locating words in the dictionary, a child can begin to look up any new word he encounters while reading, and enter the word in a Dictionary Book (a lined exercise book). The youngster should write, first, the sentence in which the unknown word appears, the part of speech filled by the word in the particular instance, and, finally, the appropriate definition if there are several: an exercise that will often require the tutor's help.

The following entry, containing two errors (the nouns, *population* and *verge*) and omissions, nevertheless shows what an eight-year-old is capable of after two years of instruction and practice.

> In a country as vast as India with its great areas of forest land and bad communications, and with its teeming population chronically on the verge of starvation, it is easy to understand the temptations to embark on a life of crime.*
>
> vast – adjective – very great in size
> teem – verb – to become filled to overflowing
> population – adjective – the whole number of people in a country
> verge – verb – to be on the border
> tempt – verb – to dare to encourage to do something
> embark – to make a start
> chronic – always present or encountered, persistent

Grammar, Salted and Peppered with Humor

Forty years ago, when I was a captive at Pape Avenue public school in the east end of Toronto, the person who dispensed grammar (as opposed to teaching it) encouraged us to recite, "Is, am, are, was, seem, become, appear, look, taste, and smell, all take subjective completions." I memorized the chant, failed the exams, and might never have bothered with this dull subject again if someone hadn't asked me to write a book on it (*Grammar for People Who Hate Grammar*). Grammar, I finally learned, could not only be interesting; it could be useful.

Studying grammar can be hilarious for youngsters when it is made a game. Your child can have loads of laughs – as mine did – learning grammatical terms. Not that knowing the terms or "labels" is the purpose of studying grammar, but knowing the labels permits us to understand each other when we discuss correct English usage. First, you might like a quick review.

You may recall that all the words in our language can fill only eight jobs – noun, pronoun, verb, adverb, adjective, preposition, conjunction, and interjection – and that some words can fill more than one job depending on how they are used. Let's begin with nouns.

Generally, nouns are either persons, places, or things – objects with

---

*From "Sultana: India's Robin Hood," in *My India,* by Jim Corbett (New York, 1952)

144

names. One way to identify a noun is to see if the word can fit in the sentence, "Let's talk about … (noun)" – though the word *a* or *the* may be needed. A noun is singular or plural depending on whether it names one item or more items. *Man* is singular, *men* is plural. A noun is called proper if it has a capital: *Terry Fox, Toronto, Union Station.* Other nouns are called common: *native, district, tower.*

Nouns, like movie stars, have stand-ins. The stand-ins are called pronouns: *I, me, we, us, you, he, him, she, her, it, they, them.*

Adjectives are describers. They describe any special qualities nouns may possess: *big, fast, heavy, blue, spooky.*

Verbs usually tell us what nouns are doing: *sing* (present tense); and if it's still happening, *singing* (present tense, continuing action); or if it has yet to occur, *will sing* (future tense); and if it has ended, *sang* (past tense). Other verb forms don't concern us here.

Adverbs usually add-to-verbs by telling us where, when, why, how, and to what extent nouns are engaged in some activity. She sings *well* (or *often*, or *tonight*).

Prepositions tell us the situation that exists between a noun (or pronoun) and other words in a sentence: *into, on, beside, near, between,* to name a few.

Conjunctions join words, or parts of a sentence, or entire sentences: *and, but, if, whether, however, therefore, where, why,* and others.

Interjections are merely gasps or exclamations: *Oh!, My!, Cripes!*

The grammar game begins with one player, let's call him X, writing down, secretly, a sentence or two: for example, *Jack be nimble, Jack be quick; Jack jump over the candlestick.* X then asks the other players to suggest words to him, and he describes the exact grammatical job each suggested word must fill. For example, X might ask for a proper noun. Someone might suggest *Prince Charles.* X strikes out the three *Jacks* in his rhyme and writes *Prince Charles* over each. Next, he might ask for two adjectives that can describe people. *Beautiful* and *hairy* being suggested, X strikes out *nimble* and *quick* and writes one of the new adjectives above each. By successively striking out *jump, over,* and *candlestick,* and asking for a verb (present tense), a preposition, and a common noun (singular) X would write in each word suggested. Finally, X would read aloud what he had first written, then read his revised version of it: *Prince Charles be beautiful, Prince Charles be hairy; Prince Charles fly into the wallpaper.*

The end product can send children into fits of giggles, and therein lies the delight for parents. The game becomes especially funny for youngsters when the text deals with family or friends. For example, *Uncle Andrew and Aunt Debbie visited Niagara Falls in their trailer* easily becomes comical so long as the relatives' names are left in. One possible result: *Uncle Andrew and Aunt Debbie shouted Mickey Mouse in their golfball.*

Start your games by changing just nouns, then when your youngster has a clear understanding of nouns, gradually begin adding the other parts of speech. Subjective completions? We might tackle them another time.

Composition

Parents needn't be writers themselves to start children writing. Children need just a little instruction and lots of practice. Two sorts of writing will be considered here: fictional writing and factual writing.

Encouraging children to write fiction helps develop their imaginations; and imagination is the trigger of inventiveness. Simple plot ideas for stories can be found in several ways. One method is to compose a chain of words, each word beginning with the letter with which the preceding word ended. For example, starting with *cat*, the next word must then begin with a *T*; perhaps *tomato*; and now the next word must begin with *O*. In such a way, the following arbitrary chain of plot words might be formed: cat-tomato-owl-lake-elephant. The child now composes sentences, each containing a plot word in the correct order of progression, and he strings the sentences together in the form of a story. To illustrate:

A cat named Harold lived in the country. Harold didn't eat mice, but he loved tomatoes. One day while he was munching a juicy tomato, an owl hooted. Harold thought the hoot was the sound of the ferryboat on the nearby lake. He raced down to the wharf expecting to have a chat with the captain, a friend of his, who happened to be an elephant.

Nonsense is, of course, essential if the exercise is to charm children.

Another device for creating simple plots is the "fortunately-unfortunately" form of story in which statements alternately express fortunate and unfortunate events. Here is a ghastly tale that will delight most children.

One day the Queen of Zazu used a special dye conditioner to make her hair blond.
Unfortunately, it made her hair fall out.
Fortunately, her eyebrows and eyelashes stayed in place.
Unfortunately, her ears dropped off the following week.
Fortunately, her hair grew back in and hid the space where her ears had been.
Unfortunately, the new hair was blue-green in color.

A child can then be shown how each of the plot lines might be enlarged, and extra sentences added, to make a more interesting story. For example:

One day, Her Majesty, the Queen of Zazu, decided she would like to change the color of her hair, which happened to be blue-green; so she had a special dye conditioner brought in from a distant land. But when she applied the conditioner to her hair, her hair fell out. Luckily, her eyelashes and eyebrows didn't fall out.

A week later, while trying to put on an earring, the ear came off in her fingers. The other dropped off shortly after lunch. A few days later, her bluish-green hair grew back in. (Occasionally, the King of Zazu suggests that the Queen dye her hair a different color, but she has no ears for his suggestion.)

Show your youngster how to write in stage-play form, and he will be able to write plays that members of the family can enact and read into a tape recorder. An example:

Mother: Here, Waldo; here, Waldo. Now where's that dog gone? Nancy, have you seen Waldo?

Nancy: Yes, Mommy, I saw him going down to the basement a minute ago.

Waldo: Oh-oh! She saw me. Here we go. Another bath. How I hate baths!

Mother: So there you are, Waldo. Come on, now, you little scamp. Time for your bath.

Waldo: Time for your bath. Time for your bath. That's all I ever hear. Why can't she just let me smell like a dog for a change?

Nancy: Do you think that Waldo perhaps doesn't like having baths, Mommy?

Mother: Nonsense. He loves baths, Nancy. Why, whenever I put him in the tub, he always licks my hand.

Waldo: That's because I can't get my teeth around it.

Fire the child's imagination by considering the ways a dime might travel in just a single day; first, by being spent at a store, then being handed out in change, perhaps to travel a great distance, only to be spent again; and so on. Have the child compose a story of his own about the traveling dime, describing the people who owned it briefly and the things they said. Stimulate the child's thoughts about what antics a magician might engage in when he goes shopping or when he visits the circus or zoo.

The child might pretend he is a doctor or veterinarian and describe some of the duties he must perform in the course of a day: how he treated an elephant's runny nose, an alligator's toothache, a lion's dandruff. Or a youngster might describe his experiences as a firefighter when the chocolate factory was ablaze. Similarly, the adventures of a police constable, a nurse, a detective, or captain of a ship provide material for first-person recounting.

Children delight in writing stories that grant them unusual powers. Here are four suggested themes:

What I'd do if I were invisible.
What I'd do if I had a million dollars.
What I'd do if I had the strength of ten people.
What I'd do if I could float on air.

Factual Writing

The writing of reports from the encyclopedia provides a simple yet doubly educating way of encouraging a child to express himself in written form. The steps for writing a report, given here, might be simplified until the child gains ease and speed in composing and entering reports in his "Encyclopedia Report Book."

1. Read the entire entry on a given topic in the encyclopedia (unless, of course, it is a long one).
2. Read the entry again; this time, jot one-, two-, or three-word notes (called jot notes) about important points, noting each point on a separate slip of paper.
3. Arrange the slips of paper in whatever order is desired (which may be quite different from the order in which they were presented in the encyclopedia).
4. Expand the jot notes into sentences and join these sentences together on another piece of paper. The result is called an outline.
5. Rewrite the outline, elaborating on each point mentioned. The result is called a first draft.
6. Read the draft. Mark corrections or additions. Check the spelling and grammar.
7. Write the finished report.

Your youngster might start with reports of just twenty or thirty words, gradually increasing in length as he gains confidence with the exercise. The child's reports should be, of course, on topics of his own choice.

Geography

Knowing the Earth's physical features, and the names and locations of land and water masses, is tool knowledge, because it permits children to understand daily events better. For example, the news that a strange creature had been sighted in a strait in the Aleutians will not mean much to a child who doesn't know what a strait is or that the Aleutians are islands in the North Pacific Ocean.

Children don't usually study geography until they are nine or ten, the main reason being that they can't read well enough before this age to distinguish the names of various geographical locations. But any pre-schooler able to read well can begin learning more about the Earth. And because geography lends itself to the playing of games, its study can be captivating for youngsters. Literate four- and five-year-olds have had a whale of a time playing the following games.

First, if you haven't a globe of the world, buy one. An inexpensive ten-inch globe is adequate. Set the globe in the middle of your supper table and you'll be ready to begin teaching geography.

Explain that the globe is a model of our Earth, except that the Earth doesn't have colors, lines, and names on it. Explain the meaning of *model* by referring to toy trains and cars.

Show your youngster the map (Fig. 26) and tell him that an island is a piece of land surrounded by water; that a strait is a neck of water; that a peninsula is a piece of land jutting out into water; that an isthmus is a neck of land; and a bay and a gulf are bodies of water partly surrounded by land.

Point out, on the globe, some of the larger islands: England, New Zealand, Cuba, and others. Mention that both Florida and Baja California are peninsulas. Indicate the Strait of Gibraltar, the Isthmus of Panama, a few bays and gulfs, and the principal seas and oceans. Explain what the north and south poles are, and the equator, too. You will then be able to make a game of locating places.

To begin, one player picks a country and asks the others to find it. For example: "Who can find Cuba?" The player on his right tries to find Cuba on the globe. If he can't find it in a specified time, another player takes a turn, or the original player takes a second turn, depending on what rules

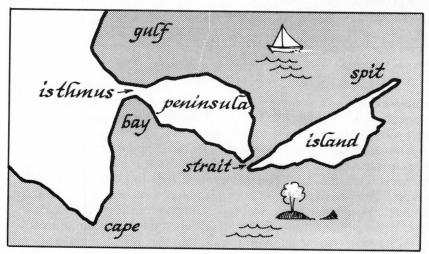

Figure 26: *A map for teaching geographical terms.*

you establish to ensure a smooth-running game. Playing the game for a week or two will teach your child the location and relative size of many countries.

Supply your youngster with a lined exercise book to serve as a Geography Book, and have him enter the names of geographical locations as he learns them. This procedure will also exercise the child's printing or writing. For entering the names of a few locations in his Geography Book, the youngster might be given a self-adhering sticker with which to label some item around the home.

Teach children, first, the larger or better-known areas of land and bodies of water; working gradually down to smaller countries, seas, gulfs, and bays. You might choose to learn countries one week, bodies of water the next, and islands another.

As the seven seas of your globe become dotted with uncharted islands of peanut butter or mashed potato, your youngster will gain considerable skill in finding places.

A geography game featuring an element of surprise is played with a chart, one red die, and one white die (or dice that can be distinguished in some way). Make a chart similar to that shown in Figure 27, filling in the

1	*2*	*W H I T E* *3*	*4*	*5*	*6*	*RED*
EGYPT	PORTUGAL	ISRAEL ˣ	TURKEY	SWITZERLAND	VENEZUELA	*1*
ENGLAND	CHINA	AUSTRALIA	U.S.A.	FRANCEˣ	ITALY	*2*
GERMANY	CANADA	RUSSIA	IRELANDˣ	SCOTLAND	BELGIUM	*3*
N.ZEALAND	MEXICO	BRAZIL	HOLLAND	ARGENTINA	IRAN ˣ	*4*
ETHIOPIA	POLANDˣ	SWEDEN	NORWAY	FINLAND	ICELAND	*5*
INDIA ˣ	JAPAN	S. AFRICA	GREENLAND	N.GUINEA	SPAIN	*6*

Figure 27: *A sample chart for the geography game.*

names of thirty-six countries, bodies of water, or islands. Spend two or three days teaching the child how to find the thirty-six places on the globe, and you will then be ready for the game.

One player rolls the dice. Let's say he rolls a four on the white die, and six on the red die. The junction of white four and red six indicates Greenland on the chart. The player must then find Greenland on the globe. Then the next player rolls. Establish whatever rules you want about the length of time allowed for locating a place. Rectangles containing the Xs add an extra dimension of delight: the player wins a treat.

A globe serves better than a wall map for a beginning study of geography because continents are shown without distortion, and because the child learns to think in terms of the world's roundness. But for the

150

study of small countries, small island groups, mountain ranges, lakes, and rivers, large wall maps are better.

Attach a large map of the world to the wall in your dining area. (Inexpensive wall maps are obtainable in larger stationery stores.) You might explain to your child that if the globe were to be cut from the north pole to the south pole, unwrapped, and flattened, the result would look something like the wall map of the world. Despite this explanation, your youngster may still be puzzled to see that a country positioned at the right edge of the map also appears at the left edge. Don't despair; and don't spend too much time on this point. The child will understand the matter in his own good time.

Use of a wall map instead of the globe permits you to include in your geography game a feature that delights youngsters: the use of pointers. Pointers permit the players to touch various locations on the map without leaving the table. Yardsticks can be used for pointers. Even curtain rods might be used. On the other hand, if you buy pieces of quarter-inch wooden dowel from a lumber dealer, the pointer will be sufficiently light that even a three-year-old will be able to manipulate a four-foot length of it.

Once your child sees the pointers and understands how the new game is to be played, he'll be eager to get started. You might then mention that cards bearing the names of geographical locations are needed to play the game. Supply the youngster with blank business cards and a list of locations so he can letter one location on each card. He'll be sure to have them ready for the next mealtime.

To play, the cards are turned face down. One player turns up the top card, reads the location, and touches that spot on the wall map with his pointer. He places the card at the bottom of the pile, and it is the next player's turn. Three or four of the cards should bear a distinctive mark, which will win the player who turns one of them over a treat or special privilege.

If two children are playing the game, a parent might merely fill the role of adjudicator, turning cards and letting the children see who will be first to touch the location with his pointer. At our own supper table, the excited *click-click* of pointer on pointer sometimes resembled a fencing match. So pleased were the children in wielding their long sticks that when one or other was dismissed from the table for misconduct, she found greater punishment in missing geography than in missing the rest of her supper. In fact, supper was sometimes ignored anyway, and it became necessary to introduce a one-minute timer to the game. The timer was activated following each play of the geography game, and for sixty seconds the children were obliged to concentrate on eating.

Selection of geographical locations by cards rather than by grid and dice offers an advantage: when a place becomes well known, its name can easily be removed from the game and a new location can be substituted.

A child will play the geography game contentedly even by himself, under a tutor's guidance, the youngster finding sufficient delight just in turning up an occasional treat card.

Eventually, you will be able to teach the child longitude and latitude. But don't teach them together. Of the two, latitude is easier for children to understand, so begin with it. Explain to the child that the lines of latitude aren't on the Earth itself; they are merely make-believe "streets" marked on maps and globes so we can give "street addresses" to countries. Explain that the equator is Zero Street, or zero-degree latitude; and trace around the globe so the child can see some geographical locations situated on this street. If the lines of latitude are shown every fifteen degrees on your globe, show the youngster Fifteenth Street North, or fifteen degrees north latitude; Thirtieth Street North, or thirty degrees north latitude, and so on. Don't introduce the south latitude until the child has worked with the north latitude lines for a few days.

To play a latitude game, one player, after studying the globe for a few seconds, might request the name of a country starting with *C* that is situated on the thirty-degree north-latitude line. Another player would then study the globe, and might deduce that only China fitted the requirement. The game would continue in this way with players taking turns finding places. Islands, lakes, or other bodies of water might also be incorporated in the game.

When the child understands north and south latitude, the game could be transferred to the wall map, where, depending on the calibrations shown, places might be located within a few degrees of latitude.

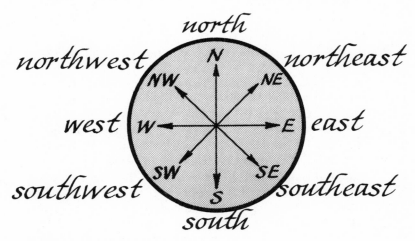

Figure 28: *The points of a compass.*

When the child can easily locate places by latitude, teach him the lines of longitude, and ignore latitude for a while. When, eventually, the youngster can easily locate places by east and west lines of longitude (which may take a week or two), the game will become more interesting because players can then begin to ask for countries, islands, or bodies of water situated at so many degrees north or south latitude and so many degrees east or west longitude.

You may find, though, that the calibrations on your map or globe are too widely positioned to permit an exact latitude-longitude fix for some smaller geographical locations, so teach your child the eight points of the compass shown in Figure 28, and you will then be able to request places situated in an exact direction from an exact junction of latitude and longitude. To illustrate, a player might request the island that is northwest of 30 degrees north latitude and 150 degrees east longitude. This island would be Japan.

Psychology and Reasoning

Understanding why people act as they do is valuable basic information. If parents explain to children their reasons for reaching various decisions, they will equip their youngsters with a basic understanding or reasoning. Whenever your child asks a question, the answer to which entails a decision, explain the factors that influence your decision. To the child's enquiry about whether or not you intend to visit Aunt Abigail, instead of just saying no, give your reason for not going. "Not today, Johann, I've got a headache. You know how you feel when you bang your knee? Well, that's how it feels in my head. And when I don't feel well, I'd rather stay home." Or again, "Can't Ophelia; Hanover's are delivering our new lamp today. Mrs. Nelson would take a delivery, but she's gone to the doctor's with little Jasmine; and Mrs. Hurd is visiting her sister in Niagara Falls."

When a child is introduced to routine reasoning, he begins to see that events do not result from mysterious forces but by the resolution of ordinary, easy-to-understand problems.

Parents can strengthen a child's elementary grasp of psychology by alerting the child to the fact that just as the child thinks he and his problems are very important, so other people think they and their problems are very important. Books that reveal the workings of the human mind might be read aloud at some convenient moment, the parent explaining any unknown word to the child or elaborating on any point made. One book worth consideration, *How to Win Friends and Influence People* by Dale Carnegie, isn't a scholarly work – nor was it intended to be – but a perceptive study of human motivation presented in an engaging and easy-to-understand manner.

Another book, *The Big Steal* by Pierre Berton, dealing with confidence tricksters, and revealing the ingenious, unconscionable ways they steal people's money, helps protect children by alerting them to the practice of deceit. The purpose here isn't to protect children's money, but their well-being; and to do so by letting them see that friendly strangers may not really be friendly at all: a message of importance to all children, but of particular importance to female children.

Latin

Knowledge of Latin is helpful in puzzling out the meanings of words that have a Latin origin, and in acquiring a more precise use of language, though these are, admittedly, advanced matters.

My children and I studied Latin briefly as an alternative to studying restaurant murals when we were obliged to travel. Temptation to study Latin took the form of a small thin book entitled *Latin With Laughter* by Mrs. Sydney Frankenburg. The book presents a light-hearted approach to Latin. A second thin book, *More Latin With Laughter*, takes beginners on to a higher level of proficiency.

The skills and abilities that have been considered in this chapter are all *cerebral* skills; skills of the mind. But motor skills – the quick and accurate movement of the body and its parts – are important too, for they permit children to perform physical tasks more effectively. Sometimes those who have possessed very high intelligence have lacked manual dexterity, as John Stuart Mill did, or have been physically clumsy, as Norbert Wiener was. The skillful coordination of small muscles (needed for manual dexterity) and the coordination of large muscles (needed for agile body movement) are dealt with next chapter.

13

Toys, Games, and Other Diversions

This chapter and the next, which deals with television, are to a great extent interdependent because if parents fail to control their children's TV viewing by the methods described in the next chapter, children aren't likely to have either the time or the inclination to engage in the pastimes described in *this* chapter. Conversely, the activities described here can help parents wean their youngsters from watching so much television.

In *Some Thoughts Concerning Education*, published in 1693, John Locke said: "I have always had a fancy that learning might be made a play and recreation to children; and that they might be brought to desire to be taught if it were proposed to them as a thing of honor, credit, delight, and recreation, or as a reward for doing something else."

John Locke's suggested games-approach to education took a long time to catch anyone's interest. Only in the last couple of decades has the educational potential of games been widely recognized by toy makers.

Almost all games and pastimes teach children *something*. And some of those things children learn while playing games have an observable long-term effect on their behavior. For example, the classic game of jackstones (commonly called jacks), an ancient game, promotes manual dexterity and hand-eye coordination: skills that children will carry with them into adulthood. Some games, however, influence thinking. For example, games that require role-playing can, depending upon the role that is played, influence children beneficially or adversely. Playing the role of nurse, mother, cowboy, or space-age rocket gunslinger is unlikely to result in any enduring adverse effect. They may even exert a beneficial influence. But some of the other roles children are called upon to fill in the course of playing certain table games deserve concern.

Table or board games rarely encourage generosity, loyalty, kindness, or thoughtfulness, though they sometimes excite greed, cunning, and guile in filling the role of speculator or hard-nosed businessperson. Indeed, some games even oblige players to lie. If children learn that lying can be condoned – even justified! – while playing a game, how can we expect youngsters to believe that lying is abhorrent in real life?

Here we will consider just those games and activities that influence children's thoughts, conduct, and abilities in a positive manner.

Pastimes for a Single Child

The first activities to be considered are those that can be pursued by an only child, by a child without siblings close to him in age, or simply by a child who wishes to play by himself. When engaged in solitary diversion, a youngster isn't dependent upon the presence and mood of a second child, nor is he competing with anyone: a feature of considerable worth in homes where children are constantly competing for parental attention.

Some manufactured toys, devices having knobs, dials, and cranks that youngsters can twist and turn, promote early skill with the fingers. Other toys, requiring the placement of objects in appropriately shaped receptacles, sharpen a child's visual discrimination. At age three—perhaps even sooner—a child can learn how to piece together simple jigsaw puzzles having twenty pieces or less. For very young children, jigsaw puzzles made of wood and those with knobs on each piece are better than those made of cardboard because the thicker pieces are easier to grasp and less likely to bend.

Children enjoy putting together the same puzzle again and again. When your child can complete a simple puzzle quickly and easily, turn the pieces over and show him how the puzzle can be put together using only the shapes of the pieces for a clue.

As a child grows older, he can be encouraged to complete increasingly difficult jigsaw puzzles. When a child begins working with puzzles containing hundreds of pieces, special recognition may be needed because the final reward—completion of the puzzle and satisfaction in having finally triumphed—is too distant to hold a five-, six-, or seven-year-old's continuing interest. The youngster might be rewarded in some way for every five or ten pieces of the puzzle he correctly positions, or, to help him along, the parent might position one piece for every piece the child positions; in that way, the triumph becomes a joint venture.

In solving jigsaw puzzles, children not only acquire a greater perception of color, tone, pattern, and shape, they develop an important character trait: persistence, the ability (and, ultimately, the compulsion) to stay at a task until it is completed.

A seemingly simpler, though equally challenging, form of puzzle is the Chinese tangram, a puzzle demanding close attention to shape and size. The tangram consists of geometric shapes that are combined in various ways to form patterns resembling specific objects. Tangrams can be found in larger toy stores.

Children's toys needn't be costly. Some of the best pastimes cost very little. If a child is shown how, by careful placement, ordinary playing cards can be used to build two- or even three-level structures, the youngster will have the means of whiling away many hours, gaining, in the process, a precision of movement with the hands. A child equipped with a quantity of toothpicks or popsicle sticks (obtainable at educational toy stores) and non-toxic glue can be shown how to build various structures.

Children can be shown how to lace borders on special boards by thrusting a piece of cord into ready-made holes and pulling it through. Later, they can progress to lacing pictures and stringing beads, or work on leathercraft items that can be laced together. A number of other kits are available that permit children at each level of development to fashion or decorate objects.

A good apparatus for developing hand-eye coordination is the ball-in-the-labyrinth puzzle – not the small hand-held types, but the large open game, about twelve inches square. In this, the player must guide a steel ball around the complex, twisting circuit without letting the ball drop into one of the many holes along the route. This puzzle, difficult even for adults, demands great concentration and deft hand movement. Weeks may pass before a five- or six-year-old gains enough skill to complete, in one turn, the entire circuit. Inducements may therefore be needed to keep a child's interest alive. Some sort of special recognition might be planned for each successively advanced position reached by the youngster around the circuit.

At least three types of labyrinth games can be found in stores. In the least difficult, the ball is maneuvered around the board by manipulation of two long forked arms that cross each other, imprisoning the ball between them. In a more difficult version, the labyrinth board can be tilted in any direction by turning two knobs. In the most difficult type, the board remains on a fixed incline, and the player raises, lowers, or alters the angle of a stick along which the ball rolls.

In their first attempts with a labyrinth, youngsters may be close to tears whenever the ball drops in a hole. But with gentle encouragement, they soon learn to brush defeat aside unconcernedly and begin again with greater determination.

Knitting provides an excellent way to develop hand-eye coordination. So, too, does corking (kits are obtainable at toy stores), which yields lengths of attractive cord that can be wound in a flat spiral and stitched together to form a place mat or pot holder, or stitched in lengths to make a belt. And various decorative cords can be plaited or woven from an inexpensive ball of butcher's string.

Knitting and working a labyrinth develop *small*-muscle skills. But children also need be able to coordinate the movement of large muscles if they are to be physically robust and able to move with ease and grace. Outdoor activities are called for: throwing and catching a ball or Frisbee, running and kicking a ball, jumping a rope, playing baseball, riding a tricycle or bicycle (even a four-year-old can be taught to ride a small bicycle), or a skateboard. Children rarely need much encouragement to engage in these or other physically demanding activities.

Pastimes for More Than One Person

Most games meant for two or more players are unsuitable for preschoolers to play together. The game rules are often too complicated. Moreover, very young children can't bear to lose in a contest. Of course, if the second player is an adult, then some sort of handicap can be introduced to ensure that the child wins most of the time. Then, Snakes and Ladders, Parcheesi, and simpler card games such as Fish and Old Maid, can be enjoyed by even four-year-olds.

The game of Memory, also called Concentration, described in *Hoyle's Rules of Games*, has been traditionally played with an ordinary deck of cards. Each player turns over a pair of cards; if they match, he keeps them and takes another turn. If not he turns them face down again. However, if a special deck of picture cards is used, the game becomes easy for even a four-year-old. In fact, once a four-year-old gets the hang of the game, he has as much chance of winning as an adult. A packaged version of the game (manufactured by Milton Bradley) contains fifty-four pairs of picture cards. By starting to play with just three or four pairs, even a three-year-old will enjoy the game.

Scan (by Parker Bros.), though recommended by the manufacturer for ages nine to adult, provides an interesting and valuable exercise for children as young as four in distinguishing between color, shape, pattern, and position. There are four different games on the one set of cards. The game that deals with color might alert parents to any tendency their youngster has toward color blindness.

A few table games require careful placement or management of objects; pick-up-sticks is a classic example. Find a toy store where the owner or operator takes pride in his knowledge of toys, and you will gain considerable help in finding toys that will contribute more to your youngster's life than mere passing entertainment.

Children of five and six can be taught to play rummy, dominoes, Chinese checkers, and ordinary checkers. Having learned checkers, a child might progress to chess. However, children are sometimes taught chess for the wrong reason. Chess is usually associated with deep thought and, for this reason, with intellectuality. And, by ascribing cause to effect, chess is sometimes thought to be an intellectual conditioner, doing for the mind what lanolin does for the scalp. But there is no evidence to support the notion that playing chess sharpens the intellect. Chess champions, generally, do not appear to possess a superior intellect, or any observable skill we might particularly want our children to have. Playing chess appears to reward chess players with no other advantage than the possibility of playing the game a little better next time. Nevertheless, chess is a fascinating game, and so long as children are taught the game for the correct reason, no harm is done.

When children reach an age when they might begin playing chess, they are able to play Mastermind (by Parker Bros.), a more briskly paced, easier game that nevertheless taxes a player's deductive power. Though intended for two players, two children can form a team against an adult; or one child and one parent can play a second child and the other parent.

Some fascinating games require only a deck of cards and Hoyle's book of game rules. Eight- and nine-year-olds can enjoy cribbage, Oh Hell!, and Hearts. And Fantan (or Sevens), though originally a gambling game, is fun even without stakes.

The claim might be made that some card games encourage the development of cunning. Possibly this is the reason some religious groups forbid the playing of cards. But one might claim, conversely, that the bickering and maneuvering for advantage that routinely occurs between siblings extends an influence of negativism far beyond what will ever likely be reached by card playing. In any case, parents will need take into account the age of the child and the general climate of the home when deciding whether card games are to be played, and if so, which ones.

Some manufactured games are merely packaged versions of parlor games that have been around for years. For example, Reversi, a game that bright five-year-olds can play – and now on the market under two names – is fully described in *The Illustrated Book of Table Games*, edited by Peter Arnold. Two other little-known, but excellent, games described in the same book are Hex and Go, the latter having been played for thousands of years in the Far East. All three games can be constructed in a matter of minutes with paper and cardboard.

Most packaged games cannot, of course, be manufactured easily at home, and the purchase of a few games is justified. But buy carefully. Box covers are sometimes misleading. Parents can avoid purchasing unsuitable games for children by getting a professional opinion of a game before buying it. Most of the packaged games available in stores today are described in *A Player's Guide to Table Games* by John Jackson and are accompanied by a frank estimate of each game's entertainment worth.

Electronic Games

Electronic games are the lowest rung on an electronic stepladder (or, better, escalator) that rises from pure play, to play combined with instruction, to purely instructional programs. The games range in design from hand-held models, to tabletop consoles, to typewriter-controlled models. Complicated and costly electronic educational equipment is beyond the scope of this book, so we will consider just the popular hand-held devices.

Electronic games, able to fascinate youngsters for hours at a time, usually demand quick visual assessment and speedy digital response. They develop in children, not surprisingly, quick visual assessment and speedy digital response; and for this reason, they usually fit players for little more than playing the game better next time. As games, they are harmless. As teaching devices, they probably add less to a child's total skill than knitting would. The preferred sort will pit the child against the machine instead of another player.

The more that an electronic device instructs, the more will it call for deliberation instead of a speedy response. Devices that help children gain skill in computing and in other academic tasks, or otherwise challenge youngsters' thinking, can contribute greatly to your home-education program.

The Arts

Writing, the commonest art, has already been considered. Drawing and music deserve passing attention, first, because a knowledge of these subjects adds dimension to a person – regardless of whether it adds to their intellectuality (as some claim it does); and second, because if parents don't trouble to influence their child's aesthetic sense, that sense will be shaped randomly by whatever children see and hear on television and outside the home.

MUSIC

Teenagers show more interest in music than probably any other age group. Unfortunately, the range of teenage taste in music is often narrow, given to loudness, exaggerated beat, and raucous singing; and one waits in vain to hear, issuing from the outsize speakers of their suitcase radios, the strains of a classical piece, an operatic aria, or one of several jazz forms.

The child who has been exposed from an early age to a range of music, and who can, in consequence, enjoy Beethoven and Bernstein, boogie-woogie and ballet music equally well, will, on becoming a teenager, be able to take thump-and-shout music – or whatever equally simple musical form is in vogue then – in his stride and enjoy it for what it has to offer, without having his musical horizons limited to it.

Children's musical education needn't be expensive. Records and tapes can be borrowed from the public library. Sing-along recordings of traditional children's songs are popular with youngsters. Some LPs are accompanied by booklets that contain the words to the songs. One series of Disney records combines the telling of a story with songs; the words of the story are contained in an illustrated booklet, providing a read-along feature that children enjoy.

Three records that introduce children to the names and sounds of various musical instruments in an entertaining way are Benjamin Britten's *Young Person's Guide to the Orchestra*, St. Saen's *Carnival of the Animals*, and the narrated version of Prokofiev's *Peter and the Wolf*.

The recording *Classical Music for People Who Don't Know Anything About Classical Music* is ideal for parents who rarely listen to this musical form. On hearing the surprising number of classical melodies that have been plagiarized and presented in popular form with very little alteration, the listener discovers that he is more familiar with classical music than was first thought.

The radio remains the cheapest source of music. In most areas, selective tuning will provide music to satisfy every musical taste.

Television can advance children's musical knowledge quickly. Musicals provide an engaging means of enlarging a child's listening repertoire. If a film musical is viewed (rather than a made-for-TV production), the sound track can be purchased or borrowed for further enjoyment, and to permit the youngster to learn the lyrics. *Mary Poppins* and *The Sound of Music* are particularly captivating for youngsters.

Once children are accustomed to the format of the musical drama, they can easily be introduced to light opera. In one home where opera music was seldom heard, Donizetti's comic opera *Daughter of the Regiment* (in English) prompted giggles by an eight- and nine-year-old and won their affection. Excerpts of the opera, recorded while the children viewed it (the microphone of a cassette recorder being placed near the TV loudspeaker), were replayed a number of times during meals, and fired still more the children's enthusiasm for the presentation. This, followed by Strauss's *Die Fledermaus* (also in English), excerpts of which were similarly recorded, served to completely win the children over to light opera.

A compelling reason for recording the music of a TV opera that your children like rather than buying a recording of it is the fact that operas originally written in a foreign language (as most of the operas were) sometimes have several different English versions, the words of each being slightly different. Furthermore, any recording available in stores is unlikely to feature the singers seen in the TV presentation.

Parents should keep an eye open for English versions of light opera. Two such operas that children particularly enjoy are *Hansel and Gretel* and *The Magic Flute*.

The Boston Pops programs present a pleasant and educating musical mixture. Camera close-ups of the soloist, or section of instruments playing the lead passage, help youngsters match sounds with the appropriate instruments. By recording Boston Pops presentations for later replay, parents can quickly endow children with a familiarity and an appreciation of basic popular classical works.

161

Television provides an easy means of introducing youngsters to ballet. The traditional Christmas ballet, *The Nutcracker Suite*, delights all children, as does *Sleeping Beauty*. Two other ballets holding special appeal for youngsters are *La Fille Mal Gardée* and *Petruchka*.

Teaching children to play a musical instrument effectively increases their interest in music. Even very young children can be taught to play a rhythm instrument—a tambourine, a triangle, a drum—and encouraged to keep time with music heard on the radio or record player. Children can also be shown how to pick out simple melodies on a toy xylophone.

A more advanced, though equally inexpensive instrument, is the flageolet, or tin flute. Fingering for "London Bridge is Falling Down" on a simple six-hole flageolet is shown in Figure 29. White circles indicate holes covered by fingers. The top three holes are controlled by the left hand, the lower three by the right hand.

A number of tunes can be played on the flageolet if one takes the trouble to discover which note of the instrument a particular melody must start on to fit in with the intervals of the instrument. Three songs that begin with all holes covered are "Twinkle, Twinkle, Little Star,"

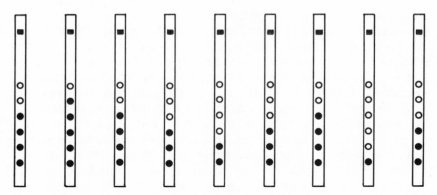

Figure 29: *Fingering for "London Bridge is Falling Down" on the flageolet.*

"When the Saints Go Marching In," and "Row, Row, Row Your Boat."

When your child is able to play a number of simple tunes and develops confidence with the flageolet, he might then begin playing a regular flute; though for this, music lessons would be required.

DRAWING

Drawing is more than a pastime; it's an activity that promotes a useful skill. The purpose here, in dealing with drawing, isn't to mold potential entrants for art colleges, but to equip youngsters with an ability that will increase their appreciation of the visual arts, and sharpen their sense of visual proportion and perception of detail: faculties that will be of value to youngsters when they deal with other academic studies and with crafts.

Though the ability to draw is commonly thought to be a gift – a mysterious, unexplainable, perhaps even divine endowment – investigation usually shows that those who draw well had, at the beginning, no more native ability than others. They were, however, encouraged by parents, prompted by circumstances, or both, to draw, and they drew more often than other children and in so doing gained better control of a pencil and a sharper power of observation: a combination of abilities that others eventually chose to call a "gift." The contention here is that children gain skill in drawing pretty much in the same way they gain skill at most things: by doing a great deal of it.

Helping children to draw well, then, is less dependent upon instruction than upon encouragement to do a lot of drawing. The ways in which children might be prompted to draw aren't much different from the ways they might be prompted to pursue any activity. Praise, and plenty of it (and a minimum of criticism), will send a youngster hurrying back to his drawing corner to produce more and better drawings. But accuracy in drawing isn't achieved in a month or a year, and the value of praise alone is limited; therefore longer-lasting inducements are needed if a child is to gain a high level of skill.

What objects should children begin drawing? Copying comic-strip characters is a pastime children enjoy and one that has endowed many artists with their initial drawing skill. The book *Animation* by Preston Blair provides cartoon characters for children to copy and explains the underlying principles of that art.

If a child isn't motivated to draw, there is an alternative to shrugging and accepting defeat: motivate him. At one time, my own children were paid for housework, but were merely encouraged to draw. This yielded a tidier home, but few drawings. So we switched. The children were then expected to tidy the home for nothing, and were paid instead for their drawings.

Drawings were occasioned, too, by the sale of TV-viewing privileges. Quality TV programs were always free; however, the viewing of Saturday-morning cartoons, situation comedies, and second-rate movies was secured by additional drawings.

Parents can therefore encourage the development of a skill that fluke circumstance alone has bestowed in other homes. To illustrate: a child raised in a home having no TV set, having parents who make little effort to engage him in activities, and having few other children his own age, may turn, for solace, to drawing, or perhaps to playing a musical instrument, and may acquire considerable skill.

14

Television: A School All Its Own

Television is a major educating force, for good or bad, in most children's lives. To ignore the great body of knowledge youngsters gain from watching TV, or to ignore the great amount of time they spend acquiring that flood of knowledge, would lessen parents' understanding of the challenge they face in educating their children and would, in consequence, reduce the effectiveness of their teaching.

The function of television in most children's lives is that of a pastime. But whereas most pastimes – reading, playing games, engaging in hobbies, and so on – channel away just a trickle of time, TV channels away a torrent of time. Even preschoolers average 23.5 hours of TV viewing each week.

The influence of TV on children's behavior is difficult to assess. First, not all TV programs are a bad influence on children. Second, the various ways in which TV can influence children aren't easily seen. Both these factors frustrate the formulation of any simple policy on TV viewing.

The question of TV and its place in the home is suitable material for a book rather than a chapter. Still, the matter can't be bypassed here if parents are to make a responsible judgment about what part television is to play in their children's lives.

Violence on Television

The great body of evidence that has now been collected, totaling more than 2,000 studies and reports, shows an indisputable link between TV violence and the frequency of real-life crimes. Assaults seen on TV often trigger an outbreak of similar assaults in real life. A TV "victim," doused with lighter fluid and set ablaze, inspired similar assaults against humans and domestic animals in Boston and Miami. A bizarre form of sexual assault depicted on TV prompted three California girls to imitate the assault on a nine-year-old. In one program a cat was hanged on a clothesline. During the following week dozens of cats were hanged on clotheslines. For every televised crime that is reenacted in real life, we might wonder how many other reenactments of that crime were seriously considered, but abandoned for want of courage or opportunity. In one study, the American Broadcasting Company found that twenty-two of 100 juvenile offenders admitted they had patterned their crime on a TV depiction of a similar crime. So intimate is the link between TV violence and real-life emulation of that violence that Michael Rothenberg, children's psychiatrist at the University of Washington, after reviewing the fifty most comprehensive studies on TV violence (studies spanning twenty-five years and encompassing 10,000 children), considered the freedom with which violence is purveyed on television to be nothing less than a national scandal.

The antisocial behavior fostered by TV is a natural legacy of the strange people who inhabit the land of the picture tube. The great collective TV "family" is disproportionately afflicted with neurotics, cutthroats, and rogues. Professors George Gerbner and Larry Gross, of the University of Pennsylvania's Annenberg School of Communications, reported in 1979, in their tenth annual *Violence Profile*, that crooks make up 17 per cent of all television characters; whereas, in real life, they constitute only 1 per cent of society: a distorted representation of humanity that afflicts children with what Dr. Gerbner terms the "mean world syndrome." The more television children watch, Dr. Gerbner and his associates contend, the more fearful, anxious, and suspicious they become of the world around them, and the more likely they are to condone aggressive behavior in themselves and in others.

When we consider that the average fourteen-year-old has watched, during the years, the assault or destruction of an estimated 18,000 human beings, we can hardly wonder that youngsters regard violence as normal daily behavior. "Television has profoundly affected the way in which members of the human race learn to become human beings," Professor Gerbner asserts. "The lesson of most TV series," child behaviorist Robert Liebert contends, "is that the rich, the powerful and the conniving are the most successful." Dorothy H. Cohen, specialist in child development, says: "When young children watch programs of crime and violence, they take literally the message that violence is a primary method of solving all kinds of problems."

Children are particularly vulnerable to the influence of antisocial acts seen on TV – ranging as those acts do from simple discourtesy to the most repugnant and vicious of crimes – because youngsters haven't the great backlog of personal daily experiences adults possess, experiences that would make them aware that, though unsavory events *do* occur in daily life, they don't occur with anywhere near the frequency seen on the TV screen.

Despite the wealth of evidence testifying to TV's damaging influence,

TV executives have dismissed the idea that television viewing adversely affects children, and they have done so even when their own studies proved the opposite. In 1972, Columbia Broadcasting System commissioned William Belson, a sociologist at the London School of Economics' Survey Research Centre, to conduct a six-year-study of 1,565 London teenage boys. Dr. Belson concluded, in the $290,000 study, that long exposure to television noticeably increased the extent to which children engaged in serious acts of violence: a revelation that CBS officials then dismissed as adding "nothing of consequence" to the truth of the matter.

The link between TV viewing and antisocial behavior would be better known but for the ability of those in the TV industry to influence fact-finding commissions and, when the facts are in, to suppress reports that might be embarrassing to those in the industry. A 1972 investigation, prompted by Senator John O. Pastore, served to show the power of the TV industry's muscle. Senator Pastore reasoned that if the surgeon general could, in the interests of public health, take a stand on the ill effects of cigarette smoking, he might also study and assess the possible ill effects of TV viewing.

The surgeon general accepted the challenge and began his study; however, the TV networks were allowed to reject any nominee to the Advisory Committee they thought might be hostile or unsympathetic to the industry. Seven such people were disqualified. The final report of the surgeon general's study expressed, not surprisingly, the message that the TV industry leaders wanted to hear. It was considered a whitewash.

Undaunted, Senator Pastore held his own hearing and called on the principals of the surgeon general's study to clarify their thoughts and state them in less ambiguous terms than had been contained in their report. They did so, whereupon the surgeon general stated: "It is clear to me that the causal relationship between televised violence and antisocial behavior is sufficient to warrant appropriate and immediate remedial action." Few television newscasters troubled to report his statement.

A fog is sometimes created by the "catharsis" theory: the notion that, when children's natural violent feelings are enacted on TV, they themselves are less likely to act out those feelings in real life. But in 1976, a Canadian study, a Royal Commission on Violence in the Communications Industry, after sifting through the evidence, reported: "The majority of studies which have been done ... indicate that the catharsis theory does not appear to be accurate. In fact, the conclusion that is drawn is that media violence raises, rather than reduces, the level of post-viewing aggression."

School Performance

Poor grades in school are another risk of too much TV viewing. A 1969 survey conducted for the Institute for Development of Educational

Activities revealed that backward pupils watched more television than did the high achievers. In fact, some teachers claim they can tell how much TV a child watches each week just by his reading ability.

The stunting effect of TV on this or that ability or aptitude is sometimes difficult to prove, let alone measure. Still, reports come in occasionally that hint at unguessed costs TV exacts on human performance. During a week without television, conducted with the parents' cooperation at Friend's Central Public School in Philadelphia, children borrowed far more books from the library, many dealing with creative pastimes: crafts, sewing, and other interests that encourage the development of worthwhile abilities.

Psychologists claim that habitual viewing stifles the imagination and thwarts creativity: losses for which TV may eventually be most condemned. Teachers report that some children are unable to understand stories that aren't illustrated. "TV has taken away the child's ability to form pictures in his mind," asserts Dorothy Cohen, child-development expert at New York City's Bank Street College of Education. Small wonder that some Grade 1 pupils question the worth of learning to read. Why, indeed, bother with a skill that projects only faint, ill-defined images on the unsensitized inner screen of the child's mind?

Television is seen to have a similar adverse effect upon perseverance, the ability to stick at a task and complete it. Accustomed to seeing on television every problem resolved in thirty to sixty minutes, children develop a low tolerance for the frustrations that accompany learning. Projects that require diligence for their solution are apt to be avoided. If undertaken, they are apt to be abandoned at the first difficulty. Teachers lament the way children dissolve into tears if a task *looks* hard. Meccano Ltd., once the king of toymakers with annual sales of $300 million, almost went out of business before someone realized that the Meccano concept was too abstract and too time-consuming for today's impatient child. The company has now switched to quick-assembly kits.

Television is said to have redeeming educational values. It *has*. The Cousteau program, *National Geographic* specials, "Stationary Ark," "Botanic Man," "Life on Earth," "Nature of Things," "Vista," "Nova," and programs of this caliber are above reproach. But when such programs are hailed by educators as exciting new ways in which the obligations of school can be filled outside classrooms, one squirms. No less a person than the U.S. Commissioner of Education, Ernest Boyer, stated in 1978: "It [TV] has caused children to travel around the world.... They've gone to the bottom of the ocean, to the top of the greatest mountain ... and we've seen the moon, and we've looked at Earth from outer space." They certainly have. But televised views of the Earth's surface, or space, are merely an education of facts, whereas the paramount concern of educators is, properly, to give children access to that immense body of information that doesn't come in picture form. To acquire this knowledge, children must be able to read, write, spell, and compute. If youngsters are led to believe that visually opulent television presentations are acceptable – even equable – substitutes for basic academic skills, then the geography, zoology, oceanology, and astronautical lessons they watch become costly diversions indeed.

Moreover, the value of television as a teaching instrument is deceptive. The rich color, sound, and background music, and the sometimes highly literate narration, often overwhelm the senses with splendor, but less often overwhelm the mind with information. If one troubles to jot down, while viewing even the best of documentaries, the total information imparted during the hour, one may find the educating content could have been conveyed equally well by a couple of hundred words and a few colored photographs. Furthermore, had the information been presented in print, the reader would then have been able to control the speed of presentation, would have had the opportunity to pause and consider, and would have had the opportunity to reread any matter for a clearer understanding or for reinforcement.

Truth-bending "Docu-fables"

A point frequently overlooked is that TV is sometimes *mis*educational. In the murky world of "docu-drama" (documentary dramatizations), fiction is often indistinguishable from fact as scriptwriters tailor history to fit their needs. The television program "Collision Course" presented a detailed account of President Harry Truman's firing of General Douglas MacArthur. A key point in the drama is their meeting in a Quonset hut on Wake Island during the Korean war. But no one witnessed this meeting, so the scriptwriter invented a conversation. In "Truman at Potsdam" the writers took the liberty of giving the impression that Truman ordered the atomic bombing of Japan not merely to end the war, but to frighten the Russians.

Scriptwriters put words in John F. Kennedy's mouth for "The Missiles of October." In fact, more than 100,000 copies of the script were distributed to Philadelphia schoolchildren in advance of the airing date as a reading (and possibly history?) assignment. "Washington Behind Closed Doors" was a free interpretation of John Ehrlichman's novel. After the scriptwriters had added their part fiction to Ehrlichman's part fiction, and sprinkled in a few facts from the Watergate trial and the Nixon tapes, the result was a sensational twelve-hour spoof that most people accepted as fact rather than fiction.

Distorting the truth is, of course, a Hollywood tradition. One went to see a movie for entertainment, then read the book to find out what really happened. But children watch so much TV that they have little time for reading. Indeed, they may not even have gained sufficient skill to read a long book.

Palate Tickling

Television has greatly affected the nation's eating habits. Widescale promotion of junk food—foods low in nutritive value, high in starch and sugar—encourage high caloric intake, which leads to obesity (and the social problems that accompany overweight), promote tooth decay, and generally lower the body's resistance to disease. Many of the commercials presented on Saturday and Sunday mornings peddle sugar-coated cereals, candy, chewing gum, and similar edible materials that help turn youngsters into what has been termed "sugar junkies." This form of selling is particularly pernicious because, throughout the sales pitch, which continues hour after hour, children are glued to their seats, perhaps even stuffing themselves on the mouth-watering, nutritionally-devoid edibles being advertised. Ideally, perhaps, children might be given unlimited use of pedal-powered TV sets, but until such a device is marketed, parents might follow the example of another, who obliged his overweight children to walk six times around the block—a total of 3½ miles—for every hour of cartoons they wanted to watch.

Hidden Costs

In the final assessment, the greater price TV exacts may not be those dysfunctions that can be measured, or even observed, but the unmeasured, unobserved childhood activities that get squeezed out of a youngster's life simply because TV leaves no time for them: playing games, working out puzzles, collecting stamps, coins, or rocks, building toys and contrivances, reading, reflecting on recent events, wondering about the future, or perhaps just daydreaming.

Another regrettable consequence of too much TV viewing is its stifling influence on family communication. In some homes television dominates much of the conversation, family members getting a chance to chat only during the commercial breaks. One veteran primary schoolteacher reports that nowadays her pupils are unusually talkative when they arrive for class. She suspects they are starved for conversation at home. According to Dr. David Pearl of the National Institute of Mental Health, TV has upset normal parent and child relationships by disrupting the routine give-and-take that is essential for children's full development.

Television provides easy, instant escape from boredom. But boredom isn't necessarily a bad condition. Boredom sometimes prompts thought, fires imagination, and encourages resourcefulness. And resourcefulness is of the same metal from which problem solving and inventiveness are forged.

However, in examining the trees, we may miss the woods. Perhaps, overall, the most pernicious element of TV is the insidious way it turns youngsters into viewers by habit. When children enter Grade 1, having then watched an estimated 4,000 hours of TV, they are well habituated to TV's fascinating spell. Can we really expect six-year-olds to suddenly kick the habit of a *lifetime* to accommodate school and social activities? During their week with no TV, some children at Friend's Central Public School reacted as addicts do when suddenly deprived of a hard drug. They begged, cried, and screamed for TV, and tried to figure ways around the ban they had pledged to honor.

Quitting TV isn't necessarily any easier for adults. In 1977, the Detroit *Free Press* offered 120 families $500 to give up TV for a month. Ninety-three families refused. The five that were finally selected for the experiment – all heavy viewers – reported an increase in smoking, in edginess, and in family quarrels throughout that memorable month. In Germany, 184 volunteers were paid to give up TV for a year. None made it past six months.

How Much Viewing?

The purpose here isn't to present a definitive condemnation of TV, but rather to sort out and examine the several, sometimes subtle, ways in which television viewing can influence your child. Members of the TV industry have been taken to task for the amount of violence aired; but, as we now see, there are other important reasons for restricting a youngster's viewing. Because of the several obvious dangers of TV viewing, plus a few suspected dangers, parents have an obligation to protect their children from excessive viewing in the same way they protect youngsters from sharp knives and strong corrosives. Yet studies show that only 40 per cent of parents exercise any control at all over their children's TV viewing.

How many hours of television should children watch each week? Dr. Victor Bailey Cline, who a number of years ago pioneered studies on the relationship between TV violence and children's behavior, limited his children to one hour a week. A one-hour-per-week limit would be difficult to justify today with cablevision now bringing several stations into the home, and public broadcasting stations providing a wealth of quality programming. On the other hand, the national average can't sensibly serve as a reference point, either. Indeed, the fact that preschoolers today average twenty-four hours of TV a week isn't reason to believe that even *half* this amount – twelve hours – shows excellent restraint. The amount of TV that other people's children watch isn't an appropriate benchmark for determining how much TV your children and mine should watch.

Parents must regard their children's time as a precious commodity (it is!), and help youngsters budget their expenditure of moments watching TV. How big a problem is TV in your home? Begin by finding out exactly how much time your child spends watching TV. Keep an accurate record for one week, noting the day, the time, the name, and duration of every program your youngster watches. When you have completed your log you can then begin snipping away – as you would prune dead limbs and parasitic growths from an unkempt shrub – those programs that sap more from your child's life than they contribute.

How extensive should your pruning be? For one- and two-year-olds, the question hardly applies. The only television that might be justified for children of this age would be musical programs. Even then, youngsters' musical education might be advanced just as well – perhaps better – if the children heard selected works on a record player or tape recorder as was suggested in Chapter 13. Indeed, there is little justification for even three-year-olds to watch television, except for special programs thought to contribute to their education.

If a preschooler is able to read, his time might be divided between reading and watching selected TV programs, provided, of course, that neither activity consumes more than an hour or so each day.

School-age children, already sitting for several hours each weekday in classrooms, shouldn't be encouraged to sit for hours more each day at home watching TV. What *is*, then, a sensible limit for TV viewing? Suppose, for the purpose of comparison, that TV hadn't been invented, and that, aside from toys, games, and puzzles, children's main source of entertainment were reading. The question might then be: how much time should children be allowed to just sit and read each day? How long might they spend reading and still participate in other important indoor and outdoor activities: hobbies, schoolwork, playing with friends, visiting others? If children were to read for a short time after school or early in the evening, then read a little more in bed before the lights were turned out for a total of one hour or an hour and a quarter – without infringing upon their other activities – would this be acceptable? Possibly. And perhaps twice this amount of reading would be acceptable on weekends, giving, altogether, a total of about eleven hours of reading a week. A child who read more than this amount might be considered, for our purposes here, bookish, and might be leading an imbalanced life.

If, in the absence of TV, eleven hours of *reading* each week would be considered acceptable, should we, with the advent of TV, consider eleven hours each week an acceptable amount of viewing? No, because then there would be no time left for reading; and reading is, after all, more than just a pastime. Reading is a valuable skill that must be practiced if children are ever to read quickly and easily. Then, should the eleven hours be divided equally between reading and TV viewing? Indeed, does the eleven-hour limit even make sense? These are questions that parents must answer for themselves. If the reasoning here fails to provide an easy, universally acceptable answer for fixing children's TV viewing, the points that have been raised may help parents narrow the acceptable range of viewing time for their youngster.

The limitations that parents eventually place upon youngsters' TV viewing will be easier to implement and enforce if two niceties are observed. First, parents must set a good example for their children. If parents themselves watch ten or fifteen hours of TV a week, they can hardly expect children to be satisfied with five. (According to statistics, adults average *twenty-nine* hours of TV viewing a week.) Second, parents should discuss a child's TV habit with him and point out that there are good reasons – whether he understands them fully – for watching less TV; not that such a talk will delight a child or win his enthusiastic support.

Reducing TV Viewing

A giant step will be made toward less TV viewing if parents forbid channel hopping in search of entertainment. Children should be allowed to watch only those programs that have been agreed upon in advance and entered in a viewing schedule for the week. The way in which this schedule is composed will depend on the age of the child and on the regime in the home. If your home is run on the order of a benevolent dictatorship, you will only have to study a television guide once a week, compose a list of approved programs the child may watch, hide the TV program guide, and the matter is closed.

A more democratic approach would be to let the youngster read the television guide himself and tick programs that interest him, then hold a meeting to discuss which programs are acceptable. The youngster might then print the titles of approved programs in a TV log book (a lined exercise book), and this would serve as his personal viewing guide for the week.

Another technique that gives children free choice of quality but restricts the quantity of viewing is to make a simple chart and keep it near the TV set. Numbers across the top stand for ten half-hours of TV viewing. Numbers down the side represent successive weeks. After watching TV, the child or parent ticks off the appropriate number of boxes for the amount of TV watched.

One way to let children select their own TV programs, while encouraging them to choose wholesome presentations, is to establish different

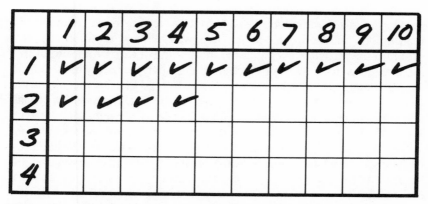

Figure 30: *A chart that allows ten half-hours of TV viewing each week.*

ratings for different programs. For example, a violent police program might require the ticking off of two boxes for every half-hour watched, whereas a quality documentary of one-hour duration might require only one box to be ticked off.

Children might, too, be offered incentives for reducing the amount of TV they watch; if the rewards they receive help to make their moments away from TV more enjoyable, all the better. Hobby shops are full of interesting ventures children can engage in: model building, beadwork, fretwork, sculpture, and others. Children need—and deserve—special attention while they are going through the stress of adjusting to less TV viewing. Parents might purchase a new table game; perhaps even an expensive toy such as an air-hockey game, a slot-car-racing set, a pool table, or a table-tennis set.

These same items might, on the other hand, be purchased as a fringe benefit in a system of "pay TV," an arrangement that is best suited for children seven or eight years and older. Suppose a child's weekly allowance is fifty cents. Parents might raise this amount to $1.50 a week, paid a week in advance. Fifteen dimes would be placed on top of the TV set. During the ensuing seven days, each time the youngster watches a half-hour of TV, he deposits one dime in a penny bank—*your* bank. For an hour of viewing, two dimes would be deposited; and so on. Whatever coins remained on the TV set at the end of the week would be the youngster's allowance for that week.

Now comes the fringe benefit. Parents might agree to double—or even treble—any amount of allowance money left that is in excess of fifty cents (the regular weekly allowance), and apply this amount toward the purchase of some special toy the youngster wants.

Perhaps your youngster was never allowed to watch much TV during the early years, but, now that he is older, is beginning to agitate for TV viewing "rights." One solution is to permit TV viewing in return for quality reading. In one home, a ten-year-old was allowed to watch any TV program she wished in exchange for the reading of worthwhile literature. And, reading 15,000 words (which she did quickly) for every half-hour of TV, she managed to glut herself each Saturday and Sunday morning with "Road Runner," "Bugs Bunny," "Sylvester the Cat," and similar trivia. For this she read S.I. Hayakawa's *Language in Thought and Action*, Vance Packard's *The Hidden Persuaders*, various books on the rise and fall of the Roman empire, several Shakespeare plays (which she had previously seen on TV), a number of biographies, and true adventures of notable men and women. (An important point: the books were read with enthusiasm. Indeed, twice in the course of reading a school text on British history – a difficult 1910 edition – the youngster exclaimed "Boy, it's really interesting!")

Another way to harness TV for educational advancement is to let children watch TV films, or series, based on biographies, classical stories, or other worthwhile works, on the condition the youngsters read the original after having seen the TV version. This arrangement not only leads youngsters to read books they might otherwise ignore, but it simplifies the reading of those works and makes the text more comprehensible and, in turn, more enjoyable.

Parents should try to watch programs with their youngsters – especially during the early years – and explain, when necessary, what is being viewed. Events that might upset or frighten children should be discussed and explained. In our home, the children, at ages five and six, were allowed to watch "Batman" because of the excellent speech and vocabulary used on the program. But some of the episodes ended with do-or-die situations – cliff-hangers – in which Batman, or Robin, or both, were fastened to some huge, improbable machine that was about to transform them into outsize doughnuts or some other absurd end product. To calm the children's alarm at these endings, they were told that the characters were just actors, and that when the actors went home each day they would tell their own children the silly things they'd done at the studio, and everyone would laugh.

Videotape Recording

The arrival of the videotape recorder (VTR for short) complicates the whole question of television viewing. On one hand, setting up the machine to record a sequence of programs requires forethought and planning – exactly what was advocated earlier as a means of reducing the amount of television watched. On the other hand, the VTR makes available such a wealth of new program opportunities that it invites *more* viewing. To understand the situation clearly, consider the capabilities of a modern VTR.

First, the VTR will record programs of varying length at any hour and on any day one wishes, recording the programs without the television set even being switched on. This means that programs you would not normally be able to watch – because they are aired during working hours or sleeping hours, or while you are traveling or on holiday – can now be viewed at a moment that suits you. And during a week that features more excellent programs than you wish to watch, some can be recorded for viewing at a time when there are no other programs that interest you.

Second, the VTR offers two features that make TV viewing generally more pleasant and more like reading: the ability to go back (in this case, rewind) to study again the material presented, and the ability to halt the presentation should there be some interruption: a knock at the door or a telephone call. And the ability to halt a presentation greatly increases the teaching worth of television; for parents can, by stopping the program with a hand-held remote-control device, explain to a child the meaning of a word, an action, or a historical or technical point.

Furthermore, material can be viewed at various slow speeds, down to one-thirtieth the normal speed. Or, indeed, the machine can be made to hold a single frame and then be advanced one frame at a time as desired (which can be highly informative when watching a performance – of magic, for example – that is more easily understood at a slower speed). Conversely, one can accelerate the machine to go through commercials at nine times the normal speed. All in all, the advantages of viewing programs via the VTR, instead of live, are so great that you may choose to tape all the programs you watch – even when they are aired at a convenient time – for later viewing.

Summing Up

Notwithstanding the case that can be made for discriminative viewing, especially when the viewing is enhanced by means of a videotape recorder, parents will wisely bear in mind that children's thoughts rarely turn to enterprising activities when the children are watching television. Model airplanes and ships don't get built; postage stamps don't get positioned in albums. Letters aren't written. Musical instruments are not played. Films and prints go undeveloped. Plants are neither seeded nor potted. Clothes are not sewn; leather isn't worked; wood isn't carved. Pictures aren't drawn, nor paintings painted. Puzzles are neither attempted nor solved. In short, the entire goal-striving mechanism unique to, and preeminent in, the human brain, falls into comfortable disuse as soon as the TV switch is flicked. This potentially dangerous switch will, in the thinking parents' home, be turned on only after the parents carefully weigh whether that which is going to be viewed is worth more than that which is going to be squeezed out of a child's life by the viewing.

To conclude: the possession of a TV set burdens responsible parents with unadvertised risks and unexpected obligations in management. Seeing the TV problem more clearly now, some parents may elect to reduce their youngsters' viewing to zero simply by pulling the plug and putting the TV set in storage: a harsh solution, but certainly the *advised* solution for parents who can't or won't be bothered to supervise their youngsters' viewing, either by the procedures that have been described, or variations of these procedures.

Though heavily committed TV viewers would find it difficult to believe, life *does* go on without TV. Indeed, in some homes where the TV set has been banished, life seems to go on in an exceptionally pleasant way. One San Francisco father decided he wouldn't replace the TV set when it broke down. His five sons, rebellious and resentful at first, championed the father's decision later. They became involved in sports, Sea Scouts, tap dancing, and reading, and developed a range of interests far wider than most children their age.

Back in 1938, E.B. White, an author and a contributing editor to the *New Yorker*, wrote, "I believe television is going to be the test of the modern world, and that in this new opportunity to see beyond the range of our vision we shall discover either a new and unbearable disturbance of the general peace or a saving radiance in the sky." Prophetic words. Who today might have suspected that, in purchasing their television set, they were automatically enrolling in a test that had been predicted forty years earlier? Tested we are. And how well we perform in this test will, to a great extent, determine how well our youngsters function now as children and later as adults and parents.

15

Electives

In school, *electives* are optional subjects that students may or may not "elect" to take. Here, the term will refer to activities that parents may or may not wish to include in their school-in-the-home program. Generally, more time, effort, or money is needed for the electives than for activities contained in the convenience-education program that has been presented up to this point. For this reason, parents may choose to engage wholly, partly, or not at all in the activities to be described this chapter. The first elective isn't a single activity so much as an adventurous approach to learning. The cost is primarily one of time.

Educational Opportunism

Almost everything that parents and children see and hear can be turned to children's educational advantage. Children's natural curiosity will, of course, prompt them to ask questions about the passing scene; but youngsters usually ask only about those objects that prick their curiosity, while other objects, though perhaps possessing equal – or even greater – inherent interest, are ignored.

Parents can add greatly to children's enjoyment of life by seizing whatever opportunity presents itself to increase children's awareness of, and interest in, the world around them. By means of this "educational opportunism," parents can turn their immediate surroundings and the passing scene to educational profit.

The delivery of mail to our door is a convenience of urban life. Does your child know that some people are not so fortunate as to have mail delivered to their doors, or to the lobbies of their apartment buildings? Why don't people in the country enjoy such service? Does your child know that the purpose of postage stamps isn't decorative, but rather to prove that payment has been made for delivering the mail? Can the child think of a couple of good reasons why letters are placed inside envelopes before they are dropped into mailboxes? Does the child understand what junk mail is? How can manufacturers afford to keep sending unrequested matter when you perhaps rarely act on their sales offers?

Time for lunch; perhaps a can of soup. Why is soup put into cans instead of jars? Why isn't jam normally put in cans? Does the child know that his can of soup is just one tiny portion of an immense batch of soup, perhaps enough to feed a thousand people? What are the stated ingredients of the soup? Does the child know that the manufacturer is obliged by law to state the contents of the soup, and to list them in the correct order of quantity, the first-named ingredient being the largest component, the last-named being the smallest?

A light bulb burns out. Don't throw it away. Does the child know what tungsten is? Put the bulb in a bag and tap it with a hammer. Let the child feel the tungsten and stretch out the tiny coils. Does the child know that tungsten is also used in toasters and in the heating elements of electric stoves?

Many are the ways in which common items can excite children's interest. And if, occasionally, the enquiry prompts the parent to glance at an encyclopedia or inspires the child to do so, then parent and child alike will profit all the more from the exercise.

Shopping trips afford many opportunities for education. First, there is the vocabulary of special shopping words: *bargain*, *discount*, *merchant*, *merchandise*, *guarantee*, *quality*, *special*, and so on. Children also have a chance to see, and sometimes touch, unfamiliar items. In the produce department of the supermarket, for example, youngsters might see items you rarely buy: turnip, watercress, eggplant, leek, kale.

Visit the fish store so the child can see lobsters, clams, eels, shrimps, and other marine creatures. Regard a department store as you would a museum. Visit the sports department, for example, and introduce the child to those items you don't have at home. Errands to almost any store – the automotive-supply house, the hardware store, the drugstore, and so on – can be turned to educational advantage. A large shopping mall with its fifty or a hundred adjacent stores is virtually a walk-in encyclopedia of objects to show and explain to your child.

Brief side trips to various other merchants, while shopping, can add sparkle to your program. Educating a child provides parents with a great opportunity to advance their own education. How many adults have seen the workbench and electronic test equipment in the back of a TV- and radio-repair shop, or the ovens and mixing equipment in the back of a neighborhood bakery, or have closely examined the tools and machinery with which old shoes are renovated at the shoe-repair store? Few adults would have the nerve to request an inspection of a merchant's premises. But when the viewing is for a *child*, neither parent nor merchant feels awkward about the request. Your youngster may be awarded a small souvenir of his visit in the form of a burned-out condenser or resistor, or a remnant of leather.

Of course, if all parents were to impose upon merchants in this way, merchants would never get any work done. The truth is, though, that few parents are sufficiently interested in their children's education – or in their own – to make such a request. Ask your local merchants how many parents have requested an opportunity to let their child look "out back." In fact, that particular question could lead easily to your second question: "Is there a good time of day when it might be possible to let young Felicity here see how you...?" The merchant may simply ask you and your youngster through for an immediate tour.

A walk around the neighborhood can provide still other opportunities for rooting out educational truffles. Can you identify different breeds of dogs? Most people with a dog will be pleased to tell you the breed, and may impart a little information about its care and diet. Do you know one type of tree from another? The person on whose property a tree stands will likely know the name of the tree and will probably be pleased to tell you. How are you at identifying flowers? If you see a flower you can't name, why not ask its owners? They wouldn't have planted the flower unless they liked it, and they'll probably appreciate your interest in the flower. In a similar way, unusual items hanging on porches or in windows might justify enquiry.

Will such enquiries arouse resentment? Here, the adage "T'ain't what you do, it's the way that you do it" comes into play. People don't usually resent a friendly, courteous question – even from a stranger. And, accompanied as you are by a youngster, people have little reason to suspect an ulterior motive in your enquiry.

A child serves as a social catalyst, setting up a unique situation that permits adult strangers to communicate more easily. For example, while waiting for a bus, a military person in line will probably be pleased to explain to the youngster the significance of this or that insignia, ribbon, or badge; whereas, were you unaccompanied by the child you might not dream of even speaking to the person next in line.

Traveling with a child provides additional educational opportunities. If you travel by public transit, you are free to observe the locale more fully and point out to a child this or that interesting feature. If you travel by car (and have time to spare) you can pull over and observe, or even turn around and drive back to study more leisurely something seen too briefly.

Regard each locale as your own special classroom. Let its principal features set the subject. Your cost is one of time. But this needn't be excessive. One day, at the start of a trip home from a rural community in United Empire Loyalist country, we came upon a church that had been built by Americans who crossed Lake Ontario to remain loyal to George III. The plaque read:

HAY BAY CHURCH 1792 –

In 1791, William Losee, an itinerant preacher, organized in this district the first Methodist circuit in Upper Canada. This Meeting House, Upper Canada's first Methodist chapel, was built in 1792. Enlarged in 1834 – 35 it was used for worship until about 1860 after which it served as a farmer's storehouse. In 1910 in recognition of its historical significance, it was reacquired and restored by The Methodist Church and is still used for annual services by The United Church of Canada. Erected by the Ontario Archaeological and Historic Sites Board.

Aside from its stock of quaint facts, the text provided many words the children – then seven and eight – hadn't encountered before. A look inside the church permitted an introduction to the words *pulpit*, *lectern*, *gallery*, and *mullioned windows*. The adjoining graveyard contained a stone inscribed: HUFF – IN MEMORY OF PAUL & SOLOMON – UNITED EMPIRE LOYALISTS TRUE TO KING & COUNTRY, which prompted mention of the Boston Tea Party as we continued our trip. The entire episode had lasted about twenty minutes. That was the *total* cost. But that wasn't the total *reward*. Memories count, too.

Creating Fond Memories

A program of educational opportunism (or impromptu enquiry – whatever name we might give to the practice) will endow your youngster with many broadening experiences. But more: *both* of you will gain a more memorable day, a day tagged for easy recall a year, two, or ten years later. Each such day becomes like a bead in a string of rich moments shared with your child: "Remember the time when we...?" Parents will wisely grasp the opportunities of the moment and make a memorable occasion of each.

Perhaps while driving along one day you may notice an object of interest too late to draw your youngster's attention to it. If circumstances permit, you might turn around and return to the vantage point, or perhaps even park the car and approach the object on foot. The expenditure of a mere ten minutes can, in this way, sometimes yield a moment of pleasant enquiry that will shine long in your memory, and in your child's memory.

Museums and Sights

The worth of taking children to museums hardly need be mentioned. A common error, though, is to delay children's first visit because they won't know many of the objects there. But *that* is the most important reason for taking them: so they will encounter objects they don't know and haven't seen before.

A second common error lies in not taking youngsters to the museum often enough. Two and three times a year isn't too often. Your youngster will soon be racing excitedly from each familiar display or apparatus to the next in the manner of one greeting old friends.

Even war museums have a role to fill in your child's education. Here the child will see a flintlock musket, a helmet, a shield, a sword, a scabbard, a spear, and similar items he reads about. Equip the youngster with a pad and pencil so he can jot down the names of new items he encounters.

Museums, art galleries, conservatories, aquariums, exhibitions, and fairs are all good places to take children. Look in the yellow pages of your telephone book. You may be surprised at the number of museums listed there.

Some people who live in a city never trouble to go to see attractions that are a visitor's first interest. Pick up a tourist guide to your city and take your youngster to see its special attractions.

Though television takes youngsters into many buildings and settings, a TV picture doesn't compare with a visit. Here are a few places a child will enjoy visiting.

The fire station, perhaps the nearest point of interest to your home, is also one of the most fascinating for a child. Step in for a minute and let your youngster shake the hand of a real firefighter. The child might mention that he knows better than to play with matches. The firefighter might take over from there and let the youngster stand on the running board of the fire engine.

Step into the local police station and introduce your youngster to the constable on duty. Depending on how busy he is, the constable might chat about pedestrian safety rules.

Perhaps you visit the public library occasionally with your child. If not, drop in from time to time and let him learn to feel comfortable with walls full of books.

Visit the main train depot. Your youngster will be fascinated by the hustle and bustle, the red caps, the baggage check. Depending on the layout of the depot, you might be able to take the child onto the platform to inspect the train at close range. A large bus depot will be similarly interesting for a child. And perhaps the most fascinating depot of all is the airport. Point out the control tower and explain its purpose. Perhaps there is a windsock for the pilots of smaller aircraft. You aren't likely to gain entry to the control tower, but if the meteorological office is situated in the airport complex, you might find a ready welcome there. If, after your visit to the airport, you are able to park the car on a nearby road over which the ascending or descending aircraft pass, the youngster will thrill to the noise and immensity of the large planes.

If you live near a port, there will be a dock area to visit with your child. The large ships, long wharfs, their machinery and fittings will fill the youngster with wonder.

A large farmer's market that has, in addition to produce, live rabbits, pigeons, or chickens, will captivate a child. And another kind of market, the flea market, will permit youngsters to see many items not commonly found in homes today: kerosene lamps, statues, and so on.

You may have visited the supermarket dozens of times with your youngster, but have you ever visited its back door? Your child will be awed by the immense trucks in the loading bays and the ceiling-high stacks of food containers.

Let your youngster experience the unique sounds and smell of a lumber yard. Perhaps the child will have the opportunity to watch a circular saw in operation.

A construction site – fascinating enough for adults – is doubly fascinating for a child. Visit a new building site where the bulldozers are at work far below clearing out the subterranean levels. Then visit the site again periodically to let your youngster see each step as the structure gradually takes shape.

Visit the tallest building in your city and take the elevator to the top. The receptionist on any particular floor probably won't mind your taking the child over to a window for a panoramic view.

The Extended Home Curriculum

The electives described so far have been of a sort that turn ordinary occasions to educational gain or take the parent and child out of the home to pursue a plan. Let's consider now those home activities that parents can engage in by plan.

As was stressed earlier in the book, of all activities in which parents might engage their youngsters for intellectual advancement, reading skill and vocabulary growth are the most valuable. Here is yet another way children's vocabularies can be enriched while satisfying still one other important need.

Books on Tape

Children enjoy being read to at bedtime, and they frequently enjoy hearing the same story over and over again. Parents, on the other hand, may find repeated readings of the same story boring. The child will, however, be able to hear the same story several times if the parent records his or her reading of the story. By selecting stories employing a rich vocabulary, the parent can help the child's ear become attuned to the new words. One parent taped *The Wind in the Willows*, *Kon-tiki*, and other books that formed part of the children's vocabulary growth program.

Such taped readings shouldn't, of course, completely replace live readings, but as long as the child gets sufficient hugs and affection at other moments he shouldn't miss the body contact he loses by recorded readings.

Word Games

Installation of a blackboard in the dining area permits parents to chalk up new words and engage in other educating diversions. If you haven't room for a blackboard-stand, fasten the board to the wall. Three- and four-year-olds who can read and print enjoy puzzling out anagrams; moreover, the child will get good exercise in problem solving. The parent might print on the board the letters ETO, REA, GLE, RAM, which the child would then try to unscramble and rearrange into *toe*, *ear*, *leg*, *arm*. Or, your youngster may prefer a simplified sort of anagram, one with partly completed answers. The following might be chalked up: $CONAB = B\_\_0\_;$ $ERIC = R\_C\_; GESG = E\_G\_$ (bacon, rice, eggs).

Parents may find they haven't enough wall space in the dining area for both a blackboard and the large wall maps necessary for geography games. This was solved in our own kitchen (which had but one small wall suitable for the attachment of items) by affixing the top edge of whatever map was being used to a five-foot horizontal length of wood (Fig. 31). Strings from the ends of the wood ran up through metal eyes screwed into the kitchen ceiling, and then down to bottles filled sufficiently with water to counterbalance the weight of the map and wood. Raising the map to the ceiling permitted use of the blackboard. Lowering the map in front of the blackboard permitted the children to play the geography games.

Films

Films may be borrowed from the public library at no charge, or for a small rental fee. Projectors can be rented too. But to take full advantage of the many films available, you might consider buying a sixteen-millimeter sound projector. A new projector is costly, but a good second-hand machine can often be purchased cheaply from a firm that rents projectors.

Films may be borrowed from several sources for only the payment of shipping charges, costing, at most, express charges both ways, or costing as little as return postage. Since films are heavy, even one-way postage

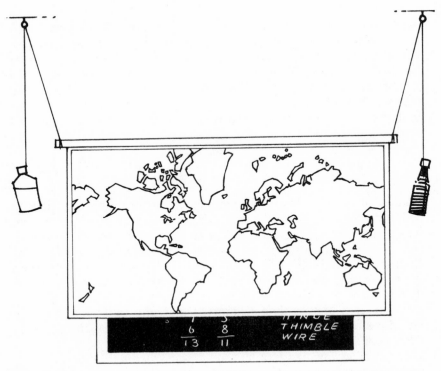

Figure 31: *If space is limited, a map can be hung in front of a blackboard.*

could cost several dollars. Families might therefore view the films together and share the costs.

Several foreign embassies lend films under the shipping-charge arrangement offering, collectively, almost a thousand films. Embassies will send a descriptive list of their films on request. Their addresses can be obtained by consulting the telephone book for either Ottawa or Washington in the reference section of your public library.

The U.S. Coast Guard has two dozen films available for the cost of return postage. A pamphlet describing their films can be obtained by writing National Audiovisual Center, General Services Administration, Washington, D.C. 20409. The U.S. Department of Commerce has fifty films available on oceanic and atmospheric matters.

The National Film Board of Canada offers the loan of about 3,500 films from their centers in each Canadian city, plus New York, Chicago, and Los Angeles. A catalog can be obtained by visiting or writing any of the centers.

The Board of Education in any city or town will have its own collection of films, often numbering thousands. Parents teaching their children at home *may* be able to borrow films from this source, depending on the local policy and how sympathetic the film librarian is to the novel educational program you are giving your child.

Thanks to the several sources of films, we were able to view more than 500 films over a three-year period. All free. The films, averaging about fifteen minutes in length, covered a wide range of subjects: geography, history, meteorology, music, general science, electricity, aerodynamics, human physiology, psychology, biology, zoology, botany, icthyology, entomology, even ESP; and, in the area of self-preservation: health, nutrition, advertising humbug, dangers of smoking and of drugs; safety in the home, in the neighborhood, in the wild, and on water.

Slide presentations on a variety of subjects can sometimes be borrowed, without charge, from photo clubs. The clubs are often listed in a community-service book that some libraries keep. If such a club isn't listed, contact the manager of a large retail photo store; he will likely be able to name one or two clubs. A few phone calls will then lead you to a source of slides. Such slide presentations may be accompanied by a script to read aloud, or by a tape cassette of narration; or the text itself may be on slides interspersed in the presentation.

Kits

The contents of a well-stocked hobby shop will suggest other ways to engage a youngster in worthwhile activities: simple crafts for preschoolers, model building and scientific kits for slightly older children.

Parents frequently underestimate what children can accomplish when they are encouraged and helped by an adult. A youngster of seven might not be able to build a model airplane unaided, but he will be able to contribute greatly to the task if encouraged to do so. Just turned seven and eight, my two built various devices in an electronic kit, among them, a Morse-code sender, a metronome, an automatic light switch, a buzzer activated by a lemon-juice battery, a two-transistor radio. Though the children needed much supervision, they positioned many of the components unaided, and I gradually sat back and let them pore over the circuit diagram to puzzle out where parts had to be connected.

Kits aren't always necessary for experiments. Books can be borrowed from the public library showing various simple experiments that can be performed with items found around the home. Or you can purchase your own book at a small cost.

The extent to which your school-in-the-home program may be enriched is limited only by the amount of time and effort you wish to devote to your youngster's education, bearing in mind that moments of quiet and inactivity also have an important part to play in the child's development.

16

Bright, Likable, Happy Children

Many ways have now been presented to advance children's intelligence, to sharpen their powers of observation, their manual dexterity, and their persistence. Let's turn off the intellectual advancement and motor-skill development switches now and consider a matter more important than either. If parents proceed with just a few of the educational activities that have been presented – indeed, if they merely teach their youngsters to read, and make a small effort to enlarge their youngster's vocabulary – their children will have higher-than-average intelligence.

As we saw earlier, bright youngsters get along better with others and generally lead a happier life than do children of average intelligence. But not *all* bright children do. High intelligence, like wealth and physical strength, is a power. And power, ineptly used, is abusive. Were a child to use his intelligence ineptly he would not make friends easily, and the fuller purpose of this book would be unfulfilled, for, as stated in Chapter 1, parents don't want to turn their children into brainy brats. Parents have an obligation to see that their youngster has a sufficient number of likable qualities so he will be able to attract friends easily and generally enjoy life more fully.

The characteristics that make children likable are learned to a great extent from the example their parents set. Children will have more or less respect for others, for their rights and their property, and be more or less prone to gentleness, kindliness, and generosity, to the extent these traits are valued and exemplified by their parents. Even children's concept of honesty, sometimes interpreted differently from home to home, will be established mainly by parental example. One might wish to see qualifications added to some of the following postulates (written by an unknown author), but would anyone deny that they contain considerable truth?

Children Learn What They Live

If a child lives with criticism,
He learns to condemn.

If a child lives with hostility,
He learns to fight.

If a child lives with ridicule,
He learns to be shy.

If a child lives with shame,
He learns to feel guilty.

If a child lives with tolerance,
He learns to be patient.

If a child lives with encouragement,
He learns confidence.

If a child lives with praise,
He learns to appreciate.

If a child lives with fairness,
He learns justice.

If a child lives with security,
He learns to have faith.

If a child lives with approval,
He learns to like himself.

If a child lives with acceptance and friendship,
He learns to find love in the world.

The formation of a child's character and code of ethics is largely the result of parental thought and action, no less so than is the child's intelligence. Whereas all children have need for social grace, brilliant children who lack this skill tend to pay a higher price in unhappiness. Average children, having failings common to most children, don't attract undue scorn to themselves for possessing those faults. But brilliant children are more conspicuous. And foibles that, in average children, might pass unnoticed, stand out, like a boil, for all the world to see and to criticize. In short, whereas most children are graced with a protective screen of obscurity to camouflage their failings, brilliant children are often called to answer for those same failings. And peccadillos that, in average children, would be shrugged off with, "Well, he's only a kid," may, when the child is bright, be attributable to "that smart-aleck brat."

Too, the bright child is often better equipped to work his mischief. In choosing to be impudent, such children are efficiently so. And adults find such needling the more vexing because it is often knowledgeable and challenging.

This is not the place for a sermon. Every thinking adult knows that if one is to attract affection, admiration, respect, loyalty – the requisites for a happy life – one must be affectionate, admirable, respectful, loyal, and *humble*. Few people like braggarts. The child who has an inflated opinion of his own worth will repel children and adults alike. And parents who try to direct attention to their children's intelligence will arouse resentment for themselves and their children too.

In raising a brilliant child, it is too easy to raise a conceited child, one acutely, perhaps intolerably, aware of his superior mental ability and general knowledge. A child this badly trained will be burdened with social disadvantages that far outweigh any intellectual advantage he has gained by early intellectual stimulation. Consider one such individual: Norbert Wiener, a child prodigy who eventually originated the science of cybernetics.

The boy's father, Leo Wiener, a professor of Slavic languages and literature at Harvard University, wanted his eighteen-year-old son to study under the renowned philosopher-mathematician Bertrand Russell. How might we expect the parent and child to behave on meeting this learned man they had crossed the Atlantic to see? Probably quite differently from the behavior Russell described in a letter. The father, Russell wrote, began with a eulogy on his child's virtues and on his own; then,

> While this information was being poured out, his son – after a period of dead silence – suddenly woke up & began an equal torrent, on the subject of his Doctor's thesis – pulling out books from my shelves & pointing out crucial passages, pointing out, kindly but firmly, where my work is one-sided & needs his broad view & deep erudition to correct it. Both went on at once, like children shouting "look at the castle I have built." "No, look at *mine*" – I believe the young man is quite nice & simple really, but his father & teachers have made him conceited. I asked him what he had read in philosophy – he at once reeled off the names of *all* the great philosophers, tho' he couldn't remember the titles of their books. Mathematics of course he professed to know pretty well, tho' he admits it would be as well to know more.

And later, Russell wrote, "The youth has been flattered & thinks himself God almighty – there is a perpetual contest between him and me as to which is to do the teaching."*

If the teenage genius performed this badly with a co-author of *Principia*

---

* *The Life of Bertrand Russell*, Ronald W. Clarke. Jonathan Cape, 1975.

Mathematica, we might wonder how he performed with others possessing less reason for respect.

Those who have raised spectacular children, though readily accepting credit for their children's commendable intelligence, have rarely accepted blame for any failings in the children's characters or for their social ineptitude (if, indeed, they even deigned to recognize such failings). Yet obsession with high intelligence and complete disregard for social grace can lead only to the development of bright oddballs.

Parental Pride

Parents who try to attract notice to their youngster's brilliance—as Jeremy Bentham's father did—invite problems. To his credit, young Jeremy rebelled against making a show of his learning. Many children might not have the wisdom or the strength of character to do so, and fall, instead, into the parents' trap.

One naturally feels satisfaction when an offspring's high intelligence is seen to be a direct result of parental involvement and effort. But parents will wisely moderate their show of pride lest it alienate their child from others, or give him a false understanding of his own importance. Different individuals have different strengths, and among desirable human characteristics, high intelligence isn't the most important. Moreover, it is mere parental duty to give offspring whatever advantage one can. Parents don't look for kudos for feeding, clothing, or sheltering a child. Why should they seek special attention for educating their youngster?

To the extent that parents involve themselves with the program presented throughout this book, so will their children be intellectually, perceptually, and physically advantaged. The purpose here is to help children reach a little closer to the intellectual limit they, as possessors of ten billion brain cells, are equipped for, not to provide parents with the means of turning this phenomenal thinking organ into an instrument for self-aggrandizement. When the priorities get mixed, not only are children's relationships with strangers disturbed, the relationship between parent and child can be unsettled; for, on reaching maturity, children are then able to ponder and assess the parents' motives and estimate the possible cost in lost happiness they themselves paid in fulfilling the parents' plan.

Boris Sidis, the Harvard professor who predicted that his offspring would be spectacularly brilliant, paid a bitter price for putting his own ambitions before his son's needs; namely, a balanced educational program that would permit the youngster to get along easily with others. His son, William James Sidis, you will recall, was the child who lectured at the Harvard Mathematical Society at age eleven.

The boy had been subjected to the greatest of academic disciplines, but to almost no social discipline. Norbert Wiener, who attended Harvard at the same time as Sidis, made this comment in *Ex-Prodigy: My Child-hood and Youth*:

> There was likewise no question that Sidis was a child who was considerably behind the majority of children of his age in social development and social adaptability. I was certainly no model of the social graces; but it was clear to me that no other child of his age would have gone down Brattle Street wildly swinging a pigskin bag, without either order or cleanliness. He was an infant with a full share of the infractuosities of a grown-up Dr. Johnson.

Lacking elementary social graces – politeness, consideration for others, and such – Sidis easily attracted scorn. Newspaper reports ridiculed him every time he did something odd, and eventually, the boy began to realize that other people viewed him as no more than an intellectual freak. Sidis became so incensed at the lopsided education he had received – an education that brought him only unhappiness – that, on graduating from Harvard, he renounced all interest in intellectual matters, and thereafter, moved around the United States working as a fruit picker, heavy laborer, and helper in a shipyard, trying all the while to be a regular fellow. His sole joy was to collect streetcar transfers from around the world.

So bitterly resentful was Sidis of his father's bizarre educational experiment, that he cut off all contact with the father, refusing, in fact, to even attend the man's funeral. He himself died in 1946 of undisclosed causes, at age forty-eight, in a rented room in Boston.

The tragic case of W.J. Sidis reveals the danger of equipping children with high intelligence while ignoring their social needs. The purpose here is to help parents raise children who are bright, likable, and happy – attributes that are in no way inconsistent with each other. Let us consider, first, guidance that will help make children likable.

Tolerance, Patience, Humility

Those with superior physical abilities, more sensitive perceptions, and higher intelligence sometimes can't understand why other people experience difficulty with problems they themselves find simple. To illustrate: while the average person gropes his way slowly through a problem, the active mind has already raced ahead, defined and resolved the problem, and waits, perhaps restlessly, for the slower mind to catch up. Unless the bright child is practiced in showing tolerance and patience, his life, both as a youngster and as an adult, can be frustrating.

The advantaged child will note and perhaps report (especially after he begins school) the difficulty other children have in coping with tasks he finds simple. Possibly, the best a parent can do in this situation is to point out that if the other children had received his early education, they too would probably find these matters simple.

190

Manners

Manners and etiquette are almost beneath mention here. Some have viewed with contempt the common insistence upon mouthing please and thank you. However, these time-honored lubricants for frictionless dealings are but verbal handshakes, or the nearest thing to a hug that our society permits between strangers.

They are, too, highly communicative words, often conveying immeasurably more by the *tone* in which they are uttered than they can convey in print. For example, depending on how "Thank you" is uttered, it might mean, "You are gracious, charming, thoughtful, and truly wonderful," or "Okay, Buster, but just wait until you want a favor from *me!*"

Indoctrination in table manners is wise, for the child who eats noisily or messily may not be invited a second time to dine with those who eat differently.

The parent who, in the name of love, ignores – or, worse, caters to – a child's immoderate or self-indulgent conduct harms the child; for, by raising an unrestrained child, the parent thoughtlessly seals off many opportunities from the child. Doors that open readily to the mannerly, courteous child close quickly to the ill-mannered child. Worse, and less-often noticed, doors also sometimes close to the parents of such children.

Etiquette in conversation is important, too. Brilliant children, having more knowledge and often more eloquence than other children, are more easily able to participate in adult conversation. And they should be encouraged to do so, provided they are alerted first to certain niceties that characterize mannerly conversation, chief among which is the fact that we don't interrupt someone while he is speaking. Children will quickly develop a sensitivity for the observance of non-interruption if they are rewarded, in some way, each time they catch their *parents* violating this important rule.

For other features of gracious conversation – suited to, say, an advanced nine- or ten-year-old – we can't do better than turn to Benjamin Franklin. Franklin's conversational manners were so offensive at one time that even his friends avoided him. Yet he ultimately became one of the most adroit diplomats the world has ever seen. How? In his own words:

> I made it a rule to forbear all direct contradiction to the sentiments of others, and all positive assertion of my own. I even forbade myself the use of every word or expression in the language that imported a fix'd opinion, such as "certainly," "undoubtedly," etc., and I adopted, instead of them, "I conceive," "I apprehend," or "I imagine" a thing to be so or so; or "it so appears to me at present." When another asserted something that I thought an error, I deny'd myself the pleasure of contradicting him abruptly, and of showing immediately some absurdity in

his proposition: and in answering I began by observing that in certain cases or circumstances his opinion would be right, but in the present case there appear'd or seem'd to me some difference, etc. I soon found the advantage of this change in my manner; the conversations I engag'd in went on more pleasantly. The modest way in which I propos'd my opinions procur'd them a readier reception and less contradiction; I had less mortification when I was found to be in the wrong, and I more easily prevail'd with others to give up their mistakes and join with me when I happened to be in the right.

We can hardly expect young children to exercise the restraint that characterized Franklin's conversation, but we can start youngsters in that direction by teaching them the difference between "You're wrong," and "I think you're wrong," progressing, eventually, as the child grows and matures, to "You may be right, but consider this other matter."

Selflessness

Selflessness goes out the window when hedonism – a fashionable philosophy today – marches in the door. "Do your own thing," "Be good to yourself," self-indulgence: the edicts of what has been termed the Me Generation encourage a preoccupation with self that is barely distinguishable from what was at one time called selfishness.

The word *service* has almost entirely been expropriated by vendors of gasoline. Luther Burbank, the "plant wizard" whose friendship was sought by eminent people of his day, had this to say of service:

Perhaps a naturalist, with seventy years of work and observation behind him, can be forgiven if he preaches a little, and it seems to me this is a good time to preach briefly on the theme of Service. . . . I will bet a straw hat to a felt one that, if you are tired of your job and discouraged with life and down in the mouth about the way you are treated, you have got a little mixed about your importance to the scheme of things, but I will bet an entire new suit of clothes against a poor necktie that, if you are happy, capable, liked and trusted, you are giving the world or your family or your employers or your employees a little more than is expected or than you are paid for or than you get back.

Luther Burbank invested hundreds of thousands of dollars in money and effort to perfect new strains of plants, then gave many of them away, and did so without resentment. "We plant inventors cannot patent a new plum," he said, in *The Harvest of the Years*, "though the man who makes an automobile horn not [much] different from the ram's horn with which Joshua blew down Jericho can get a patent and retire to Southern

California and wear silk underclothes the rest of his life! ... As regards my own work I have long since ceased to think of it as anything more than a contribution to the whole body of knowledge and an addition, in its results and conclusion, to the technique and practice of plant development."

Children indoctrinated with even a smattering of this philosophy will never lack friends.

Instinctive Helpfulness

For children to help others instinctively, they must develop a liking for people. Fortunately, alerting youngsters to reasons for liking others is as suited to a mealtime game as any other subject. If your youngster is now able to print or write, engage him in the following game. Pick someone you both know or have observed – a friend, a relative, a neighbor, or a merchant – and help the child compose a list of that person's likable traits or characteristics.

PARENT: What about the lady who sits at the information booth at the shopping mall, Abdul?
CHILD: She looks nice.
PARENT: Yes; well, that's because she's *neat*. And that means everything about her is tidy. Put down *neat*. [Spell it.] Anything else?
CHILD: She smiles a lot.
PARENT: Right! She's *pleasant*. What else?
CHILD: She asked me why my hand was bandaged.
PARENT: Yes, indeed. She's *concerned* about others. And that's because she's both *kind* and *considerate*. Anything else?

With just a little help, your youngster will be able to compose a list of a dozen or so pleasing and desirable attributes possessed by the person you are describing. And what if, on your next visit to the shopping mall, the youngster were to hand his list to the lady? The list might top her day, if not her entire year.

While driving, you might play Who Can Say Something Nice About..? Pick someone you know, or had recent dealings with, or perhaps a group of people: police constables, firefighters, garbage collectors, doctors, and so on.

Encouraged to see the best in people, children will develop a giving nature. And those who give readily, share willingly, and help others instinctively make friends quickly and easily.

What have children to give, to share, and how can they help others? Children's drawings make welcome gifts. Alerted to the courteousness of the person who works in the produce department of the supermarket, a youngster might be encouraged to create a drawing, in appreciation for the person's prompt attention and thoughtfulness. The drawing, suitably inscribed, "From Arabella, with love, because you're always nice to us," might be remembered, if not treasured, by its recipient for years.

On those occasions that delight children – Hallowe'en, Easter, and such – a youngster might be taken to a local hospital and allowed to distribute a few small toys (rather than edible treats, which may not be welcomed by the staff) to child-patients. At Christmas, a child might be alerted to the afflictions of others and encouraged to contribute a small amount from his savings to their help: an amount the parent might see fit to add to.

Compliments

By teaching a child that others value words of appreciation no less so than he himself does, the youngster can be encouraged to voice his approval: a practice that might begin at home: "Mommy cooked a delicious supper, right, Driscol? Let's hear it for the cook. Hip-hip...."

Once children begin to see the pleasure their appreciative words arouse, they will warm to the procedure. In fact, encouraging children to express their appreciation may help parents overcome their own inhibition about giving compliments: an inhibition possibly based on a fear of rebuff, or a fear that the compliment may be misinterpreted. Here, too, the child's presence provides a unique social catalyst between adults. Imagine, for example, knocking on someone's door and saying: "Hope I'm not disturbing you; but my daughter, Enid, here, said she thought you had the nicest front garden on the street. And we've got a special little program going between us this week in which Enid and I have agreed to express our appreciation to people. Well, again, I hope we haven't bothered you. Thanks for your time." Try to dispense two or three compliments for a couple of days. Thereafter, certain days – perhaps every Monday – might be designated as compliment day, the day's quota of two or three to be duly filled.

The thought might occur to you that the suggestions given here in some ways also further the goals of other chapters, by prompting the child to print and spell, by encouraging him to draw and to form closer links with people who may, in turn, add to the youngster's knowledge. Indeed, should parent and child engage in a mealtime reading of some book that deals with getting along with others – a natural complement to the youngster's training in social skill – the youngster's vocabulary will also be enriched. And what if, while learning to count, a child were to endow neighbors with an unusual gift by taking out a plastic garbage bag and picking up fifty pieces of litter – a logical and practical extension of the "Don't litter!" theme so popular today, coupled with an early application of the boy scouts' pledge to do a good turn each day. Similarly, eight-, nine-, or ten-year-olds might be encouraged to erase or expunge graffiti in apartment elevators and halls. The superintendent's job? Yes. But the fact that the neglected chore is allocated to someone else needn't cheat your youngster out of an opportunity to do something nice for everyone.

Those children who learn the inner satisfactions of serving others are less apt to take example from what other children do or fail to do; and, tapping the meandering spring of individualism thus, they may follow its flow to leadership.

Matters considered to this point have only touched the threshold of happiness. Let's consider now the other requisites for a contented life.

Happiness

Of the factors that make children's lives happy or less so, the amount of affection youngsters receive has been found to play a preeminent role.

AFFECTION

Children's greatest need, after food, clothing, and shelter, isn't intellectual stimulation, but affection. So great is this need that if children are young enough and the deprivation of affection is severe enough, children simply die. Such cases, though rare today, were common sixty-five years ago in orphan asylums. When the lack of affection isn't severe enough to kill, it often leaves children mentally retarded. Dr. René Spitz of New York compared the development of babies in two different institutions. In one, infants were cared for by their mothers. In the other, foundling infants were cared for by overworked nursery personnel. Over a two-year period, the Developmental Quotient of the foundling infants dropped from 124 to 45. Indeed, these children never learned to speak, walk, or feed themselves. And a study conducted at the Cleveland Jewish Orphans Home revealed that when the lack of affection isn't severe enough to stunt children's intelligence, it can still stunt their physical growth.

Criminal, neurotic, psychotic and other forms of asocial behavior can be traced, in most cases, to lack of early love or emotional instability. In *Delinquency and Human Nature*, Dr. Denis H. Stott reports the close relationship that was found to exist between early lack of affection and crime in his study of 102 persistent criminal offenders aged fifteen to eighteen.

Child development researcher, Dr. John Bowlby, contends that all children younger than the age of three who lack affection will be permanently damaged, as will most children between the ages of three and five, and even some children between the ages of five and eight. But damage to children resulting from insufficient love isn't simply a black or white condition; it is one of infinite grays: some children being slightly damaged, and others more so. Absence of warmth and affection, Dr. Bowlby found, could result in acute anxiety, excessive need for love, and powerful feelings of revenge leading to a sense of guilt and depression.

The enduring effects of meager affection, or maternal deprivation as it is called, was determined by Dr. Harry Harlow at the University of Wisconsin. There, baby monkeys had access to two dummy mothers made of wire mesh. Inside each, an electric light bulb emitted a semblance of body heat. The nipple of a feeding bottle protruded from one mesh form. The other mesh form had no feeding facilities, but the mesh was covered with soft cloth.

The experimenters found that though the baby monkeys received their nourishment from the naked mesh form, they always returned, between feedings, to the cloth-covered mesh form. From this, Dr. Harlow concluded that the infant's need for contact comfort is more powerful than the hunger drive in forming bonds of affection.

But an equally important discovery was made when the monkeys reached maturity. All showed little interest in sexual activity, and when the females finally mated and bore offspring, they either ignored their babies or cruelly mistreated them; this, the result of having been reared by unresponsive mothers who neither patted, cuddled, nor played with them.

Young children's first needs are primitive. The animal kingdom is, therefore, a good reference point in how to raise offspring. The outstanding quality, we note, in the mother and cub relationship is, initially, not education, but physical contact. Infants thrive on body contact with the mother, and clamber contentedly over her as if measuring the great mass that protects them from an alien world. Body contact of this sort with the parent makes offspring feel not only protected, but loved. Human young are no different.

But human parents aren't disposed to lying on the floor to let offspring clamber over them; so bouts of body contact between parent and offspring are normally negotiated with the parent sitting or kneeling. And that's what cuddling is all about: a primitive animal need that has no less value for human young than for lion or bear cubs. Children aren't lovable 100 per cent of the time. And parents can, in anger, do or say things they afterwards regret. Cuddling acts as an antidote for the venomous remarks that a parent may spit out at a child.

Children won't be happy unless they believe they are loved. Nor will such children be adventurous. Nor will they be able to show affection easily to others. The child raised in an emotionally upsetting atmosphere,

196

devoid of love, can become an emotional cripple, no less handicapped – indeed, perhaps more so – than a lame child. For a child to feel loved, parents must constantly reassure the child of that enduring affection by hugs, cuddles, pats on the head, a gentle brush of the cheek, and kisses. Parents should miss no opportunity to show, by expression and touch, the great warmth they feel for their child.

When children need affection, they don't announce, "I need hugging." Indeed, they often express their need ineptly and grumpily, thereby arousing in parents feelings inimical to affection – at least until parents are able to interpret children's sign language. One youngster known to me coupled grumpiness with faked imbalance that sent her stumbling gently into the wall. A moment of hugging and her grumpiness disappeared and her sense of balance returned to normal.

FEARS

Children will be happy and adventurous only to the extent their lives are free from fears. Some parents have filled their children's heads with fearful thoughts as a means of making the children more dependent on them: an unwholesome conditioning that can exert a lifelong negative influence upon youngsters. Such parents are, fortunately, rare. Less rare, though, are parents who teach their children, as a joke, that a fearful monster lurks in a cupboard or in some dark place: an error that, once made, is difficult to correct; for having taught a child to fear something that doesn't exist, the parent has no means, later, of proving the bogey is nonexistent.

And many parents unintentionally pass on fears to their children: fear of snakes, insects, and bats being the most common. If one lives in an area where certain dangerous creatures abound, children must, of course, be alerted to such danger.

Every thinking adult knows that the common house spider is harmless, yet parents routinely pass on to youngsters their own abhorrence of the creatures. If you, because of fearful early example, can't bring yourself to pick up a caterpillar, beetle, or snail with your bare fingers, be sure not to show revulsion when your youngster picks one up. (You may be thankful sometime to have someone around to pick up and remove such creatures from the house for you.)

Police constables sometimes come off badly in children's training: "Don't throw that wrapper on the road, Wolfgang, or a cop'll take you away." Not only is a wrong and unfounded fear of police introduced to the child's thinking – *mis*education – but a great opportunity for education is lost. A child who is, instead, taught that it is wrong to make a mess, especially on ground used and owned by everyone, won't litter even when no police constables are around.

SENSE OF HUMOR

The child with a sense of humor will find life more entertaining. But what *is* a sense of humor. Certainly not the ability to enjoy a joke. Almost everyone can do that. Rather, a sense of humor permits one to see humor where it isn't obvious or intended – in everyday circumstances and in the play of words; this latter being the vehicle for wit. Possession of a sense of humor, then, combines a sensitivity to appropriateness or inappropriateness, and a sporting attitude toward life.

Life is more entertaining for the individual who is alert to, and perceptive of, the day's offering of comical windfalls. So, to whatever extent parents can teach children, by their example, to see more than the obvious, serious side of matters, children will be more disposed to good humor.

ATTITUDE

Abraham Lincoln once remarked that "Most folks are about as happy as they make up their minds to be." Everyone can find reasons to justify being miserable because fate has apparently short-changed him in some way. On the other hand, people may, instead, focus their attention on the various ways fate has granted them a more pleasant life than others. Everyone has this conscious choice. Attitude, and state of mind then, play an important part in determining how much your youngster enjoys life. By encouraging children to notice reasons for being contented with their lot, instead of alerting them to reasons for complaint, we endow youngsters with the nearest thing to a "happiness key" that exists.

VOCATION

One's work can profoundly influence one's general contentment. With modern labor-saving devices, physical drudgery is rare. But spiritual drudgery is, unfortunately, common; workers being present in body but absent in spirit, yearning daily for a change and new challenges.

What vocation will your child follow when he grows up? Such a decision may be a long way off, but parents can help their youngster choose; they can, in fact, influence his choice.

Different professions require different skills and aptitudes. A lawyer must be able to express himself well in speech; a surgeon need not be able to speak well, but must, instead, have exceptional manual dexterity.

History is rich with stories of parents who have unwisely obliged their children to pursue some profession though the children's interests lay elsewhere. The main purpose of endowing children with a well-rounded education isn't to predispose them to this or that vocation, but to equip them for dealing effectively and wisely with life's problems; chief among which is earning a living. If parents have a strong preference about which career their child eventually chooses, they may encourage the youngster to acquire knowledge and develop abilities that are valued in that field rather than blatantly impose their preference. The story is told of a mother who stole into her child's darkened bedroom each night to whisper in his ear, "I want to be a lawyer." We might hope that one night, the child, still wide awake, might have rolled over and asked, "Well, Mom, why *don't* you be one?"

The child, or, rather, the emerging adult, is often the best one to decide what profession to follow. If parents think the young-adult's choice is starry-eyed, they might then arrange for him to meet someone in that field so he will clearly understand the advantages and disadvantages of the job.

What if the academically advanced youth wants to be an auto mechanic or engage in employment that doesn't call for great learning? Happiness in one's work is of first importance. Parents will wisely curb their own ambitions for their youngster and let him make his own decisions. The child's first decision may not be his final one, but merely a leaning in the general direction of some yet-to-be-defined or discovered vocation. The active, inventive mind won't abide inactivity. And the child who begins as an auto mechanic, hungering for challenge, may discover important matters in the design of automobiles that have so far been ignored. Henry Ford started by repairing watches and clocks. The Wright brothers began by building printing machinery, then bicycles. Louis Pasteur was just a chemist. Enquiring, innovative minds balk at the apparent imposition of limits to man's ability, and, embarking on a small problem, they sometimes find it to be a tributary leading to a larger, more important problem, which they, with their unusual abilities and grounding, are uniquely suited to solve. And they solve it.

17

The Early Education of Jason Kauppinen

This book was in the final stages of writing when I first heard of Jason Kauppinen. Jason invented a portable battery-powered traffic light for police to use when regular traffic lights fail. The battery-powered light spares policemen from standing at intersections – perhaps in a violent storm – to keep traffic moving. Jason has also invented special battery-powered eating utensils for the handicapped: a knife that holds the meat while it cuts, a fork that rotates to gather spaghetti, and a spoon that turns toward the diner's mouth. Jason is four years old.

Discussing Jason's early education with his mother, Ann-Marie Kauppinen, was, in a way, unsettling, for the mother's program of early instruction so outpaced the speed of educational advancement suggested in this book that, turning to architecture for metaphor, it was as if I had been telling the builders of mud huts how, with bricks, mortar, and wood, they could now build two- or even three-storey structures – only to glance over and find someone quietly constructing an edifice on the order of the CN Tower.

Geniuses of the past have accomplished no less than Jason in those areas in which they received special training. But their parents have left little information about their child's education. We know, for example, that Jeremy Bentham, at age four, was reading and writing at an adult level. But what method of teaching had the father employed? Would his method be as effective in our present age with its many electronic distractions? And what about the phenomenal William James Sidis, who, at age four, was reading and writing both English and French at an adult level, and who almost two years earlier had devised his perpetual calendar? How had he been taught? An intriguing question that may never be answered.

Parents of manufactured-to-plan geniuses – Bentham, Mill, Witte, Wiener, Stern, and all the rest – went about their self-appointed tasks with great vigor; though none with more vigor than Ann-Marie Kauppinen. But then her reasons were unusual. Resentful of the experimental educational program she had been exposed to in primary school (one in which the alphabet was not taught), Ann-Marie wanted to make certain her son would not, and could not, be damaged, as she had been, by any similarly absurd educational program that might be in vogue by the time he started school.

Jason's education is presented here not as a model for other parents to emulate, but rather to provide parents with an additional choice of activities, to include or not, as they see fit, in their own child's education.

Ann-Marie had no special plan in mind when she began Jason's education. She hadn't studied the lives and education of eminent historical figures; nor had she any formal training as a teacher. Her sole source of knowledge and experience derived from having tended, at an early age, six younger brothers and sisters.

Throughout history, the parent-educators of geniuses and prodigies have been male scholars. Ann-Marie makes no pretense of being a scholar, nor even of being well-read. Ann-Marie's education, which she describes as "the pits," ended when she left school at age fifteen. Unqualified to pursue the vocation of her choice, surgical nurse, Ann-Marie began studying to become a hairdresser. Strangely, though, the study of cosmetology at that time (before 1960) paralleled, in some ways, the study of nursing, and Ann-Marie was obliged to learn the principle parts of the brain; the muscles of the eye and ear and their function; the liver, its function and diseases, and how these diseases could be recognized by skin tone; the significance of changes in appearance of the eye; and different heart disorders that can be recognized by changes in the appearance and structure of the fingernails. In short, she received – by an educational back door – an unusual knowledge of human biology: knowledge that fitted her well for teaching Jason at least one important subject.

When Jason was born, Ann-Marie lost no time in starting his education. Jason was introduced to the first subject on the curriculum, reaching and grasping exercises, even before he and his mother had returned home from the hospital. Ann-Marie held an object in front of the child. When his attention was fixed on the item, she placed his hand upon it; when he relinquished his hold, the procedure was repeated again and again.

Next, Jason was taught the rudiments of body rolling. He soon learned how his hand had to be positioned beneath him to permit him to roll over. And he was taught to find his daily bottle of fruit juice when it was hidden beneath a fold in the blanket or under a cloth: a problem he was successfully solving at age one month.

The mother's ideas about speech instruction were unique. Why, she wondered, when encouraging children to imitate simple speech sounds, were youngsters not shown the letters of the alphabet that correspond with those sounds? In other words, why not teach children the letter code so they could learn to read at the same time they were learning to speak? Finding no reason against the idea, Ann-Marie began teaching Jason the letter sounds when he was two months old. She held up a large letter A, patiently repeated many times the sound as it is heard in the word *at*, and encouraged the youngster to voice his approximation of the sound. When Jason finally learned A, Ann-Marie showed him the letter B (sounded as in *ebb*). Additional letters were gradually introduced, and eventually short, simple words that employed those letters.

Jason's physical progress kept pace with his academic progress. At three months of age he was able to turn over without help. By the fourth month, the youngster was able to move around the home, traveling, though, in an unusual manner: not crawling, but moving forward *on his back* by pushing with his feet. The youngster's newly-acquired mobility, coupled with his now-advanced skill in locating hidden objects, permitted the mother to engage him in a new game while she tended to housework. Ann-Marie hid various toys around the home—under chairs, pillows, in cupboards and drawers—and Jason delighted in finding them.

At six months of age, Jason was speaking and reading about twenty-five words; among them, *apple, ball, cat, jam, doll, ring, sun,* and *baby.* (Educators might ponder here how a six-month-old infant would have scored on a reading-readiness test.)

An exercise in problem-solving was created at this time by cutting a word—*cat*, for example—into its component letters, then scrambling them, and asking Jason to put *cat* back together.

Jason was able to stand unaided at ten months. At eleven months he was speaking and reading simple sentences. About that time, Ann-Marie (who was not known to me at that time) discovered my book *Teach Your Child to Read in 60 Days.* Having, until then, no book to guide her, the mother had wondered whether her approach to reading was the best one; especially when Jason sometimes seemed confused. The book reassured Ann-Marie that her teaching method was as good as the best used in schools and provided an easy, stepped program that helped Jason advance more quickly.

Aside from his academic activities, Jason spent many hours playing with the usual sorts of toys that interest children of that age: play dough, blocks, stuffed toys, a coloring-book, and a toy telephone among them.

Each day was, for Jason, a series of impromptu study sessions prompted by his own inquisitiveness. To Ann-Marie, the practice of telling children they will learn about this or that matter when they are older was reprehensible. She backed her belief with an unswerving principle; namely, that whenever Jason asked a question, she would stop whatever she was doing and give him as detailed an answer as she could, teaching him, in addition, whatever other information was needed for him to understand her reply. Her fidelity to this principle is seen by an incident that occurred when Jason was a year old. While Ann-Marie was scrubbing the floor one day, Jason indicated by his expression and the word "wet" that he was puzzled why the insides of the windows were moist. Afraid lest she misinform the child, Ann-Marie abandoned the half-finished floor (fastidious though she is), dressed Jason, and hurried off to consult the encyclopedia at the public library about the laws of condensation. In this way, Jason gained his introduction to science. Two months later, by means of his mother's simple drawings, he knew all about the water cycle: the evaporation of a puddle, rising in the form of warm, moist air, forming a cloud, followed by saturation, condensation, then rain forming puddles again. The youngster learned, too, how the water cycle was altered by the seasons.

Jason also learned the cycle of trees, from seed to shoot, to sapling, to mature tree, to bloom, and back to seed. Ann-Marie taught Jason the life cycle of animals, particularly apt at that time because she was pregnant with a second child. Jason learned how the egg traveled down the fallopian tube to be fertilized, and how the baby grew. The youngster thought the nine-month gestation period to be an incredible delay in the birth of the baby until he learned that the gestation period for elephants was almost two years.

Jason was able to spell in two ways by fifteen months: with magnetic letters affixed to the refrigerator or a tray, and by printing with a pencil. He spelled phonically; that is, in composing the word *cat*, he sounded the letters "kuh, a, tuh" rather than "see, ay, tee." Ann-Marie constantly challenged his spelling ability; in consequence, he was soon able to spell not only his full name, but a variety of other difficult words. Indeed, when Jason printed the word *spaghetti* one day, an adult questioned his spelling of it. A dictionary was brought, and the adult was found to be wrong.

When Jason was eighteen months old, Ann-Marie introduced him to a game that sharpened his power of recall. She placed three items on a tray, then, covering them with a cloth, asked Jason to name the items. Gradually, Ann-Marie added more items to the tray until Jason was able to recall upwards of twenty objects. A second benefit from the exercise was his growth of vocabulary and of general knowledge; for, in adding new objects to the tray, the mother taught the youngster not only their names but their uses.

Jason's progress was a curious mixture of quickness and slowness.

Although the child was able to speak twenty-five words at age six months, and able to stand unsupported at ten months, he still wasn't able to speak more than twenty-five words or walk at *nineteen* months.

For Jason, the television set was a perpetually open book, but only for the educational presentations of PBS in Buffalo and for TV Ontario. The child didn't spend long periods watching TV, preferring to play with his toys, turning to television periodically whenever the subject caught his interest.

Attending to the housework posed a considerable challenge for Ann-Marie, with Jason, age twenty-two months, beginning to clamor all the more for intellectual stimulation. To keep him occupied, Ann-Marie gave him a pencil and newspaper, circled a high-frequency word – *the*, for example – and asked the youngster to circle every other *the* he could find on the page. This he did contentedly, not only marking the words, but counting them in groups of ten, marking the first ten *the*'s with horizontal strokes of the pencil, the second group of ten with vertical strokes, the third with horizontal strokes again, and so on, then counting up the groups of ten.

In many of the tasks set for Jason, the important pervasive exercise was that of problem-solving: a skill to which Ann-Marie attached great importance. She taught Jason how to solve simple wooden jigsaw puzzles with large pieces, progressing gradually to the cardboard type with many small pieces. Another exercise in problem-solving at that time was to have Jason locate specific words in a children's dictionary containing sixty entries.

One toy Jason enjoyed playing with required the insertion of geometric shapes through appropriately shaped apertures. However, the youngster, on learning the shapes had names, then wanted to know their names, and Ann-Marie, having almost no knowledge of geometry, was required, once again, to scurry for the necessary information.

Ann-Marie bought Jason a 2,300-word children's dictionary for his third birthday. Now he could find words for himself: an exercise he engaged in with increasing frequency because of the words used on one of his favorite television programs (called "Science International" in the U.S., and "What Will They Think of Next?" in Canada), a program that piqued the youngster's interest in solving scientific and mechanical problems. The program featured inventions that had been devised to fill specific needs; the original problem or need was described first, and then solutions or temporary solutions to the problem were shown. Sometimes, a day or two after watching a program, Jason would disclose why he thought a proposed solution to a problem seemed inneffectual, and what changes might be made to solve the problem better. Soon, Jason demonstrated his problem-solving ability in a practical way.

Driving home in a storm one night, the family passed a policeman directing traffic at a busy intersection where the traffic lights had failed. Mulling over the policeman's apparent discomfort in the wind and rain, Jason, then age three and a half, fell to thinking about a better way to solve the problem. Quizzing his mother about electricity (which she hastily began to study) the youngster was soon working on a portable traffic light that could be easily transported to a trouble spot.

Progressing deeper into a study of electricity, Jason began to find his new dictionary inadequate, so an adult dictionary was acquired. With greater word-power as an ally, Jason was soon solving the technical problems in his traffic light, and by his fourth birthday, the device had been perfected and tested.

His interest now whetted by the wonders of electricity, Jason's questions increased in frequency and difficulty, so Ann-Marie began an evening class in electrical drafting. With her help, Jason was soon able to read a schematic diagram for a stereo radio. Though he didn't understand the workings of every component, he understood the flow of power through the circuit.

Jason's next major challenge in problem-solving occurred one day when his babysitter, a mature woman, mentioned to Jason's mother the problems of being partially incapacitated because of a stroke, especially how demeaning it was to have to rely on someone else to cut her meat for her. Jason, the ever-present, ever-silent observer, drank in this information and his brain rapidly followed the problem through to a logical solution. The youngster fetched a piece of paper and a pencil and quickly explained, with drawings, the function of a special knife, fork, and spoon for handicapped people.

Jason's vocabulary was, by this time, becoming awesome, for he had learned many new words from his extensive reading. One day, in a moment of exasperation at an adult whom, he felt, had overstepped the bounds of good manners, Jason called the offender a "curmudgeon," adding that he would no longer tolerate the totalitarian dictatorship that had persisted, and that though he was a mere plebe, he demanded respect.

An Overview

In attempting to explain Jason's uncommon intellectual advance, it is easy to say, "Oh, yes, but he was different almost from birth," dismissing entirely the fact that his training was, thanks to Ann-Marie, different almost from birth; and that if the mother hadn't initiated, and persisted with, her program of special instruction, Jason today would probably be as ignorant and mentally undeveloped as any other four-year-old.

Some of the factors that contributed to Jason's emergence as an exceedingly advanced youngster are easy to see: early intellectual stimulation, and a mother who would give unstintingly of her time at his every request and would go to considerable trouble to gain whatever information he wanted.

Consider, too, what Jason's education lacked that might have worked to his disadvantage; for example, the absence of less knowledgeable peers such as he would have encountered in a day-care center or a nursery school. Furthermore, he saw little television other than educational programs.

Being the first-born child gave Jason the usual advantages, yet, strangely, less an advantage than his younger sister has gained. Two-year-old Lori-Ann is receiving an even better education than her older brother received – thanks in no small part to Jason himself, who has taken up her education with as much enthusiasm as his mother: listening to his sister's reading, marking her printing and affixing either a gold star for complete correctness, a blue one for being almost perfect, or a red one for trying very hard. (Tested at age two years, eight months, by the Durham Board of Education, Lori-Ann was found to be reading and computing with the skill of a child half way through Grade 1.) And the mother, more experienced now in educating children, has discovered better ways of teaching. For example, one important new exercise – which may ultimately win a spot in the cereal hall of fame – is called Stacking Cheerios. The game requires the careful placement of Cheerios breakfast food on top of each other to build as high a column as possible (Lori-Ann's present record is six inches). The mother attributes her daughter's exceptional manipulative skills solely to the child's long practice with these edible building blocks: an exercise she began at eighteen months of age.

The story of Jason and Lori-Ann is just beginning. The true worth of their unique early education may not be fully apparent for years.

18

Finding a Group for Your Child to Learn With

If there are no children nearby for your child to play with, you may consider placing your youngster where he or she can meet, play with, and learn from others in a spirit of cooperation. On the other hand, if both you and your spouse work outside the home, you may be *obliged* to place your child in group care. (You might, of course, place your youngster with someone who cares for children in the home, but this wouldn't avail the group experience to your child.)

Group child-care takes two forms: day-care centers and nursery schools. Each type of establishment serves a different purpose, though both provide common important experiences for children: learning to get along with others, learning to give and take graciously, learning to wait one's turn, learning, in fact, that the universe doesn't revolve around one small person who might easily acquire that notion in the absence of other demanding youngsters his own age.

Much of my knowledge about day-care centers and nursery schools was gained, at the beginning, as a parent looking for suitable child care for my own children, for a service that would permit me, a single parent, to work each day undisturbed. To this initial knowledge has now been added the experience of setting up and directing the Early Learning Centre, in Don Mills (an area of metropolitan Toronto). The program and facilities at the Centre, described later, will serve as a guide to the amenities you might look for – or hold out for – when seeking child care for your own youngster. If, however, your child already attends a day-care center or nursery school, you might discuss with the supervisor or owner the possibility of introducing some of the ideas in this book. Let's begin by considering the basic distinctions between a day-care center and a nursery school.

Day Care and Nursery Schools

A day-care center differs from a nursery school principally in that it provides child care for the entire day, beginning sometimes as early as six o'clock in the morning (for parents who must get to work early), and running as late as six o'clock at night. The services of a day-care center, therefore, are intended primarily for parents who work all day. A noon meal is normally provided for the children unless they bring their own lunch. A snack is provided in the morning and another in the afternoon. And provision is usually made for children to have a nap in the afternoon. The main purpose of a day-care center is, therefore, that of child *care*.

A nursery school, on the other hand, provides not so much child care as preschool education, hence use of the term *school*. Children usually attend a nursery school for two or three hours a day, either in the morning or in the afternoon, but not both. Some parents, though working, prefer to send their child to a nursery school rather than a day-care center because of the emphasis given to education. Such an arrangement becomes practical when one parent works half-days and is able to take care of the child at home the other half-days; or when there is a relative or a housekeeper to look after the youngster during the half-day he doesn't attend the nursery school.

Briefly, then, a day-care center provides supervision and care for the whole working day, whereas a nursery school provides tuition and care for just two or three hours a day. Day care is usually a necessity for those parents who enrol their child in such a program, whereas a nursery school is usually the choice of parents who do not require child care.

Parents seeking, primarily, a group educational service will therefore, if circumstances permit, choose a nursery school. But parents, particularly those who have engaged their youngster in the various stimulating activities described throughout this book, may not find a nursery school that offers the kind of program they would like. Most nursery-school programs are patterned after kindergarten programs, which are themselves often unchallenging.

A good day-care center and a good nursery school will have some characteristics in common despite their different goals. Any establishment is, of course, only as good as its staff who, generally, will reflect and propagate the philosophy and sentiment of the director. Day-care centers and nursery schools are generally of two sorts: those operated privately – whether for profit or not – and cooperatives run by the parents themselves. On the whole, there aren't riches to be made in operating either a day-care center or a nursery school. Often, the venture is a labor of love; the operator being driven primarily by a maternal (or paternal) desire to raise her (or his) extended family. At least this is the driving force behind the best child-care facilities. Some operators, though, driven by other motives, have found that the profit picture can be brightened considerably by employing various forms of misrepresentation: forms that will be considered presently.

Montessori Schools

In the pursuit of quality nursery-school service, the name Montessori naturally arises, so a word about this large network of schools would be in order.

First, use of the word *network* is misleading. In fact, use of the name Montessori is misleading, too, because the name is not protected by copyright. Almost anyone, with or without skill, with or without knowledge, can open a nursery school and call it a Montessori school. One need not subscribe to the philosophy of Maria Montessori, nor even use her materials. One cannot therefore generalize when speaking of Montessori schools, but must always distinguish between one particular Montessori school and another.

Then, too, even among the Montessori schools that profess fidelity to Maria Montessori's teaching, the question of accreditation can be confusing, for there are two different Montessori organizations, each of which has its own standard of excellence, and neither of which recognizes the other. Rather than get caught in the web of comparative accreditations and their respective merits, we will simply accept the fact that there are *good* Montessori schools in business, and there are others that shouldn't be in business.

Reading instruction is an advertised feature of better Montessori schools. The reading method is usually a phonic one, which, as in primary schools, may or may not be correctly and effectively taught depending on the teacher's knowledge and expertise.

Limitations of Child-care Establishments

The failings commonly encountered in child-care establishments (both day-care centers and nursery schools) are of two types: honest failings, and dishonest failings. We'll consider the former first.

Mention has already been made of the simplified kindergarten curriculum that passes for preschool education in many child-care establishments. This program usually features what is called "peer group interaction" or, in plain English, learning to get along with others of the same age. A child's social development is vitally important in any program of preschool activities; however, social development sometimes receives so much stress that it serves as an excuse for teaching children little else; as if by teaching children to be cooperative and mannerly, management and staff are then freed from any need to engage children in intellectually stimulating subjects or skill-enhancing activities.

My own children had two full years of this blinkered training; they did not learn to tie their shoes, to count, to tell the time, or to accomplish any other useful skills during their 4,000 hours of attendance. Fortunately, I balanced out their loss by teaching them at home; first, reading, then various other activities described throughout this book.

Slowly it dawned on me that the few moments of instruction my two received at home each day were of infinitely greater educational worth than the instruction they received during their daily eight hours at the center.

Of course, the children brought home hundreds of free-expression drawings and paintings over the years: a collection that swelled as they eventually sallied into kindergarten and Grade 1. By sheer volume alone, the works they produced should have guaranteed them artistic excellence if, indeed, the skill could be acquired in this way. But it can't. The production of free-expression drawings and paintings, having possibly some therapeutic value for disturbed or backward children, is of little artistic value to other children.

This, an unpopular notion, probably won't pass unchallenged. I state it both as a former commercial artist, and as a portrait painter whose works have hung in major competitive exhibitions in Canada, England, and France. I know of no artists – and I know many – who trace their skill back to free-expressionistic artwork, whether executed during the preschool years or at any other time. Artistic ability requires more discipline than is needed for free-expression works.

The concern here, then, is the disproportionate time and attention given to social skills and to arts and crafts in most nursery-school and day-care programs: a lop-sided emphasis that often leaves little time for intellectually stimulating activities.

This, then, is the disservice done to children by well-intentioned conscientious teachers: an honest failing. Let us now consider dishonest failings.

Inspecting a Child-care Establishment

Have someone accompany you if you can. Four eyes are better than two, and two minds are better than one. Your companion might think of an important question to ask, one you might miss.

Of first concern is your child's physical and emotional well-being. Do the children at the establishment seem happy and relaxed – even the smaller ones who might be tyrannized by bigger, stronger children in a poorly managed establishment?

What is the child-to-teacher ratio? Some operators have plausible explanations for "temporary" large ratios. And some operators are not averse to pressing the cook, bookkeeper, or janitor into the momentary role of teacher to give the appearance of a low ratio while visitors are present.

Are there plenty of play materials for the children, and have they any educating value? On visiting some establishments, parents might be impressed by the great range of toys and their new appearance, failing to notice that the toys are on shelves too high for the children to reach. Such toys are not intended for children to use; they are merely to impress parents.

Are there first-aid materials? Does anyone know how to use them? Are fire drills held regularly? When was the last one?

If a noon meal is served, is the menu posted for the day? Might you examine the menus for the past week or for the next week? Bear in mind, though, that a menu can provide a deceptive description of the meal that finally ends up on a child's plate, and with only your child as a witness to what is served, you may never really know whether the lunch measures up to the menu unless you visit while the children are eating.

Asking for an opportunity to watch children at their daily activities is, surprisingly enough, one request from which an operator may justifiably demur *if the staff has specific teaching goals to reach each day*. In an establishment where children spend much of their time playing with plasticene and blocks and scribbling with crayons, there is little reason to bar parents from the classroom. But if teachers are attempting to teach youngsters advanced skills, they need the children's full attention. The presence of parents would be a detrimental distraction.

Does the management provide periodic reports to parents on their child's progress at various skills? Are there, in fact, any stated goals in physical or intellectual activities?

The purpose here isn't to parade the gamut of unethical practices a sharp operator can perpetrate on parents. Such an operator, possessing the advantage of forethought and experience, can spin a web of tricks and artifices that are difficult to detect and too numerous to list. Often the swindle takes the form of proclaiming nonexistent features of the program—for example, reading instruction, French as a second language, musical or dance instruction—when, in fact, there is no one qualified to teach the proposed activity. Because the parent is reliant solely upon a child for a report, the scam is hardly detectable.

Probably your best course is to ask parents of the other children there what progress their child has made in areas you consider important.

Rather than expose your youngster to a program of uncertain worth, you may prefer to organize, with the help of other discriminating parents, child-care facilities that meet your own specifications: a cooperative day-care center or nursery school. Or you might prefer a venture that fills both functions: full day care for parents who wish it, and half-day school for others.

Establishing Your Own Child-care Facilities

Operating a cooperative establishment doesn't necessarily oblige you or other parents to teach, or even to care for the children. Teachers can be hired to take care of that. You and your cooperating members might concern yourselves only with setting up and managing the venture: choosing a location, renting premises, hiring staff, planning a program of activities. Parents may or may not take turns as teaching assistants under the guidance of a paid professional. And, of course, to whatever extent parents help out in ministering to children's needs, so the costs go down. On the other hand, children behave quite differently when their parents are present, and this is often the bane of a cooperative venture.

How do you go about finding interested parents? Post notices on bulletin boards in local churches, community centers, and shopping plazas. Insert an advertisement in a neighborhood newspaper. Type a brief announcement several times on a sheet of typing paper, get photocopies, cut the announcements apart and pay youngsters to deliver the slips around the district.

A direct approach can be effective. Knock on doors to find homes with preschool-age children. As soon as you find your first interested parent you will then have someone to share the task of finding more parents. And as each additional parent is found, the task becomes easier.

Once you have five or six interested parents you can begin looking for a suitable location and begin contacting the appropriate government department for information on licensing. The inspector for your area might be persuaded to visit your group and explain the requirements. Too, he may have a selection of free literature on how to deal with the various problems of setting up and operating a child-care establishment: how to find teachers, what accreditation they should have, what recreation and hygiene facilities are required, and so on.

Toys and equipment needn't cost a great deal of money. Parents can probably donate an educational toy or two that perhaps sees little use in their own homes. Toys and puzzles can sometimes be picked up inexpensively at church bazaars and flea markets.

If chairs and tables are too costly for you at the beginning, purchase rectangular samples of discontinued carpet lines at a carpet outlet. Children can sit on these and work on the floor. Paint for decorating the rooms and furniture can be purchased cheaply from the paint department of stores where colors are mixed to order. Often the mix doesn't come out the way it's supposed to, and the store is stuck with quantities of various colors they must then sell for whatever amount they can get.

Does someone know a printer? The unprinted side of a spoiled printing run – on colored paper or card stock – provides a good surface for collages. If the printer has a hole-punch machine, its bin will be a treasury of paper circles of different sizes and colors that are just thrown away. Children can glue these on sheets to create pleasing patterns.

A good, low-cost activity that enhances hand-eye coordination skill for children requires only the purchase of a hammer, one-inch roofing nails, and a two-inch thick sheet of styrofoam from a building supply center. If the hammer has claws, cut them off with a hacksaw or bind them with foam so children can't harm themselves on the sharp edges. Cut the styrofoam into manageable pieces about a foot square. Children have a whale of a time driving nails into the soft styrofoam. The large heads on this type of nail permit their easy removal for re-use. We take this activity a step further at the Early Learning Centre by affixing, to the styrofoam, paper bearing large printed words. Circles indicate where children are to drive in the nails (Fig. 32).

A great potential source of low-cost materials is the business associates of your working parents who, with their diverse contacts in various businesses, may be able to secure all manner of materials and supplies cheaply.

The content of your proposed program will be the first matter to discuss with any teacher you consider hiring. You will want to select someone who is sympathetic to your goals, someone who knows the letter code and can use it to teach reading, *or* someone who will make the effort to learn it (see Chapter 7). Ideally, the teacher would be able to suggest ways your goals might be made easier to reach, or even ways in which your goals might be extended.

Discipline

A major concern in the running of a child-care program is holding children's interest and gaining their cooperation. With skillful management, children pose few disciplinary problems, or do so only for a short period while they are learning how much self-advancement will be tolerated in a group. Youngsters soon learn that to get the attention they crave, they are expected to cooperate and to show concern for others. Children learn, too, that some techniques they may use effectively at home to get what

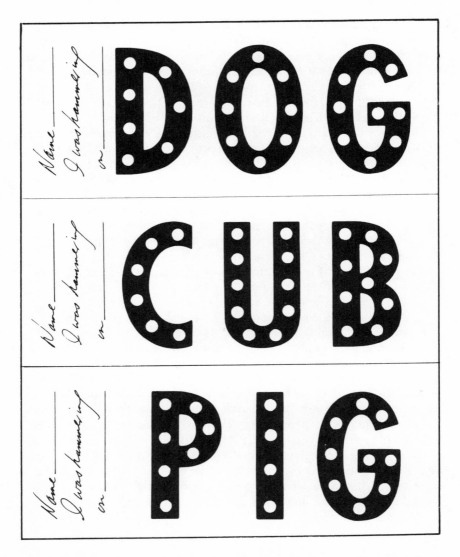

Figure 32: *These words, shown half-size, are affixed to styrofoam and the children drive nails into the circles.*

they want are both ineffective and unacceptable in the group.

Corporal punishment has no place in group care. Indeed, it is unlawful. An obstreperous child must learn that antisocial behavior wins only segregation from the group, the child being placed at some distance from the other children and denied, if necessary, participation in certain group activities.

The Sidney Ledson School
(formerly the Early Learning Centre)

The development of children's sociability is, properly, the first concern of any educational program. When treated courteously by people who do not raise their voices, children learn to behave courteously without raising *their* voices. The most important element in social instruction, therefore, is the example set by the staff.

Our second goal is to stimulate children's thinking; achieved first by teaching children to read, an activity that takes just a few minutes each day. All our children—two-year-olds included—learn to read, beginning first with a few letter sounds and short simple words, then on to simple sentences, progressing finally to advanced sentences that employ words containing new letter-combinations.

When a child reads his first word, a diploma is sent home. The diploma is dated, and the child's name is hand-lettered in script (Figure 33). Printed on bright orange paper, with a happy-face drawn on a combination of gold and red notarial seals, the document is both colorful and impressive—which is, of course, the intent. When affixed to a wall in the child's home, the diploma attracts the comments of visitors. In this way, the child's interest in reading is fanned.

Figure 33: *A reading diploma from the Sidney Ledson School.*

A second happy-face seal is sent home for affixing to the diploma when the child reads his first sentence. And when the child begins our first reader, the third and final seal is sent home.

Most of our children are younger than six; some are as young as two. Children can attend half-day or whole-day, five or fewer days per week. School hours are from 9:00 A.M. to 4:00 P.M.; however, children can be brought as early as 8:00 and picked up as late as 6:00.

Our children's ages and abilities differ greatly from those children in public schools, so rather than separate them by grade, we divide them into three general groups: Juniors (ages two and three), Intermediates (ages four and five), and Seniors (most of whom are five and six).

Our purpose is twofold: first, to advance children's intellectual and social skills; and second, to find improved ways to advance those skills. Functioning thus as a laboratory school, our program changes constantly as better ways are devised to make the various activities more interesting, more entertaining, and more educational. For this reason, any description of the program must be qualified by a date. The description that follows—appropriate for April 1986—may serve as a source of ideas for use at your own school or day-care center. This is the schedule for our Seniors.

9:00–10:15 Children are taught reading and vocabulary growth individually or in twos and threes while the others work quietly at puzzles, mathematics, printing, writing, tracing, drawing, language-skill sheets (that deal with punctuation, sentence structure, and spelling), and French vocabulary; or they engage in various tasks and games that develop manual dexterity, hand-eye coordination, visual acuity, memory skill, and problem-solving ability. Use of an electric typewriter reinforces reading skill. Quiet classical music provides a background for the children while they work and play, thus helping to attune their ears to one form of quality music.

10:15–10:30 Tidy-up time, then children engage in an exercise of body balance, "Follow the Bear."

10:30–10:50 Children exercise on the outdoor apparatus in the back field (weather permitting) or in the gymnasium.

10:50–11:05 Snack time. Some parents prefer that their child not be given confections, so cake, cookies, and sweetened drinks are not served. Instead, children receive simple foods: peanut butter and crackers, cream cheese and crackers, portions of apple, banana, or carrot. Milk, the standard drink, is periodically replaced by apple juice.

11:05–11:30 Special-activity time. See below.

11:30–11:40 Circle and song time. The children sometimes accompany themselves on rhythm instruments.

216

11:40–11:45 Queenie the puppet, Barclay her dog, and other characters make their brief daily appearance to reinforce reading instruction, rules of safety, of hygiene, and of manners.

Special activities vary from day to day. The children engage in the following activities once or more each week.

Crafts: Children construct an item to take home. Projects are chosen that are more likely to advance children's ability to handle tools and materials, and exercise their creative powers.

Music and dance: Children receive musical instruction each week. A specialist in eurhythmics introduces the children to the fundamentals of musical theory, and leads them in activities that encourage movement to music and develops their sense of rhythm.

French: The children play games that employ French words.

Science: The changing seasons, variations in weather, and plants and animals provide an easy introduction to the natural sciences: meteorology, botany, and zoology. Each subject permits the teachers to introduce important new words and concepts to the children.

Tours: The children visit local businesses, a shoe repair shop, a pet store, a branch of the public library, a bank, an upper story of a nearby tall building (so they view the neighborhood from on high), the warehouse area of a supermarket, and other places to learn interesting matters and new words relevant to each.

Show and tell: Every Friday, children bring some object from home— a favored toy, a souvenir of some trip or special event, an item of clothing or something they have watched a parent use—to tell us what it is, whose it is, how it works, and so on; providing thus, an exercise for children in putting their thoughts into words, and in speaking before a group.

Other: Children engage in a memory game or learn about synonyms, fractions, or any one of several matters that recent events favor the introduction of. Experts in hygiene, traffic safety, fire safety, and dental care visit the school periodically to teach the children their special subjects, often using puppets, films, and other entertaining teaching aids.

The Intermediates and Juniors engage in a simplified version of the Senior program, with emphasis being given to their first needs: social skills, motor development, and speaking and listening skills.

The afternoon program is similar to that of the morning.

Parents play an important part in their child's reading progress. An instructional folder is sent home explaining the problems children face in learning to read and how learning can be made easy (information of the sort that is presented in Chapter 6). Parents receive an audio cassette of the letter sounds so they can voice them correctly and reinforce at home the instruction their child receives at school.

Parents also receive three copies of the first letters and words their child learns to read, and they are told how to display these around the home to help ease his or her progress (providing thus, a form of "immersion" reading program for their child). Nine reading games are also sent home so that parents can engage their child in a playful review and reinforcement of the child's reading.

Each child has his or her own Reading Record Book in which the teacher inserts a brief comment about the child's reading that day. Children take their books home with them daily. Parents are then able to see what their child accomplished in school, and are themselves able to write a comment on what reading they reinforced at home. The next day, the teacher inserts a sticker-reward for the child's having cooperated with the parent in doing "homework." Parents are encouraged to contribute to their child's reading progress because we believe that literacy is too valuable and enduring—and wonderful!—a skill to be left entirely to those outside the family for its development.

Children's speech vocabulary, another priority, is enlarged by discussing objects that children are not likely to know the names or use of. Picture-sheets showing these items are then sent home so children can post them on their walls. Correct language usage—a most important skill—is continually encouraged. Teachers avoid the use of clichés and vernacular terms.

A record is kept of each child's daily performance in those activities that encourage the development of hand-eye coordination, visual acuity, and manual dexterity. Progress can then be noted from month to month. A brief description of two such activities may suggest other challenging exercises to include in your own program. The purpose here isn't to specify what equipment to buy, but merely to suggest the *type* of equipment you might fit to your own needs.

The *Labyrinth,* manufactured by Brio, of Sweden, provides excellent training in hand-eye coordination. The child alters the tilt of a tray by adroitly turning two knobs, and by doing so, is able to make a steel ball follow a twisting path without the ball falling into a hole. Insert-trays (also made by Brio) can be purchased to simplify the challenge for beginners and very young children.

The placement of shapes in appropriate apertures or slots provides a good challenge in both visual acuity and manual dexterity. The game called *Perfection* (Parker Bros.) provides such an exercise. The game includes a timer and a pop-up feature that very young children may find intimidating, in which case these elements of the game would not be activated.

By consulting a catalog issued for nursery schools and day-care centers, you will find a wealth of challenging games that are rarely found in regular toy stores. And the government department in charge of licensing child-care centers will probably be able to give you the names of game and equipment suppliers.

One important activity of our school, which you can easily provide

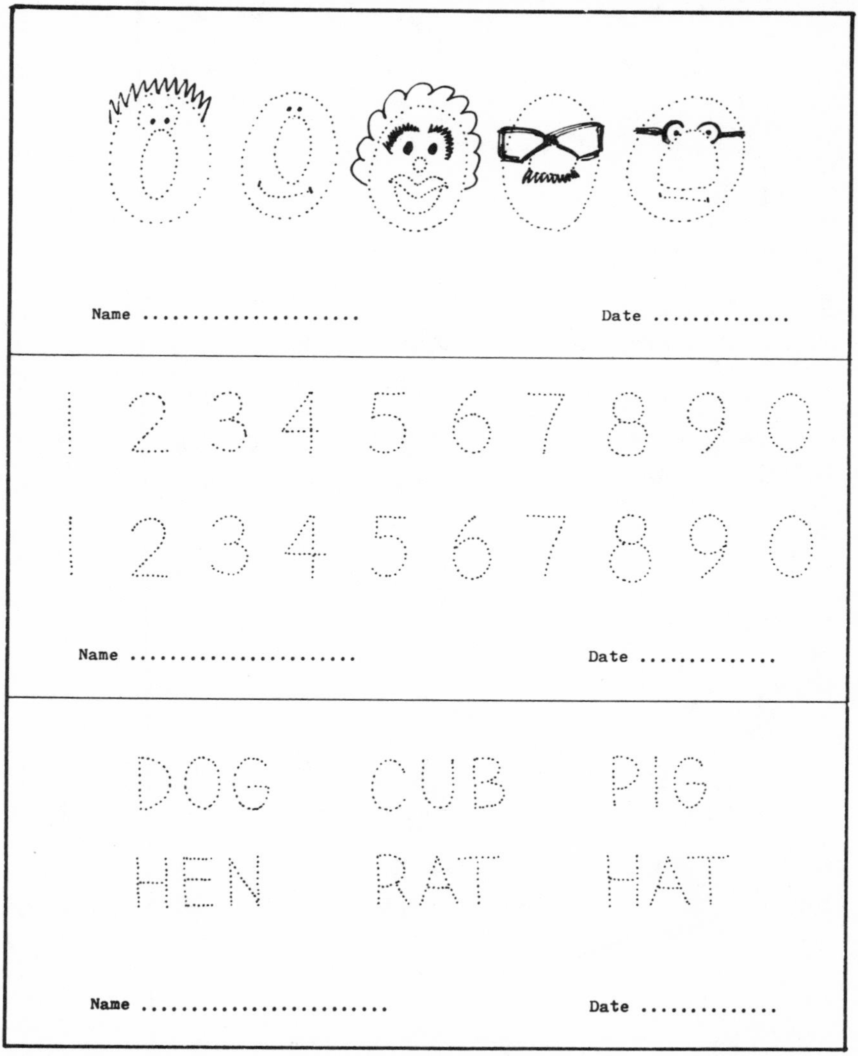

Figure 34: *First tracing faces, then numbers and letters, and finally words develops skill in manipulating a pencil.*

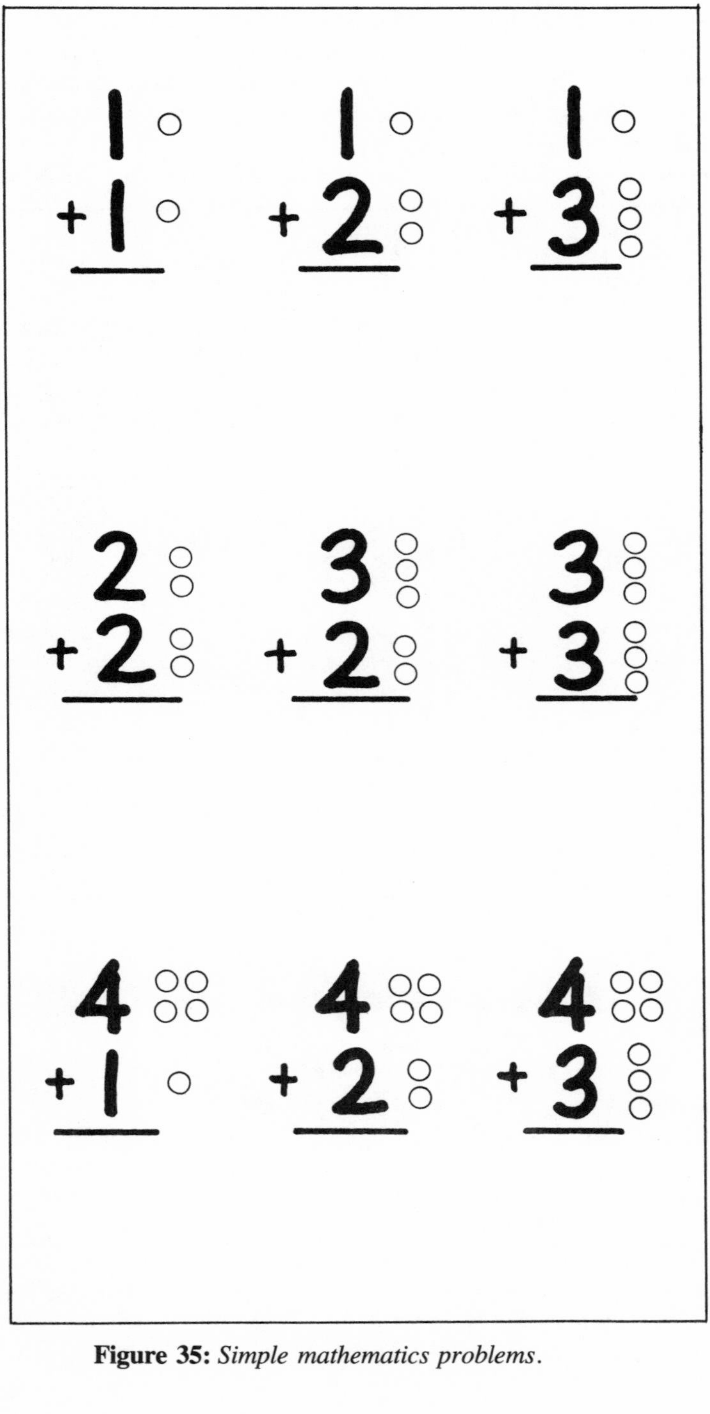

$$\begin{array}{r} 1 \\ +1 \\ \hline \end{array} \quad \begin{array}{r} 1 \\ +2 \\ \hline \end{array} \quad \begin{array}{r} 1 \\ +3 \\ \hline \end{array}$$

$$\begin{array}{r} 2 \\ +2 \\ \hline \end{array} \quad \begin{array}{r} 3 \\ +2 \\ \hline \end{array} \quad \begin{array}{r} 3 \\ +3 \\ \hline \end{array}$$

$$\begin{array}{r} 4 \\ +1 \\ \hline \end{array} \quad \begin{array}{r} 4 \\ +2 \\ \hline \end{array} \quad \begin{array}{r} 4 \\ +3 \\ \hline \end{array}$$

Figure 35: *Simple mathematics problems.*

for your child at home, is tracing. Merely draw a set of letters, another of numbers, and another of faces on a single sheet of typing paper (Fig. 34); photocopy them in quantity, cut them apart, and you will have an inexpensive and highly rewarding daily exercise, one that advances children's skill in using a pencil. We date the children's tracings and send them home daily.

Arithmetic problems, for the advanced children, are also marked and sent home daily. Simple problems (Fig. 35), progressing to four columns of figures, can be reproduced in the same manner as the tracing exercise.

Our children progress at these various activities at their own speed, not the speed of the group. Instruction is therefore often individual; and while a few children are engaging briefly in these closely supervised activities, the rest pursue activities of their choice, working alone or with others at various challenging puzzles or, in the case of the Juniors, simply building with blocks or with pieces of a plastic construction set, or modelling with play-dough.

Parents are kept well informed about their child's social and intellectual advancement. Parents have an opportunity near the end of any day to watch their child engage in group activities without being seen themselves. A special one-way viewing screen permits parents to see how their youngster behaves in the presence of other children when the parent is thought to be absent. Parents receive frequent verbal reports on their child's progress, plus the written comments of their child's teacher in the Reading Record Book. In addition, parents are invited to visit during class hours once each month to watch their child engage in various activities. The record books for these activities are consulted, and parents can note and discuss their child's progress. Finally, a detailed, written progress report is sent home twice a year.

An Overview

The motto of our school is "More than education, intellectual growth." Our stated goal is to raise children's intelligence, and our program has been designed specifically for that purpose. We encourage children to think and we advance their intellectual power. With what success?

Advanced intelligence in young children is difficult to measure in a wholly scientific manner. However, we can get some idea of an individual child's standing by noting the standing of the group. If a group of children is seen to be more intelligent than other groups, it is reasonable to assume that the individual children in that group are similarly more intelligent.

One attribute of intelligence that our children have been seen to possess collectively is the ability to grasp new ideas or principles quickly. Mischi Thadaney, a specialist in eurhythmics, teaches several groups of children around Toronto. When she first encountered our children, she reported: "I just couldn't believe how quickly they caught on. Usually I have to repeat things over and over again, but your children get it first off. They're incredible. They've learned to listen. One can really tell they're in a special program—the way they talk and the way they conduct themselves. Their concentration is excellent. They are truly gifted."

When our children visit the public library to participate in story time and sing-along, the librarians comment on their greater attentiveness, responsiveness, and general maturity.

Admittedly, such reports are not scientific proof of advanced intelligence; however, dealing as we are with children, not mice, we are limited in the ways by which we can fairly deduce their past and present intellectual standing and what advances have occurred as a result of our tuition.

Perhaps we attract the sort of parents who, by their concern with early education, would already have advanced their children's intelligence? Possibly, but we also attract parents of slow-to-learn children who see the need for their children to receive an early boost. Most of our children are about average when they start.

The rates of progress of different children from the same home can also be revealing. A working parent whose child was driven to our school by others sent this note with a tuition fee payment: "I wanted to take this opportunity to thank you for what we believe is proving to be a most beneficial program for Sam [who was then two years, eight months]. As a writer, I am obviously a firm believer in the importance of early reading and writing instruction, but I do feel that the values of your school go beyond practical skills. Both my husband and I have observed in Sam a much keener awareness of the world around him, and a sharper grasp of basic concepts. His vocabulary has taken enormous strides forward, and he seems to have arrived at the 'Why?' stage much earlier than did my other sons [who did not attend our school]."

Most tests used to assess children's intelligence attach great importance to a child's ability to read and speak skillfully, two skills that are fundamental to our program. Though children vary greatly in the speed at which they learn to read, we find that, generally, after a year of instruction, a child—now at age three and a half—will be reading at a Grade 1 level; children four and five will be reading at a Grade 3 or 4 level; and a six-year-old will be reading at a Grade 4 or 5 level.

Some parents drive great distances to bring their preschoolers to us (some have driven 56 miles, 72 miles, 90, and even 120 miles each day); however, parents cannot endure this regime for long. In consequence, these children usually attend our school only until they learn to read—which takes five or six months. Those who stay with us for longer periods reach advanced levels of learning. For example, Tamara Zimmerman was just beginning to talk when she began with us at age two. By age four she was reading a Grade 4 text. At age six she was reading Grades 6 and 7 material; this, with just half-day attendance. In early 1986, in Grade 1 of a Jewish parochial school, she was reading books of 40,000-word length.

Zahra Manji, almost three when she began with us, spoke no English. At age seven, Zahra reads Grades 6 and 7 science material with ease and complete understanding. Her computing skills are similarly advanced, and her mental multiplication—which delights her—is up to the twelve-times table. Her printing is excellent, and she is beginning to write. Her French is progressing nicely, and her memory skills are impressive.

Our school also fills the function of a remedial clinic for schoolchildren who are reading poorly. Their reading usually advances to their grade level in two to three months.

Producers of TV programs on early childhood education visit us periodically to film the special devices and methods we use to achieve quick, easy learning. Nine such television crews have visited during the past six years.

Our first commitment is to children. Our second, to parents (for whom we maintain a stock of literature on child-raising). And our third commitment is to those who work with children. We provide a three-week Reading Specialist training program that compresses into those three weeks a detailed study of the history of reading instruction and its technology, and instruction in teaching children as young as two to read. Two other programs are the Early Learning Specialist and the Home School Teacher.

Though we are in the forefront of experimental education, we are not funded by a university. Therefore, we are not able to follow and record the progress of our former pupils. We do, however, hear reports of the surprise and delight educators express when they encounter our "graduates."

Are there any children we cannot advance? No. All our children progress, though at varying speeds. Every child learns to read. Not that reading ability is the sole measure—or even the most important measure—of intellectual progress; for, assuredly, learning to behave in a responsible manner is an equally valid sign of intellectual advancement.

To reduce the burden of travel for parents who live at a distance, we have begun opening small branch schools in the homes of graduate teachers of our training programs.

19

Your Child and the School System

In due course, your child will be expected to attend school. The age at which a child is expected to attend school ranges from five to eight years old, depending on the state in which you live.

These are the ages children are *supposed* to start school. But youngsters don't have to go to school if certain conditions are met. Even if a child is already in school he can, under certain circumstances, be taken out of school for education solely at home. Whatever type of exemption you may wish for your child, other parents have already taken that route, and you can learn from their experiences. Let's suppose, first, that you plan to enroll your youngster in school in the normal manner.

Sending Your Child to School

Kindergarten is a carefree time for children no matter what their academic achievements. And Grade 1 is hardly less so. The child who has benefited since birth from the program presented in this book may enter Grade 1 with academic abilities at the Grade 5, 6, or 7 level. Such a child won't feel out of place in school so long as parents haven't disregarded the cautions described in Chapter 16. The question of "fitting in" at school was dealt with on page 28. My youngest child was reading at a Grade 6 level when she began Grade 1. This raised no barrier between her and the other children. In fact, it removed barriers, for she was able to help the others with their reading (and writing, spelling, and computing) and did so *in a courteous and unassuming manner,* here again underscoring the important message of Chapter 16.

If, in addition, parents establish a friendly relationship with teachers, a child is even *more* likely to enjoy school. Unfortunately, not all parents observe this nicety. Some parents of brilliant youngsters have unthinkingly presented their child to the teacher on the first day of school with an attitude of "Lo! my astonishing creation," then tried to wheedle—if not *demand*—every manner of concession or special attention for the youngster.

An initial encounter of this sort can spell trouble for parents and child alike. Teachers don't like pushy parents any more than they like pushy children. Though the parents are primarily interested in the education of their children, the teacher is more concerned with the education of all thirty in her care.

Finally, bright children can present a challenge the teacher may not welcome. The teacher may feel nervous about coping with a bright youngster and wonder how she will be judged as a result of her performance with the child. Should parents have been so reckless as to ignore the requisites described in Chapter 16 for the development of a mannerly, likable child, then indeed, teacher, pupil, and parent may be in for a difficult time.

Avoiding contact altogether with the teacher isn't necessarily the best tactic either, especially if she might not know that a youngster has had early instruction. In fairness, the teacher should be informed of the matter without boast or apology; perhaps in the form of a note:

Dear Ms. White:

Adelaide has been taught certain matters at home that aren't usually taught to preschoolers. If you would like to discuss her education at any time, please let me know and I'll be glad to visit you at your convenience.

Yours respectfully ...

Such a note invites friendship. Moreover, it conveys the important message that the parent doesn't intend to bother the teacher and will, in fact, remain distant until the teacher wants to discuss this or that matter.

Suppose a child were to enter a Grade 1 classroom in which the teacher was a personal friend of the parent. Would the parent or the child have any difficulty in dealing with the teacher? Not likely. Well, then, why not *befriend* the child's teacher? Instead of sending a note, a parent might visit the teacher, but—and this is important—*not* for the purpose of eulogizing the child's accomplishments, or the parent's. Visit the teacher with the primary object of befriending her. Teachers are, generally, likable people; and a parent may find, after a brief chat, a basis for friendship: common interests, concerns, or preferences. A parent will then be able to mention, almost incidentally, that the child has had early instruction, and that the parent stands ready to cooperate with the teacher in any desired way.

The parent who makes a special effort to educate a youngster eventually forms certain beliefs about education and about teaching. In fact, if a parent began teaching when the child was one, the parent would have been teaching for five years by the time the child enters Grade 1.

This *could* be longer than the Grade 1 teacher has been teaching. And because the teaching methods presented in this book are quicker than those generally used in schools, the parent could be critical of the slow, humorless educating techniques teachers are burdened with. In any case, parents would do better to keep their views on teaching to themselves unless they are asked by the teacher. And, at home, parents will wisely avoid criticizing, in the child's presence, techniques used in school, lest such criticism compromise the child's relationship with the teacher.

Enrolling a child in school doesn't mean parents should stop teaching at home. Indeed, the home will always be the more important contributor to a child's education until the child enters high school, and perhaps even until the child enters college.

Skipping Grades

Should children skip grades? Common sense would indicate that bright children should stay with those their own age rather than advance into classes of older children. But studies show this course isn't best. Researchers have discovered that high intelligence is often accompanied by qualities that make grade-skipping not only acceptable, but desirable. For example, a link has been found, curiously enough, between intellectual development and physical development; the more intelligent child often being a more physically advanced child. And the child's emotional and social development are similarly found to be advanced. Intellectually advanced children, therefore, appear to be advanced in everything but age; and age is, in itself, hardly a satisfactory reason for confining a child to the company of those below his or her level of physical and intellectual development.

Of the several studies that have been made of this matter, one, under the auspices of the State Department of Education in California, showed that of five hundred and twenty-two children who had been accelerated, only nine experienced serious problems after being placed in higher grades, and these nine had, in fact, been questionable in the first place.

If the principal of your child's school cannot, or will not, agree to acceleration for your child, and the child is bored, visit the teacher. Tell her you realize she is busy enough coping with so many children—some of whom may be obstreperous beyond belief, or agonizingly slow to learn—and ask her if there is any way you can help keep your youngster interested in school: perhaps by sending the child to school with assignments he could do in school, and you could mark at home, submitting the work later to the teacher for approval and general assessment.

Opting Out

There are a number of general reasons why parents might choose to educate their child solely at home, plus any number of specific reasons dealing with a particular school, a particular teacher, a local educational ruling, or other circumstance. If, for example, you have taught your preschooler for several years, you might be reluctant to see your teaching program interrupted by the child's attendance at school. Reasons aside, the only requirements for conducting a home-education program are that a parent have the desire to teach and that he or she be able to stay home each day.

Education solely at home isn't new. A number of notable people were taught by a parent or grandparents for some of their early years, or were partly self-taught, among them: Yehudi Menuhin, who had no schooling; Alexander Graham Bell, who had one year of private school, two years of high school; Gilbert Grosvenor, long-time editor of *National Geographic,* who began school at age ten; Gen. Douglas MacArthur, who had no schooling until he entered West Point whereupon he passed the tests with the highest score ever given an applicant; Margaret Mead, who began school by attending high school; and Franklin D. Roosevelt, who entered school at fourteen. And Abraham Lincoln was almost wholly self-taught.

No difficulty is encountered in keeping a child out of school if the family is constantly moving. The children of circus people and other itinerant families receive much of their education mainly by correspondence. But families who remain in one location, as most families do, can have problems when they opt for education at home. In fact, legal battles have been waged between school boards and parents who sought this right. Still, some parents have managed to keep their children out of school without a legal wrangle. These parents usually arranged their child's absence from school in one of two ways, the first employing conciliation.

Conciliation

You might start with the principal of your local school. Though the principal may play only a small role in a child's abstention from school, he can inform the proper person of your decision and spare your phoning various government departments. Moreover, in any amicable arrangement ultimately reached with the educational authorities, they might suggest you collaborate with the principal in your child's education: an arrangement you might welcome if it permits your youngster to engage in activities that would ordinarily have to be left out of your home program for want of expensive equipment: for example, science, gymnastics, music, woodworking, or metalworking. The principal can also extend use of the school library to your youngster. In addition, you may wish to borrow a few school textbooks to use in your home-education program. In short, it's best to make a friend of the principal rather than an enemy.

In any matter that could have legal implications (if the proceedings went sour), communication by letter is wiser than communication by telephone—at least until you can see your plan moving smoothly, uncontroversially, in the direction you wish. Keep copies of all correspondence in case more copies are needed for other authorities, or, indeed, for the newspapers. When composing letters for school authorities, one couldn't do better than to study letters that have already been written by articulate parents for the same purpose. Chapter 4 of John Holt's book, *Teach Your Own,** presents several thoughtful, inoffensive, yet powerful letters expressing parents' feelings about education at home rather than in school. The letters are models of tact and restraint, rich with persuasive logic that can work as well for you as they have already worked for their originators.

Your letter to the principal might indicate no more than that you intend to keep your child at home, beginning on a certain date, to pursue your own special program of education. You may or may not indicate a reason for your decision and action; though, in passing, there is one reason that will gain immediate understanding by all educators: namely, that the ratio of one teacher (you) to one pupil (your child) is more advantageous, both for teaching and for learning, than the regular one teacher to twenty-five or thirty-five children.

The principal might invite you to the school to discuss the pros and cons of your decision. If he does, accept the invitation and visit him expecting to make a friend and an ally.

The first important point to remember in a discussion with the principal is that any request to keep a child out of school is easily interpreted by him as being a criticism of his school, or the way he runs it, or the school system in general: criticisms he would rightfully resent. You should, therefore, get your facts straight and present those facts in a clear and forthright manner. You might simply state that your youngster is adjusted to a routine he enjoys, a routine that has given the child apparent advantages; that you or your spouse is home all day, and that you would like the opportunity to continue your home program. Presented in a friendly, unchallenging way, your proposal may well win

*John Holt. *Teach Your Own*. New York: Delacorte Press/Seymour Lawrence, 1981.

the principal's support for an unusual, but interesting, teaching alliance between you and the school.

The principal might express concern about your child's missing valuable peer group experience. You could then mention that your youngster will still be playing with his friends each day at noon, after school, and on weekends and other holidays.

The principal might, on the other hand, have completely different views about the importance of peer group relations. Indeed, the supposedly valuable social intermingling that occurs in school is sometimes cited by educators as being sufficient reason for taking children *out* of school. In answer to the question, "If children are taught at home, won't they miss the valuable social life of the school?" John Holt replies:

> If there were no other reason for wanting to keep kids out of school, the social life would be reason enough. In all but a very few of the schools I have taught in, visited, or know anything about, the social life of the children is mean-spirited, competitive, exclusive, status-seeking, snobbish, full of talk about who went to whose birthday party and who got what Christmas presents and who got how many Valentine cards and who is talking to so-and-so and who is not. Even in the first grade, classes soon divide up into leaders (energetic and—often deservedly—popular kids), their bands of followers, and other outsiders who are pointedly excluded from these groups.
>
> I remember my sister saying of one of her children, then five, that she never knew her to do anything really mean or silly until she went away to school—a nice school, by the way, in a nice small town.

But don't expect the principal—of even a ghetto school—to thump his desk top in emphatic agreement with this sentiment. He isn't likely to acknowledge—even if he secretly believes it—that he is nominal godfather to numerous rival clans of pink-cheeked warlords. So better not mention the point.

Nonattendance

Some parents, for reasons of their own, have preferred to ignore the authorities and have simply kept their child out of school. Such an action can be interpreted by government officials as a challenge to their authority. The question then easily swings from "Should this child be allowed to be educated at home?" to "Are we going to quietly look the other way whenever parents decide to take their child out of school without even consulting us?'' And, possibly miffed at the parents' cavalier handling of the matter, the legal guns are rolled out and the battle is on.

The laws concerning compulsory school attendance vary from state to state, and from province to province. The best source of information about education outside of school is the Boston-based organization Growing Without Schooling, founded by John Holt. This group tells parents that the wisest course, when considering the removal of a child from the school system, is to first find out exactly what the state laws on education say about the matter: information that can be obtained at a public library. Bear in mind, though, that laws concerning education are in the process of change. Indeed, sixteen states have revised their home-education laws since 1982; seven of them in 1985 alone! Other states are busy at this moment working out regulations that are more accomodating to the public's demand for greater educational freedom.

The laws concerning education can also be learned from your state's department of education. Ask what the regulations are for home-schooling and for operating a private school. In some states—California, Illinois, Kentucky and Indiana among them—the requirements for operating a private school are minimal; so, in these states, parents would only have to call their home a school to escape harassment and enquiry. (If you feel uneasy about revealing your identity to the state when seeking the information, have a friend phone or write for you.)

As a rule, the principal of a school or the representatives of the local school district are not reliable sources of information about home-schooling laws. Lower-rung education officials have little reason to acquaint themselves with these laws, and they may have an incorrect understanding of them. Go to people whose business it is to know the laws, or go to the legal text itself.

Another source of information is your state or regional homeschooling group. The names of each will be on the "Homeschooling Resource List"—available for one dollar from Growing Without Schooling (729 Boylston St., Boston, MA 02116). You may obtain, at the same time, a free list of books and special materials relevant to home education which you can then order from G.W.S. (But if you ask for this free list separately, send a self-addressed, stamped envelope.)

Parents who feel unsure of their ability to devise a curriculum of studies might enlist the help of a school that offers a correspondence educational program. Not only is the curriculum already worked out for you, but professionals will monitor your child's progress and offer individualized help. Two highly regarded courses are the Calvert School program (Tuscany Rd., Baltimore, MD 21210), and the Home Study International program (6940 Carroll Ave., Takoma Park, MD 20912).

The latter, run by the Seventh-Day Adventists, can be taken with or without religious instruction.

Parents who want to retain control over what their child learns, yet who would welcome suggestions for a curriculum outline plus incidental advice and legal support, might contact the Clonara School Home-Based Education Program (1289 Jewett St., Ann Arbor, MI 48104).

Another way parents have kept children out of school—more discreetly, if less legally—has been to simply avoid enrolling the youngsters in kindergarten or Grade 1. This will only work, of course, where there are no other children to report to teachers that so-and-so has a school-age child at home; and where the parents don't parade the child around the neighborhood for all to see at a time when other children are in school.

One New York City couple chose this route. Their son was reading at age two, and during the next couple of years, the youngster progressed to nature study, history, science, and so on. When the the child was five, he was allowed to look in at a few schools to see what he thought of them. Likening them to jails, the youngster wasn't obliged to attend. There being no record of his existence in the area, the child received an exemplary education at home without the school authorities ever knowing he was alive.

Finally, the neighbors. When parents keep a child out of school, neighbors can interpret their decision as, ''School may be all right for *your* child, but it isn't good enough for mine''; this, in turn, prompting feelings of resentment. Parents would do best to shrug off the matter and say, ''Well, we'd worked together at home on a program for a long time and it had gone so well there seemed no point in switching. And the principal agreed.''

Keeping children out of school is becoming an increasingly common occurrence due mainly to the work of John Holt and his associates at G.W.S. There are now about 150 homeschooling groups in the U.S., seven in Canada, a sprinkling in England, Australia, New Zealand, and elsewhere around the world (all are on the G.W.S. list). Parents of home-taught children find considerable support in the periodical ''Growing Without Schooling,'' published by that same group. In it, parents are able to compare notes on the common problems that arise in teaching children and in dealing with schools and courts while educating their children at home.

But, alas, most parents can't consider keeping children out of school because of their own need to work. Such was my own case; and as each daughter reached school age, she began attending school. Our educational program at home continued as before; and whatever contribution schoolteachers made to the children's education was considered to be a welcome supplement.

Dropouts

The final group of children to consider are those who have attended school for one or more years but who are now to be removed from the school system for education solely at home. In some ways this is the most difficult program to initiate, because the children are on the schools' records and teachers are accustomed to seeing the children around. Such a change is best made, therefore, during the summer holidays. This is a change my own daughters made, so a word might be in order about how the change was made, and why.

When my children were eight and nine, I was employed at home and was able to consider taking over the children's entire education. At the time they were, in truth, pretty much self-educating: they were able to deal with various exercises and projects, and then present their work for correction and assessment.

My contact with the principal and the children's teachers had been infrequent, brief, and cordial. What had been taught to the children during school hours was, I believed, the school's business (within reason), and what had been taught to the children at home was my business.

The children hadn't been sent to school for an education, so I had no cause to complain about what they hadn't been taught. The school had rendered me considerable service just by taking the children off my hands for a few hours, permitting me to get a day's work done. The children's report cards routinely presented their school performance as good; so teacher-parent meetings were seldom necessary.

The children liked school and fitted in well there. Their report cards for the year before they were removed from school carried the message for one child: "She is a well-adjusted happy child, eager and enthusiastic," and for the other child, "She is very cooperative, gets along well with the other students, and is always cheerful."

Though the children's marks were good—excellent, in fact—this report of excellence was, I felt, an untrustworthy assessment of our home-education program. The children's marks were excellent, yes, *when their performance was compared to children who hadn't received similar training at home*. In short, the children's high marks invited a comfortable, though unwise, complacency on my part. The more important questions were: How well were the children measuring up to their own potential? How much were they being disadvantaged by running with a slow pack?

The final reason for wanting to remove the children from school was simply that they couldn't be expected to continue, year after year. working an hour a day on our home program when they had already spent six hours in school. Worse, the elder child was beginning to get homework, and this was upsetting our studies. The choice gradually being forced upon me was to abandon, or severely curtail, our educational program, or to take the children out of school.

We discussed the matter. The children said they liked the idea of studying wholly at home each day instead of going to school. The advantages and the disadvantages of such a program were carefully explained to them: that their present curriculum of studies would have to be expanded; that the workload would have to be increased to two and a half hours a day; and that they would have to work independently (to avoid squabbling), and disturb me as little as possible.

The main advantage for the children lay in their being able to spend most of the day outside playing once their work was completed. They would, of course, be able to play with their same old friends at noon and after school each day; so there would be no social upset. Secondly, there wouldn't be any more evening work, though tutors would continue to visit on weekends to teach mathematics.

We decided to test the plan during the summer holidays to see if they really could fill their part of the bargain. An extended curriculum was drawn up and our program began. The test curriculum included vocabulary growth: seven unknown words were to be entered in a vocabulary book along with the part of speech each was filling, followed by a dictionary definition of the word. The words were to be drawn from important children's books—*Oliver Twist, Robin Hood,* and others. The exercise served, in this way, the second valuable function of introducing the children to good literature.

Three dozen multiplication problems were a daily requirement, and on three mornings a week a twelve-year-old tutor (available because of the summer holidays) instructed the children in working with fractions. Oral reading (for diction) was also on the curriculum. Five minutes of playing the flageolet and the copying of one cartoon character filled out the formal daily requirement. This was augmented by natural history at mealtimes, our continuing program of film-viewing, and conversational French lessons on weekends, handled by a ten-year-old neighbor who taught the children while playing various table games. Finally, occasional TV programs dealing with science, biology, and geography contributed to our program.

The program proceeded without difficulty through the summer, and a few days before school was to start, I discussed once again with the children the idea of their not going back to school, doing so in an unenthusiastic manner, sounding them out for any hesitancy about following through with the idea. But they had accepted the plan without reservation. The children were cautioned against making much of their abstention from school in any conversation with their friends. But this was scarcely necessary because they both recognized the need for discretion.

This occurred in 1977, before taking children out of the school system came to be championed and before any guidance was available, and I was largely ignorant of how to deal with school authorities. The fact that I succeeded may give other parents encouragement in proceeding, armed, as they would now be, with information I didn't possess. For whatever worth it may be, here is how my children's first exodus from school proceeded.

Though I had met and chatted with the principal of our local school, he had, over the summer months, left for another school; so a new man was now in charge. Knowing he'd be extremely busy the first few days of school, I didn't phone him but, instead, informed his secretary that my daughters would, this year, undertake a special program of instruction at home (thus keeping the records straight and not upsetting projected class sizes).

A few days later, the principal phoned to confirm my decision, saying that though my plan was unusual, he presumed I knew that the Ministry of Education made provision for parents to educate their children at home. He added that an attendance counsellor would be visiting to check our arrangment, and ended by wishing me well.

As it turned out, the attendance counsellor was interested only in the children's emotional well-being, not in their curriculum of studies; and, after chatting with me to determine that I had thought out the matter carefully, then chatting privately with the children for a couple of minutes to make sure their interests were being best served, he lent his support for the acceptance of our program by the school superintendent.

Surprisingly enough, no request was made by the school superintendent for a list of subjects the children were to study. Possibly the superintendent felt that the children's school performance up to that moment spoke well enough of our home program.

Our program proceeded without a snag. With the beginning of school, the Public Broadcasting System (PBS) and TV Ontario (an educational station) began showing educational programs. A teacher's guide from each network permitted us to reap even greater benefit from their teaching programs. The neighbors' children soon accepted the fact that my two didn't attend school any more, and their various friendships continued as before.

In the spring, the school superintendent asked for a report on what the children had engaged in during their ten months at home. The report (pages 244 to 246) is a copy of the one sent. The children were, at that time, eight and nine, and they would have been completing Grades 3 and 4 had they attended school.

Not all children are suited, by temperament, for education solely at home. Such was the case with one of my daughters. Yet, I rebelled at the notion of sending her back into the public school system; and, alas, I couldn't afford to send her to a private school, where scholastic standards are usually higher than those of public schools. Fortunately, a solution to the problem was provided when we moved, in September, to Scarborough (a part of metropolitan Toronto). Here, a special educational program was available through the public school system for children who were academically advanced.

Then came the bad news. The enriched program wasn't for children who were merely advanced. It was for children whose intelligence was exceptionally high. But my disappointment turned to surprise when both children passed the qualifying examination.

Until then, I had no idea what effect our home-education program might have had on the children's ability to think. They had been rated just average when, at ages two and three, our educational program had begun. At least that was the opinion of the day-care teachers who tended them, an appraisal that matched the opinion of friends and relatives.

And so, the revelation: the various activities that had given the children their advanced skills—educating artifices that were prompted by a need to ensure my peace of mind while we drove, shopped, and ate, and generally, to secure tranquility—might, it seemed, work equally well for other parents; might, in fact, be welcomed by them. And this book was started.

The special school program made me largely redundant as a teaching force, though I continued to contribute peripherally as a part-time merchant, bartering TV situation comedies, second-rate movies, and weekend cartoon shows at the rate of one hour of television for 25,000 words of quality reading; and by purchasing drawings at six for forty cents.

The children found their new school program exciting, or not, depending on their teacher any given year. I found their program acceptable, or not, based similarly on their particular teachers. Regrettably, I found the values of some teachers to be in conflict with my own—sometimes in ethical matters, more often in academic matters.

Not everyone would give first importance to my preferred subjects: psychology, semantics, vocabulary growth, and English usage. But education, like religion, is pretty much a personal matter, one in which parents should have a voice. Excellence in these few preferred subjects was, by my observation, the common trait of those we normally regard as learned. And this is what I wished for my daughters. I despaired, therefore, to see their attention being diverted to matters I considered trivial.

At the end of three years, my eldest daughter, then fourteen, went to live with a relative in Ottawa. I discussed with her sister, then completing Grade 6, the prospect of dropping out of school again to pursue an improved program of studies at home. She liked the idea, so we began planning a curriculum.

Shades of Big Brother

That fall, when we initiated our home program again, I found that the educational authorities had imposed tighter control over home educators since I had last removed a child from the system five years earlier. Though the Education Act states, "a child is excused from attendance at school if he is receiving satisfactory instruction at home or elsewhere," inspectors were now presuming to examine and assess home-teaching programs at least three times a year.

This seemed unfair. Inspectors do not visit public school classrooms three times a year to examine and assess what is taking place; though it is commonly known that little learning occurs in some classrooms. Educational authorities tend to ignore the fact that children need learn only a small amount at home each day to equal what most children learn in school.

Doubtless, there are parents who would abuse the privilege of home education; but such parents are easily spotted by a discerning eye. And they are better dealt with individually than by setting up a program of checks and restraints that unnecessarily burden conscientious parents. Parents who hold views about education that are different from views held by educators will, naturally, plan a curriculum of studies for their children that is different from the curriculum favored in schools; and an inspector who says a little more of this or of that subject is needed to win his enthusiastic support (or even grudging assent) can easily disqualify the educational freedom that the Education Act is meant to give.

So long as homeschooled children learn to read, write, spell, and compute as skillfully as children in school, authorities have little reason to bother parents. Generally, children taught at home gain a degree of skill in these basic subjects that far surpasses what is commonly achieved by children their own age in schools.

Homeschooling, with a ratio of one teacher (the parent) to one child, is obviously superior to the public school arrangement of one teacher to thirty children *provided* the relationship between parent and child is conducive to learning rather than to squabbling. Many of the factors to be considered before embarking on a home-education program are presented in John Holt's book *Teach Your Own*. The book also reveals how to negotiate a child's exit from the school system, and how to defend that move legally if the need arises.

Formulating a Program of Studies

Some children hardly need a study program from which to work. Possessing an active curiosity and great energy, they spontaneously involve themselves in a variety of projects, in pursuit of which they often seek out information that, for other children, must be presented almost as a recipe: a little math, a little history, and so on. Any judgment about whether children should follow a detailed study program can't sensibly ignore a particular child's nature and body chemistry. The child who is prompted by an innate craving to know the answers to self-generated questions will, assuredly, learn more easily and quickly than a child who is following a plan. For self-starting children, therefore, free rein is the best method.

My daughter didn't complete every project on her curriculum (described on pages 246-248). Some projects—the map-making, for example—proceeded more slowly than expected. Parents—and schoolteachers too—cannot foresee circumstances that will thwart the completion of this or that project. In presenting a proposed study program to an educational authority, though, the parent will wisely include too much study material rather than too little.

Your home curriculum might be enriched by friends or neighbors who have special knowledge in some field: an amateur (or even professional) naturalist, geologist, writer, artist, potter, or radio ham, for example, who could explain his specialty to your youngster.

The content of future TV programs can't be known; however, we *do* know that there will be a number of highly educational programs shown in the ensuing season: "Nova," and the *National Geographic* series, for example; and such programs deserve inclusion in your "paper offering" to education officials. Two rich sources of educational programs, TV Ontario and PBS, both issue a catalogue of school programs before the beginning of the fall school term. These too can be included in your curriculum.

Parents cannot always predict what journeys they will take with their child, or what interesting sights, buildings, or activities the child will see in consequence. But, such educational trips are no less rightfully a part of your home-education program simply because they couldn't be foreseen at the beginning of the homeschool year. Allow for them in your curriculum.

Include, too, any activity or project your child is currently engaged in—or will engage in or be exposed to. For example, if you intend to wallpaper a room, let the child help, and describe the activity as manual training. Do the same if the child repairs his bicycle, helps paint kitchen furniture, or tends the garden. And include hobbies—building a model ship or airplane, collecting stamps or rocks or butterflies; all can be seen to advance some important skill or trait, if not, indeed, the most consistantly ignored trait of genius: perseverance. And all these activities deserve mention in your home-education program.

By attaching appropriate—and justified!—importance to these various actitivities (and numerous others you will probably think of), and by describing them in a suitably grand manner, you will create an impressive amount of quality paperwork which, I have found, keeps school officials happy, and distant.

20

Afterword:
The Kauppinens Revisited

The text describing the education of Jason and Lori-Ann Kauppinen in Chapter 17 goes only to November 1982. Much has happened in the intervening years.

S. L., Toronto, April 1986

Bright, advanced children can be bored in school if their teachers are unequal to the special teaching opportunity fortune has handed them. And so it was with Jason Kauppinen. Bored and frustrated, he begged his mother, Ann-Marie, to take him out of public school and teach him at home as before. However, his single-parent mother had to work, so his preferred form of education wasn't possible. An unfortunate situation, yes, but a far greater tragedy would have been for the mother to ignore Jason's intellectual growth just so he would be better able to enjoy a school program especially designed for children whose intellectual growth had been unstimulated for five or six years.

Fortunately, Ann-Marie found a superb private co-op school with fees she could afford; so now Jason, age eight, and his sister Lori-Ann, six, pursue whatever subjects catch their curiosity, current among them being science, biology, Arabic writing, and Chinese ideographs. And both children are gradually working through a series of biographies on famous people; among them, Alexander the Great, Hannibal, Julius Caesar, Attila, Napoleon, Aristotle, Darwin, Braille, and Charles Babbage, originator of the modern computer.

In a sense Lori-Ann is now the more advanced of the two because she engages in all the same activities as Jason, yet is two years younger. Moreover, she is pursuing a few extra preferences of her own: jazz tap-dancing, Spanish, and ethnic cooking (having now progressed sufficiently in this latter to begin expanding her mother's knowledge).

Ann-Marie attends the co-op school periodically, too—as art teacher (when she isn't at her other three jobs: hairdresser, laboratory technician, and florist). Ann-Marie's laboratory work—which deals mainly with chemicals—has greatly expanded her knowledge of science, and the children are, in consequence, now familiar with the scientific method and with some of the special equipment she uses to measure the water content of chemicals.

The Kauppinen children continue to receive much of their education at home, and Ann-Marie's own continuing education is indivisible from the children's. Whatever she learns is passed on to them. And whatever subject they want to know more about, she studies—sometimes by taking evening courses at the community college or high school. The trio forms a tightly-knit, knowledge-hungry team.

Jason became enthralled by stained-glass windows, so Ann-Marie took a course in their design and production. Mother and children have now designed and produced a number of decorative stained-glass pieces.

When Jason wanted to know how "chroma-keying" was achieved (the effect seen on television in which an object seems to float or even to disappear), Ann-Marie took a course in TV production. The knowledge she acquired has permitted the family-team to create a new type of educational TV program for children. A local television station is interested in their producing a series, so twenty half-hour programs are in the works.

Cramped for space, Ann-Marie decided to make the back shed habitable. After taking a preparatory course in architectural drafting, she began the project, Jason and his sister handling those jobs that favored shortness. The venture gave rise to a curious spin-off. When Jason understood the workings of the floating ball in the carpenter's level, he saw how an application of that same principle could prevent train derailments—much in the news at that time. Unfortunately, his proposed solution—a hydraulic wheel stabilizer with a computer sensor—can't be tested on a model train, so the trio is looking around for an opportunity to have it tested on a real railway car.

On one occasion, Jason's inventiveness was triggered by vexation. The family received a notice from the public library asking for the return of a book purportedly three months overdue. On their next visit to the library, Ann-Marie expressed puzzlement at the apparent loss, but agreed to pay for a replacement copy. Moments later, Jason found the very same book on the library shelf and presented it to the librarian. He was then both astonished and angered when the librarian didn't offer an apology. Jason's annoyance seems to have fired a creative starburst, for he immediately puzzled out ways to improve the library service, reduce the librarian's workload, and (ahem) reduce blunders. The head librarian is scheduled to hear of his plan soon.

Psychology has become a major interest in the Kauppinen home. By reading Eric Berne's book *Games People Play,* Jason and Lori-Ann have gained a better understanding of human conduct—especially their own. And another of Ann-Marie's study-courses, newspaper advertising psychology, has given the children an insight into that manipulative art.

Each evening, one or another of the trio reads aloud a few pages of the *World Book Encyclopaedia* on some topic suggested by the events of the day. This is followed by a discussion of the subject.

Ann-Marie's various night courses and late work at the laboratory creates much work for baby-sitters. But taking care of Jason can be hazardous. One bewildered sixteen-year-old telephoned Ann-Marie at the lab one night to say Jason had just fired her. The mother asked to speak to her son. He disclosed that the girl's boyfriend had arrived and they were drinking beer. Speaking to the girl again, Ann-Marie upheld her son's decision, pointing out that, by his action, it was apparent that Jason had been taking care of *her*. (An uncle, living in the unit above, took over the sitting.)

During the March break, Ann-Marie hired a sixteen-year-old to stay with the children each day for the whole week. When, on Friday, Ann-Marie paid the girl twenty-five dollars, she turned and gave it all to Jason. It seems they had played euchre. And, unfortunately (for the girl), Jason had recently been working on a mathematical equation pertaining to probability. He tested it during the game. (Always the gentleman though, Jason then spent considerable time helping the sitter with her math problems.)

Appendix

Two Home Programs

The activities listed below (and referred to on page 234) are the ones my daughters engaged in at home when they were eight and nine. This home program replaced the curriculum of activities they would have pursued in Grade 3 (for the younger child) and Grade 4 (for her older sister) at a public elementary school in Ottawa. Despite the fourteen-month difference in the children's ages, they were equal in academic and intellectual standing, and both were therefore able to deal with the same assignments.

General Knowledge: visits to more than forty museums, galleries, displays, and educational spectacles across Canada and the United States.

Grammar and English Usage: dealt principally with the parts of speech. The TV series "Write On" was regularly viewed; each episode was seen more than four times.

Reading: selected articles from the *Reader's Digest,* and any article in the *National Geographic*. Books read included: *Loch Ness Monster, Helen Keller, William Osler, The Diary of Anne Frank, Douglas Bader, The Interrupted Journey, The Invisible Man*. In addition, the following books were read in comic-book form: the *Iliad,* the *Odyssey, Moby Dick, Arabian Nights,* and *Ivanhoe*. Three magazines, *Owl, National Geographic World,* and *Highlights for Children,* were extracurricular reading material. The younger child, a quick reader, read from 20,000 to 30,000 words each weekday; the older child, about 10,000.

Vocabulary Growth: a minimum of three words (though often more)—taken from the *Reader's Digest* "Word Power" feature or encountered in the course of general reading—were entered in vocabulary notebooks along with dictionary definitions, representative sentences actually employing the words, and an analysis of the speech part played by each new word. Neatness in both the layout of the entry and of the writing was required.

Writing: about a hundred research reports of eighty to a hundred words, and the same number of free compositions (stories made up) of a similar length.

Speech: reading aloud each day from the McGuffey Readers to develop diction (and for the ethical lessons these readers contain).

History: viewing of selected television series, most programs of which were seen twice, some three times: "The Fall of Eagles," "Ten Who Dared," and "The Fight Against Slavery." The series "H & G

Mystery'' taught Canadian history and geography. Books on the following historical figures were part of the daily reading program: Captain Cook, Benjamin Franklin, Cleopatra, Caesar, Cortes, King Charles II, Mary Kingsley, Mary, Queen of Scots, Father Lacombe, Edith Cavelle, Radisson, Frontenac, General Custer, Davie Crockett, Balboa, Isaac Brock, Hickok, Daniel Boone, Lawrence of Arabia.

Mathematics: adding, subtracting, multiplying, and dividing in decimals, fractions, and mixed numbers; working with percentages; finding the area of rectangles, circles, triangles; finding the volume of cubes and cylinders. Geometry: dissection of, and measurement of, angles.

Home economics: the children played an important role in keeping the home tidy and in running it; paying all the bills by check, mailing them, and recording these mailings. When shopping, they are able to determine prices by unit measurment, and are, in consequence, shrewd shoppers. The children know what foods to avoid; know the value of protein and which foods supply it. They are able to prepare a number of cooked meals; can bake bread and meat loaf unaided. The elder child has sewn a number of doll's clothes by hand, and has made a few items on the sewing machine.

Science: the television series ''Don't Ask Me'' was a principal source of scientific instruction. The contents of numerous science museums added considerable knowledge.

Art: various handicraft projects were undertaken, and one drawing was produced each day.

Biology, Physiology, Zoology: reading of appropriate articles, viewing exhibits in museums, and viewing the television series ''The Stationary Ark,'' ''See You,'' and ''Microbes and Men.'' Both children read the book *Where Do Babies Come From?* and the younger child read *The Sea Around Us*.

Music: daily instruction in playing the flageolet, which the elder child now plays with skill. The children have developed an appreciation for both jazz and classical music. Music from concerts watched on television was recorded on an audio tape for frequent replaying. One child read the autobiography of Beverly Sills; the other, the life of Chopin.

Languages: French instruction was given by a neighbor's child. The television programs ''The French Show'' and ''Parlez-moi'' contributed to the children's knowledge of French. They learned to read and understand simple Latin sentences, and their vocabulary of German words increased.

Pschology: study of Pierre Berton's *The Big Sell,* and Dale Carnegie's *How to Win Friends and Influence People,* plus discussion of the workings of the human mind.

Physical recreation: after daily studies of two and a half to three hours' duration, the children were able to spend their time outside tobogganing and skating in winter; they swam in an indoor pool two or three times a week, which, coupled with swimming lessons, has made them reasonably competent swimmers.

***

Whereas the preceding is a report of the work actually completed during a school year for Grades 3 and 4, the following home-study program, undertaken as a substitute for Grade 7 education in school, is a guide to what work was planned to be done if time permitted. Some of the projects were not completed; some were not started.

The program has two parts: one for weekdays, one for weekends. The numbers are minutes to be spent at each activity.

WEEKDAY STUDY PROGRAM

Grammar and English usage
   View each segment of the TV Ontario program "Write On," and complete the appropriate assignment in the study guide (purchased from TV Ontario)—30. Read *Grammar for People Who Hate Grammar* and complete the assignments presented in the book—20. As one or other of these works is completed, begin studying *Using Language Skills.*

Cartography (as an approach to geography)—15.
   Draw a street map of Toronto showing all major thoroughfares; to be completed by Christmas. From Christmas to the March break, draw a map of Ontario, identifying cities, towns, lakes, rivers, and canals. From March to the end of June, draw a similarly detailed map of Canada.

Semantics—20.
   Read S. I. Hayakawa's *Language in Thought and Action,* then re-read, making notes from each page and answering questions posed in the work. If this text is completed before the end of June, commence a study of psychology using, for texts, Dale Carnegie's *How to Win Friends and Influence People,* and works by Vance Packard.

Nutrition—20.
Study *Family Guide to Better Food and Better Health* and make notes.

Vocabulary Growth—15.
Enter in an exercise book words that have been encountered variously in other studies, giving part of speech, root source, and appropriate dictionary definition.

Typing—20.
Practice typing exercises as presented in self-teaching typing manual.

Music
Practice the xylophone—15.
Study famous composers and their works, listen to various compositions, and write a report on each composer.

Conjuring—15.
Textbooks: *Sponge Balls, Magic Digest, Learn Magic*. Practice and master the sponge-ball routine.

Art—10.
Copy cartoon characters.

Domestic arts (to be pursued at convenient moments).
Use of the sewing machine for general repairs and alterations. Tailor a pair of gauchos, a skirt, and a pair of slacks. Prepare each week one of the following dishes from a recipe; dumplings, meat loaf, Welsh rarebit, stuffed peppers, cabbage rolls, spinach salad, peanut butter cookies, roast chicken, peanut butter porridge, shepherd's pie, pecan pie, goulash, beef kebabs, whole wheat bread, oyster rarebit, rice pudding, and other dishes yet to be selected.
Purchase complete food and general household supplies, assessing each item by unit price.

SATURDAY

Etymology and vocabulary growth—45.
View the PBS program "Wordsmith" (taped), making notes. Study the "Wordsmith" manual and write a report.

Reading program—15. Continues as part of the Sunday program.

SUNDAY

Reading program—60.
Reading one of the literary works listed. Write a report giving the title, author's name, approximate word count, and date read. Tell what

the text dealt with in fewer than forty words. In the complete report—a minimum of one hundred words—tell whether you liked the
work, and why. List any words you didn't know the meaning of.
Consult the encyclopedia and give a brief biography of the author—
his date and place of birth and of death, early influences, interesting
aspects of his life, and a list of any other important works written.

Saki, "The Open Window"
Rudyard Kipling, "Rikki Tikki Tavi"
J. D. Salinger, "For Esmé With Love and Squalor"
H. G. Wells, "The Man Who Could Work Miracles"
Stephen Leacock, "I Open a Bank Account"
Stephen Vincent Benet, *The Devil and Daniel Webster*
Shakespeare, *Romeo and Juliet*
Abraham Lincoln, selected speeches and letters
Washington Irving, "Rip Van Winkle"
Ogden Nash, selected poems
W. W. Jacobs, "The Monkey's Paw"
Sir Winston Churchill, "Their Finest Hour" (selections)
Gregory Clarke, "McAllister"
Jack London, "To Build a Fire"
C. Northcote Parkinson, "Parkinson's Law" (selections)
Edgar Allen Poe, "Ms. Found in a Bottle"
Robert Service, "The Cremation of Dan McGrew"
Clarence Day, "Father is Firm with His Ailments"
Guy de Maupassant, "Looking Back"
James Thurber, "The Unicorn in the Garden"
               "The Secret Life of Walter Mitty"
W. Somerset Maugham, "The Verger"
                     "A Friend in Need"
                     "The Kite"
Sir Arthur Conan Doyle, "Adventures of the Lion's Mane"
                     "The Red-headed League"
O. Henry, two stories, to be selected
If time permits, read *Pygmalion* by George B. Shaw.

Bibliography

Arnold, Peter. (General Editor) *The Illustrated Book of Table Games*. New York: St. Martin's Press, Inc., 1975.

Carnegie, Dale. *How to Win Friends and Influence People*. New York: Simon & Schuster, Inc., rev. ed. 1981.

deBono, Edward. *Lateral Thinking*. New York: Harper & Row, 1973.

Doman, Glenn, *What to do About Your Brain-Injured Child*. Garden City, N.Y.: Doubleday & Co., Inc., 1974.

Goertzel, Mildred & Victor. *Cradles of Eminence*. Boston: Little, Brown & Co., 1978.

Hay, Henry. *Learn Magic*. New York: Dover Publications, Inc., 1975.

Hayakawa, S. *Language in Thought and Action*. New York: Harcourt Brace Jovanovich, 4th ed., 1978.

Holt, John. *Teach Your Own*. New York: Delacorte Press/Seymour Lawrence, 1981.

Ledson, Sidney. *Grammar for People Who Hate Grammar*. Ajax, Ontario: Dickson Printing, 1981.

_____. *Teach Your Child to Read in 60 Days*. New York: Berkley Publishing Group, 1986.

Morehead, Albert H., & Mott-Smith, Geoffrey. *Hoyle's Rules of Games*. New York: New American Library, 1983.

Sperling, A. P., & Levison, Samuel D. *Arithmetic Made Simple*. Garden City, N.Y.: Doubleday & Co., Inc., 1960.

Stern, Aaron. *The Making of a Genius*. North Miami Beach, Florida: Renaissance Publishers, 1971.

***

The following books provide essential information for understanding why many teachers have difficulty teaching children to read.

Flesch, Rudolf. *Why Johnny Still Can't Read*. New York: Harper & Row, 1986.

Johnson, Mary. *Programmed Illiteracy in Our Schools*. Obtainable from Clarity Books, Box 92, Station C., Winnipeg, Manitoba.

Mathews, Mitford M. *Teaching to Read*. Chicago: University of Chicago Press, 1976.

The Reading Reform Foundation is a group of concerned citizens, educators, and reading authorities working to return the phonic (or letter-code) reading system, of the sort described in Chapter 6, to public school classrooms. Anyone wishing information about which reading systems are up to the RRF's exacting standards of achievement should send a stamped self-addressed envelope to: Reading Reform Foundation, 7054 East Indian School Road, Scottsdale, AZ 85251.

Index